My
Samsung Galaxy S7
for Seniors

D0791472

Michael Miller

800 East 96th Street,
Indianapolis, Indiana 46240 USA

Real Possibilities

My Samsung Galaxy S®7 for Seniors

Copyright © 2017 by Pearson Education, Inc.

ISBN-13: 978-0-7897-5787-6

ISBN-10: 0-7897-5787-7

Library of Congress Control Number: 2016940221

1 16

Trademarks

All terms mentioned in this book that are known to be trademarks or service marks have been appropriately capitalized. Que Publishing cannot attest to the accuracy of this information. Use of a term in this book should not be regarded as affecting the validity of any trademark or service mark.

Galaxy S7 images are provided by Samsung Electronics America.

Warning and Disclaimer

Every effort has been made to make this book as complete and as accurate as possible, but no warranty or fitness is implied. The information provided is on an "as is" basis. The author, AARP, and the publisher shall have neither liability nor responsibility to any person or entity with respect to any loss or damages arising from the information contained in this book or from the use of the CD or programs accompanying it.

Special Sales

For information about buying this title in bulk quantities, or for special sales opportunities (which may include electronic versions; custom cover designs; and content particular to your business, training goals, marketing focus, or branding interests), please contact our corporate sales department at corpsales@pearsoned.com or (800) 382-3419.

For government sales inquiries, please contact governmentsales@pearsoned.com.

For questions about sales outside the U.S., please contact intlcs@pearsoned.com.

Editor-in-Chief
Greg Wiegand

Senior Acquisitions Editor
Laura Norman

Development Editor
Charlotte Kughen

Marketing Manager
Stephane Nakib

Director, AARP Books
Jodi Lipson

Managing Editor
Sandra Schroeder

Senior Project Editor
Lori Lyons

Indexer
Ken Johnson

Proofreader
Kathy Ruiz

Editorial Assistant
Cindy Teeters

Compositor
Bronkella Publishing

Cover Designer
Chuti Prasertsith

Contents at a Glance

Table of Contents

2 | Using the Galaxy S7 edge — 47

5   Connecting to the Internet and Cellular Networks   119

9 Texting Friends and Family   211

17 Shooting and Sharing Photos and Videos — 331

About the Author

Michael Miller is a prolific and popular writer of more than 150 nonfiction books, known for his ability to explain complex topics to everyday readers. He writes about a variety of topics, including technology, business, and music. His best-selling books for Que include *My Windows 10 Computer for Seniors, My Social Media for Seniors, My Facebook for Seniors, My Google Chromebook, Easy Computer Basics,* and *Computer Basics: Absolute Beginner's Guide.* Worldwide, his books have sold more than 1 million copies.

Find out more at the author's website: **www.millerwriter.com**

Follow the author on Twitter: **@molehillgroup**

About AARP and AARP TEK

AARP is a nonprofit, nonpartisan organization, with a membership of nearly 38 million, that helps people turn their goals and dreams into *real possibilities*™, strengthens communities, and fights for the issues that matter most to families such as healthcare, employment and income security, retirement planning, affordable utilities, and protection from financial abuse. Learn more at aarp.org.

The AARP TEK (Technology Education & Knowledge) program aims to accelerate AARP's mission of turning dreams into *real possibilities*™ by providing step-by-step lessons in a variety of formats to accommodate different learning styles, levels of experience, and interests. Expertly guided hands-on workshops delivered in communities nationwide help instill confidence and enrich lives of the 50+ by equipping them with skills for staying connected to the people and passions in their lives. Lessons are taught on touchscreen tablets and smartphones—common tools for connection, education, entertainment, and productivity. For self-paced lessons, videos, articles, and other resources, visit aarptek.org.

Dedication

To my family.

Acknowledgments

Thanks to all the folks at Que who helped turned this manuscript into a book, including Laura Norman, Greg Wiegand, Charlotte Kughen, Lori Lyons, and Tricia Bronkella.

Note: Most of the individuals pictured throughout this book are of the author himself, as well as friends and relatives (and sometimes pets). Some names and personal information are fictitious.

We Want to Hear from You!

As the reader of this book, *you* are our most important critic and commentator. We value your opinion and want to know what we're doing right, what we could do better, what areas you'd like to see us publish in, and any other words of wisdom you're willing to pass our way.

We welcome your comments. You can email or write to let us know what you did or didn't like about this book—as well as what we can do to make our books better.

Please note that we cannot help you with technical problems related to the topic of this book.

When you write, please be sure to include this book's title and author as well as your name and email address. We will carefully review your comments and share them with the author and editors who worked on the book.

Email: feedback@quepublishing.com

Mail: Que Publishing
ATTN: Reader Feedback
800 East 96th Street
Indianapolis, IN 46240 USA

Reader Services

Register your copy of *My Samsung Galaxy S7 for Seniors* at quepublishing.com for convenient access to downloads, updates, and corrections as they become available. To start the registration process, go to quepublishing.com/register and log in or create an account.* Enter the product ISBN, 9780789757876, and click Submit. Once the process is complete, you will find any available content under Registered Products.

*Be sure to check the box that you would like to hear from us in order to receive exclusive discounts on future editions of this product.

In this chapter, you learn how to set up and start using your new Samsung Galaxy S7 or S7 edge. Topics include the following:

→ Unboxing and Charging Your New Phone
→ Getting to Know the Galaxy S7
→ Turning Your Phone On and Off
→ Using the Galaxy S7
→ Performing Basic Operations
→ Managing Your Phone's Power

Getting Started with Your Samsung Galaxy S7

The Galaxy S7 and S7 edge are the latest models in Samsung's popular line of smartphones. There's a lot of functionality built into these phones, which means there's a bit to learn before you start using them. Just what do you find when you open the box—and how do you move around from screen to screen? That's what this chapter tells you, so start reading!

Unboxing and Charging Your New Phone

So you've taken the plunge and purchased a new Samsung Galaxy S7 or S7 edge. What do you need to do to get it up and running?

Take Your New Phone Out of the Box

If you purchased your new phone at a retail store, or from your mobile carrier, the store personnel probably configured the phone with your new or existing phone number. Thus configured, your phone is usable right out of the box—assuming it's charged up, of course!

Here's what you'll find in the box:

- Samsung Galaxy S7 or S7 edge phone
- Samsung quick charger (also known as an Adaptive Fast Charging charger)
- MicroUSB to USB 2.0 cable
- USB-A to MicroUSB adapter (also known as an On-The-Go, or OTG, adapter)
- Headphones + alternate ear buds
- SIM removal pin
- *Quick Start Guide*
- Product Safety & Warranty Information booklet
- Various informational booklets from your mobile carrier

Obviously, you should read the *Quick Start Guide* before you do anything else. The other items you immediately need from the box are the quick charger, microUSB cable, and, of course, the phone itself.

Fast Charging

The Galaxy S7 features Adaptive Fast Charging that enables you to charge your battery to 50% in about 30 minutes. To take advantage of this feature, you need to use the Adaptive Fast Charging charger included with your phone, or a similar third-party quick-charging adapter. If you use a regular charger, your phone will not charge as fast.

Connect and Recharge Your Phone

It's possible that your phone arrived fully charged. It's also possible that it didn't—in which case, you need to connect it to a power source and charge it up before you use it. You can get about four hours' worth of charge by leaving the phone connected for about 10 minutes. Keep the phone connected longer to get a full charge.

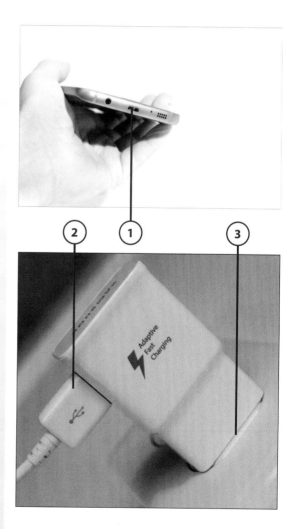

1. Insert the small end of the USB cable into the multifunction jack on the bottom of the phone.

2. Insert the larger end of the USB cable into the Adaptive Fast Charging charger.

3. Plug the charger into a powered wall outlet.

How Do I Know When It's Fully Charged?

The charging light on the front of the phone flashes red while the phone is charging and goes green when fully charged.

>>>Go Further
WIRELESS CHARGING

The Galaxy S7 also features built-in fast wireless charging. This means you can charge the phone without plugging it in; all you have to do is set it on a compatible wireless charging unit.

For this purpose, Samsung offers the $59.99 Fast Charge Wireless Charging Pad. Simply plug the charging pad into a power outlet and then place your phone on top of it; the phone charges automatically—no cables to connect!

Getting to Know the Galaxy S7

After your phone is charged, it's time to start using it! Of course, it helps to know which keys do what—and where you can find various features and functions on the device itself.

Volume up key —

Volume down key —

The Galaxy S7 has two keys on the left edge of the unit. Use these keys to control the volume level up and down—and, in some apps, change the size of the onscreen font.

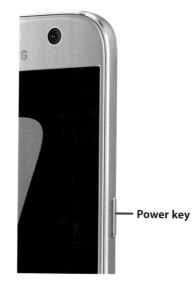

Power key

On the right edge of the unit you find the Power key. Use this key to power the phone on and off, as well as lock and unlock the phone when not in use.

LED indicator ——   —— Front camera

Proximity sensors ——   —— Receiver

Home key ——

Recents key ——   —— Back key

Moving to the front of the unit, there are three important keys on the bottom. In the middle is the Home key, which is a traditional push key you use to both activate the screen when off and navigate to the phone's Home screen. (It has other functions, as well, which come up throughout this book.)

To the left and right of the Home key are flat areas that host touch keys. These areas light up and become active when you touch them with your finger. The touch key on the left is the Recents key; tap it to display all open apps on your phone. The touch key on the right is the Back key, which you tap to go back one screen in most apps.

At the top of the front you see the front-facing camera, to the right of the Samsung logo, which you use for taking selfies. On the left side of the logo are two proximity sensors, the receiver for listening to phone calls, and a small LED indicator light. This light glows three colors: red when the phone is charging, green when it's plugged in and fully charged, and blinking blue when you have waiting messages.

On the back of the phone is the main rear-facing camera, along with the LED flash and a heart rate monitor you use with your finger. The back of the Galaxy S7 is Gorilla Glass, same as the front; only the edges of the phone are metal.

Gorilla Glass

Gorilla Glass is a special toughened glass, manufactured by Corning, designed to be thin, light, and damage resistant. As such, it's widely used in smartphones and other mobile devices.

Headphone jack

USB/charger jack   Microphone

Speaker

On the bottom edge of the phone is the USB/charger port, dubbed the multipur-pose jack, where you connect the USB charging cable. Next to that is the head-phone jack, to which you can connect external headphones or earbuds, as well as a microphone and speaker.

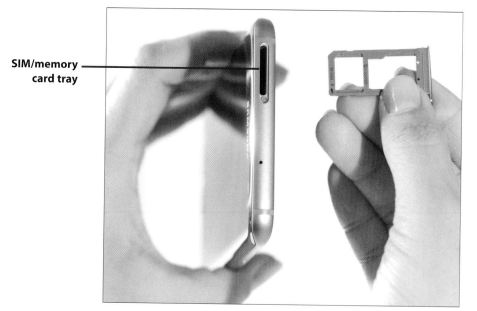

SIM/memory card tray

The top edge of the phone hosts the tray that holds the SIM and memory cards. Remove this tray to remove or change either of these important cards.

SIM Card

Information about your mobile phone account, including your mobile phone number, is stored on a subscriber identification module (SIM) card—actually, on the Galaxy S7, it's a smaller card called a nano-SIM. This card resides in the SIM card slot on the top edge of the phone. You need a special SIM removal pin, included with your phone, to access this slot and remove the SIM card.

Turning Your Phone On and Off

It's easy to power your new Galaxy S7 on and off. You can also lock the phone without powering it off, to turn off the screen and conserve power.

Power On Your Phone

Out of the box, your phone is turned completely off. To power it on, you use the Power key on the right side of the unit.

 Press and hold the Power key.

2 The screen lights up, briefly flashes the Samsung logo, and then displays the Lock screen. (You also hear the Samsung "start" sound.) Swipe right to move to the Home screen.

Setup Wizard

The very first time you power up your phone you see the Setup Wizard, which enables you to quickly set up email accounts, sync contacts that were previously backed up from another phone, turn on location services, and more. Follow the onscreen instructions to complete this initial setup process.

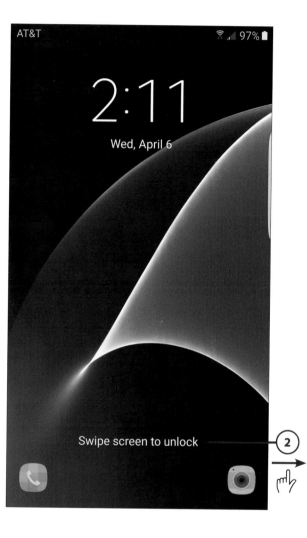

Lock Your Phone

When you're not using your phone, you should lock it. This turns off the display and pauses all running apps, but the phone is still activated to receive calls and texts.

(1) Press the Power key.

(2) The screen goes blank.

Automatic Locking

Your new phone locks itself if it isn't used for a brief period of time (30 seconds, by default—although you can change this on the Settings screen, as discussed in Chapter 3, "Personalizing the Way Your Galaxy S7 Looks and Works"). In practice this means that if you haven't interacted with your phone for that period of time, the screen dims and goes blank, and all running programs are paused. To resume whatever it is you were doing, you must unlock the phone—as discussed next.

Unlock Your Phone

Unlocking the Galaxy S7 is similar to powering on, although it's a much quicker process. That's because the phone itself is still powered on when locked, even if the screen is turned off.

(1) Press the Power key *or*…

(**2**) Press the Home key.

(**3**) The screen lights up and displays the Lock screen. Swipe right to display the Home screen.

PINs and Fingerprints

To ensure that unauthorized users can't unlock and access your phone, you can configure your Galaxy S7 to unlock only after you've entered a PIN or password, or touched your fingerprint to the Home key. All of these options are discussed in Chapter 21, "Making Your Phone More Secure."

Turn Off Your Phone

If you are not using your phone at all and don't want to receive calls or texts, you can turn it completely off. When you power the phone off, everything is powered off.

(**1**) Press and hold the Power key to display the options panel.

(**2**) Tap Power Off.

(**3**) Tap Power Off again. The screen goes blank and the unit completely powers down.

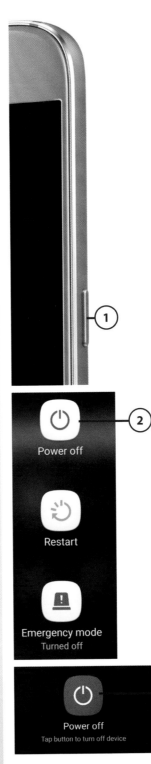

Restart Your Phone

On occasion you might want to power down your phone and then immediately power it back up. You do this by selecting the restart option.

(**1**) Press and hold the Power key to display the options panel.

(**2**) Tap Restart.

(**3**) Tap Restart again. The phone powers down and then immediately powers back up, displaying the Lock screen.

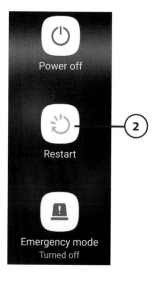

Power off

Restart

Emergency mode
Turned off

Restart
Tap button to restart device

Using the Galaxy S7

The Galaxy S7 functions much like any other modern smartphone, including its predecessors the Galaxy S5 and S6, and the competing Apple iPhone. Most operations are accomplished by tapping or swiping the screen, using a series of touch gestures.

Learn Essential Touch Gestures

To effectively operate your new Galaxy S7, you need to learn a variety of motions and gestures that you perform with your fingers on the device's touchscreen. The most common gestures are listed in the following table.

Gesture	Name	Operation	Description
	Tap	Tap an onscreen object once with your finger	Opens apps, selects menu items, pushes onscreen keys, etc.
	Drag	Touch your finger to an onscreen object, then drag your finger across without lifting	Moves an item from one location to another, activates onscreen toggle switches, etc.
	Swipe	Touch your finger anywhere on the screen, then drag your finger across without lifting	Swipe right from the Lock screen to unlock your phone; swipe left or right from the Home screen to view other panels; swipe up or down to scroll through a page or list
	Tap and hold	Tap the screen and leave your finger on the screen	Accesses available options of the selected onscreen object
	Double-tap	Tap an onscreen object twice quickly with your finger	Zooms into or out of a selected picture or web page
	Spread	Place two fingers together on the screen and then spread them apart	Zooms into the screen
	Pinch	Place two fingers apart on the screen and then pinch them together	Zooms out of the screen

There are also several gestures specific to the S7 edge. Learn more in Chapter 2, "Using the Galaxy S7 edge."

>>>Go Further

ADDITIONAL MOTIONS AND GESTURES

There are additional gesture shortcuts you can activate on the Galaxy S7 for specific applications. You activate these gestures by swiping down from the top of the screen and tapping Settings. From the Settings page, tap to select the Device tab, then tap Advanced Features. Scroll down the page and switch on or off the following:

- **Pop-up View Gesture:** Displays the current app in a pop-up window when you drag down diagonally from either the top-left or right edge of the screen.

- **Palm Swipe to Capture:** Takes a screenshot when you swipe the edge of your hand from left to right across the screen.

- **Direct Call:** Automatically calls the contact whose details are currently onscreen when you bring the phone to your ear.

- **Smart Alert:** Your phone vibrates when you pick it up if you have any missed calls or messages.

- **Easy Mute:** Mutes incoming calls and alarms when you place your hand on the screen or turn the phone over.

I find most of these options useful, except for Direct Call—which I personally leave turned off.

Navigate the Lock Screen

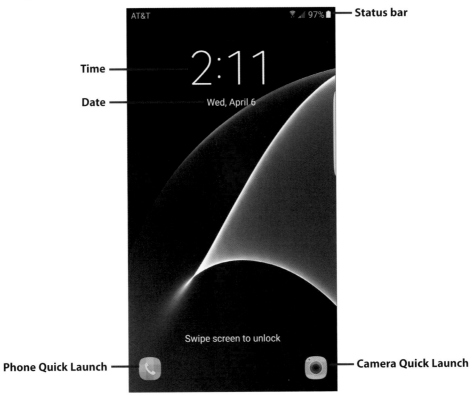

The screen you see when you power on or unlock your Galaxy S7 is the Lock screen. By default, this screen displays the current date and time. The status bar shows any notifications or messages you've received since you last used the phone.

To answer or initiate a phone call from the Lock screen, drag the Phone icon upward. This displays the phone dialpad.

To take a photograph from the Lock screen, drag the Camera icon upward. This displays the camera screen.

Quick Launching the Camera

To "quick launch" the camera from any screen on your phone, double press the Home key; this opens the camera app. You can even double press the Home key to access the camera when your phone is locked.

To unlock your phone for full usage, swipe right on the Lock screen. This displays the Home screen.

Navigate the Home Screen

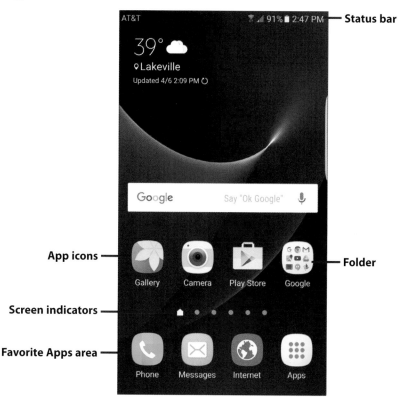

The Home screen is just one of several panels that display your apps. Swipe the screen left or right to view additional panels. The dots, or screen indicators, above the Favorite Apps area indicate which of the panels you're currently viewing.

The icons on the Home screen panels represent some of the individual apps installed on the phone. (Not all apps are displayed on the Home screens by default.) Tap the icon for any app you want to launch.

Managing Apps

Learn more about managing the apps displayed on the Home screens in Chapter 6, "Installing and Using Apps."

Some apps are grouped into folders. Tap a folder to view its contents in a separate panel. Tap the Back key to return to the standard Home screen view.

At the bottom of the Home screen is the Favorite Apps area. By default, this area displays icons for the Phone, Messages, and Internet apps, but you can customize this area to display any apps you use frequently. There is a fourth icon, as well, for Apps; tap this icon to display the Apps screen, where all your apps are listed. (You can also opt to display five icons here instead of the default four.)

To return to the Home screen at any time, press the Home key.

Understand the Status Bar

AT&T   91% 2:47 PM

At the top of the Home screen is the status bar. This area contains icons that indicate the status of various phone functions. The following table details the indicator icons you may see in the status bar.

Status Bar Indicator Icons

Icon	Description
⊘	No signal
⏀	Signal strength (more bars = stronger signal)
1	Accessing SIM card
R	Roaming (outside of normal phone service area)
4G LTE	Connected to 4G network
📶	Connected to Wi-Fi network
N	NFC (Near-Field Communication) enabled
✳	Bluetooth enabled

Icon	Description
	Mute mode enabled
	Vibration mode enabled
	GPS location sensing activated
	Call in progress
	Missed call
	New voicemail message
	New text message
	Battery full
	Battery low
	Battery charging
	New email message
	File download in progress
	File upload in progress
	App updates available
	App updates complete
	Alarm set
	Error or caution

Navigate the Apps Screen

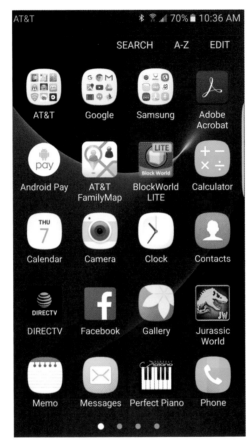

As noted, when you tap the Apps icon on the Home screen, you see the Apps screen—actually, a series of panels. These panels display all the apps installed on your phone. Use the Apps screen to access apps not displayed on the Home screen, select which apps to display on the Home screen, and uninstall unwanted apps.

By default, apps are displayed in the order they're installed. To display apps individually, tap A-Z. To search for a specific app, tap Search.

To return to the Home screen, press the Home key.

View the Notification Panel

The notification panel pulls down from any screen to display any active notifications, as well as links to key system settings.

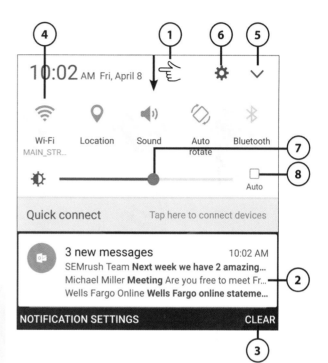

(1) Swipe down from the top of any screen to display the notifications panel.

(2) Any notifications are displayed beneath this panel. Tap a notification to read messages and perform related actions. Drag a notification to the left or right to clear it from the screen.

(3) Tap Clear to clear all notifications from the notification panel.

(4) Tap any of the Quick Settings icons to turn on or off Wi-Fi, Location, Sound, Auto Rotate, Bluetooth, Power Saving mode, Ultra Power Saving mode, Airplane mode, Do Not Disturb, or the Flashlight. (Swipe to the left to see past the first five icons.)

(5) Tap the down arrow to see additional Quick Settings.

(6) Tap Settings to display the Settings screen.

(7) Tap and drag the brightness slider to adjust screen brightness.

(8) Tap to select the Auto option to activate automatic screen brightness.

(9) Tap Quick Connect to quickly search for and connect to nearby Bluetooth and Wi-Fi devices.

(10) Swipe up from the bottom of the notification panel to close the panel.

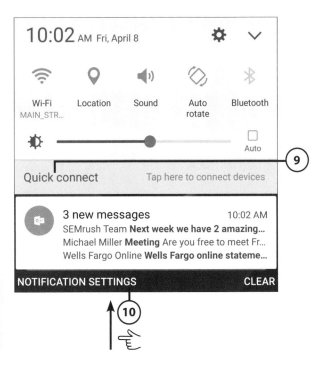

It's Not All Good

Auto Brightness

The automatic brightness function attempts to set the proper brightness level for the ambient light in your current location. This sounds good in theory, but may not be the best in practice.

The first issue is that some people find that auto brightness results in screens that are too dark. This is especially a problem for people with vision issues, where you need increased brightness to read text clearly.

The second issue is that auto brightness doesn't always work well. The ambient light sensor sometimes doesn't accurately track the outside light level, resulting in a screen that is too dark or too light for the current conditions. In addition, the light sensor might significantly lag behind any changes in lighting as you move from location to location.

For these reasons, you might want to disable the auto brightness option on your phone—or at least experiment with it before committing one way or the other.

Move from Screen to Screen

Moving from screen to screen on the Galaxy S7 is a simple matter of tapping and swiping.

1. From the Lock screen, swipe to the right to unlock the phone and display the Home screen.

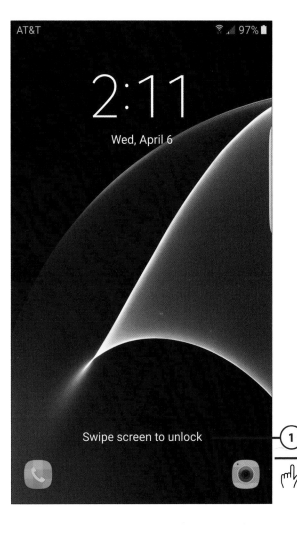

AT&T   97%

2:11

Wed, April 6

Swipe screen to unlock ————1

(2) From the Home screen, swipe left or right to display additional panels.

(3) Tap the Apps key to display the Apps screen.

4 From the Apps screen, swipe left or right to display additional panels.

5 Tap the Back key to return to the previous screen.

6 Press the Home key to return to the Home screen.

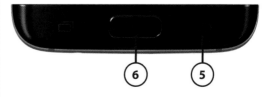

View and Close Open Apps

The apps you open on your phone stay open, but paused, until you manually close them. Use the Recent Apps key to display your open apps, navigate to those you want to reuse, and close those you no longer need open.

① Tap the Recent Apps key to display all open apps in a stack.

② Swipe up or down to view all the apps in the stack.

③ Tap an app to reopen it fullscreen.

④ Tap the X on a given app to close it, or just drag the app left or right off the screen.

Close Your Apps

In general, you want to close your apps when you're done with them. Leaving apps running in the background—even if they're theoretically paused—can use enough power to unnecessarily drain your battery.

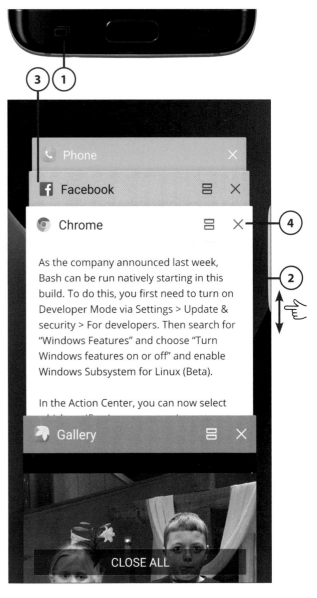

Performing Basic Operations

Your new Galaxy S7 or S7 edge can do a lot of things—run apps, send and receive text messages and email, play music and videos, and more. But there are some basic operations, such as controlling the volume and screen brightness, that apply to all operations.

Change the Volume Level

Many applications on the Galaxy S7 generate sound, whether it's the ringing of the phone, the click of the onscreen keyboard, or music that you're playing. The Galaxy S7 features volume up and down keys on the left side of the device—but there's more you can adjust than just that.

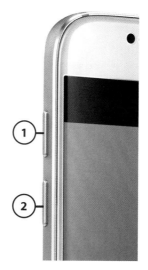

(1) Press and hold the up volume key on the left side of the unit to raise the volume level of the current application. If no application is running, this adjusts the volume level of the phone's ringtone.

(2) Press and hold the down volume key on the left side of the unit to lower the volume level of the current application. If no application is running, this adjusts the volume level of the phone's ringtone.

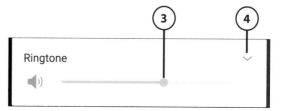

(3) When you press either of the volume keys, the phone displays a volume panel onscreen. You can drag the slider in this panel to adjust the volume level of the ringtone.

(4) To adjust the volume level of other functions, tap the down arrow in the volume panel. This displays an extended volume panel. You can make individual adjustments to the volume levels for these functions—Ringtone, Media, Notifications, and System.

5 Drag the slider in the Media section to adjust the volume level of music and video playback.

6 Drag the slider in the Notifications section to adjust the volume level of notifications and alerts.

7 Drag the slider in the System section to adjust the volume level of system sounds.

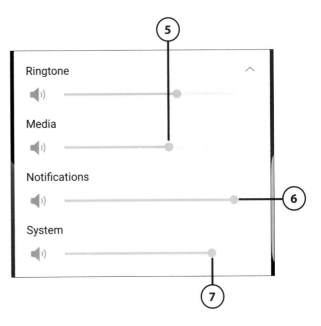

Put the Phone on Vibrate or Mute

By default, when someone calls or texts you on your Galaxy S7, the phone rings. If you're in a quiet area, however, you might want incoming calls or texts to be less obtrusive. In this instance, you can turn off the ringtone and instead have your phone vibrate or be totally silent.

1 Swipe down from the top of the screen to display the notification panel.

2 Tap the third Quick Settings icon to switch between Sound (default ringtone and the phone vibrates), Vibrate (no sound, but phone vibrates), and Mute (phone neither rings or vibrates) modes.

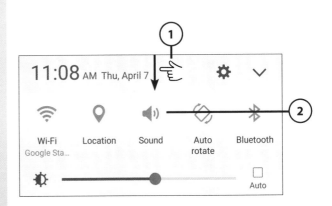

Adjust the Brightness Level

Some users find the Galaxy S7's default screen brightness to be a little too dim to comfortably read, especially in direct light. You can, however, easily make the screen brighter or dimmer.

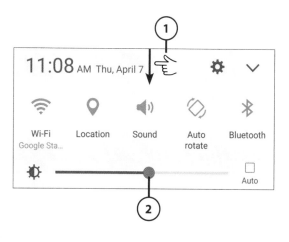

(1) Swipe down from the top of the screen to display the notification panel.

(2) Tap and drag the brightness slider to the right to make the screen brighter, or drag to the left to make it less bright.

Rotate the Phone

You can hold your new Samsung smartphone so that the longest edge is vertical (portrait mode) or horizontal (landscape mode). Although portrait mode is the normal mode for most uses, you might find that some onscreen content is easier to read or manage when you rotate the phone 90 degrees.

The Home screen itself doesn't rotate, but many apps do. Many users find that the onscreen keyboard (discussed next) is easier to type on when the phone is held horizontally; the keys get bigger to fill the wider width. You might also find that some web pages and documents are easier to read with the phone rotated, for the same reason; the onscreen text gets bigger when the screen's width is larger.

(1) To switch to landscape mode, turn the phone 90 degrees in either direction. (It doesn't matter whether you have the Home key on the left or the right.)

(2) Most (but not all) apps rotate to match the new screen orientation. Move back to portrait mode by rotating the phone so that the Home key is back on the bottom.

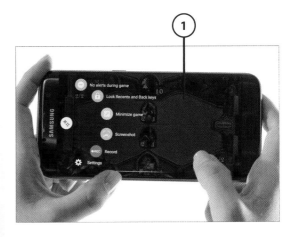

Disable Rotation

By default, the Galaxy S7's screen rotates when you rotate the phone. If you want to lock the screen into portrait view, even when the phone is rotated, pull down the notification panel and tap "off" the Auto Rotate icon.

Enter Text with the Onscreen Keyboard

When you need to enter text on your phone—to send text messages, create emails, post to Facebook, enter website URLs, work in word processing documents, and the like—an onscreen keyboard automatically appears at the bottom of the screen. Use this keyboard to enter text, numbers, and other characters.

(1) The onscreen keyboard automatically appears whenever text entry is required.

(2) Tap a letter or number key to enter that character.

3 Tap the spacebar to enter a space.

4 Tap the up arrow once to enter a single uppercase character.

5 Tap the up arrow twice to enter all-cap mode.

6 Tap the up arrow three times to return to normal lowercase entry.

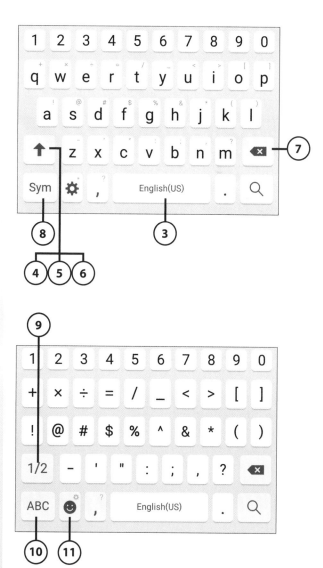

First Word Capitalization

The onscreen keyboard automatically capitalizes the first word of a sentence. It knows that a new sentence starts when you enter a period (.) or if you have entered two spaces in a row.

7 Tap the Delete (x) key to remove the previous character.

8 Tap the Sym key to display the symbol keyboard when you need to enter punctuation marks and symbols.

9 There are two screens of symbols available. Tap the 1/2 or 2/2 keys to switch between symbol screens.

10 Tap the ABC key to return to the alphanumeric keyboard.

11 To enter emoji instead of text, tap the emoji key.

Emoji

The word *emoji* means "picture letter" in Japanese. An emoji is a small picture or icon used to express an emotion or idea.

12 Emoji are organized into categories. Tap to select a category.

13 This displays the first of several screens of emoji. Swipe right and left to view additional emoji.

14 Tap an emoji to enter it in your message or document.

15 Tap the ABC key to return to the alphanumeric keyboard.

16 Tap the Back key to hide the onscreen keyboard.

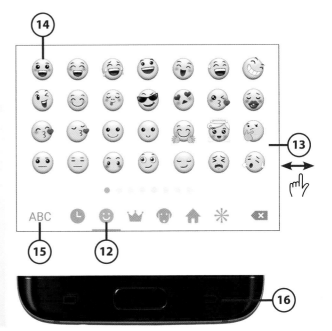

>>>Go Further

PREDICTIVE KEYBOARD

Your Samsung Galaxy S7 uses a *predictive keyboard*. This means that the keyboard looks at what you're typing and predicts what you'll type next, suggesting possible words. As you type, suggestions for the next word appear in the row space above the top row of number keys. To accept a suggestion, all you have to do is tap it.

The predictive keyboard also includes auto-correct functionality. This means if you mistype a word, the keyboard automatically inserts what it thinks is the correct word. Although this auto-correct often does a good job of catching spelling mistakes, it can also change perfectly acceptable words into something else entirely. For this reason, you still need to look at the screen when typing; you can't rely on the predictive keyboard to always make the right choices.

Copy and Paste Text

When you're entering text, you might find it more convenient to copy and paste text from one location or document to another. For example, you might want to copy an address from a web page and paste it into a text message or maps application.

| SELECT ALL | COPY | SHARE | ⋮ |

get connected and start using all aspects of the
Internet — safely and securely. Like my other "For
Seniors" books, reviewed and endorsed by the
AARP. Pick up or order a copy today!

(1)   (2)   (3)

(4)

| Search or type URL | 🎤 |

r ⋯⋯ ⋯ ⋯ ⋯ -my-internet-f ↖
n   **PASTE**   **CLIPBOARD**   iternet-for-senio

(5)

(1) Tap and hold the text you want to copy. This selects the current word.

(2) Select more than one word by tapping and dragging the blue selection bars to enlarge the selection.

(3) Tap Copy to copy the text to your phone's clipboard.

(4) Move to and tap where you want to insert the selected text, either in the current app or in another app.

(5) Tap Paste.

>>>Go Further
HOW TO TAKE A SCREENSHOT

To take a digital picture (screenshot) of the visible screen on your Galaxy S7, hold down the Power and Home keys simultaneously until the screen flashes. The screenshot is stored in the Screenshots album in your photo gallery.

You can also use a palm swipe to capture a screenshot. To do this, place the edge of your hand on the left side of the screen, then swipe it to the right.

To capture app screens that extend across multiple pages (typically by scrolling down), you need to activate the S7's Smart Capture feature. Swipe down from the top of the screen to open the notification panel and then tap Settings. From the Settings page, tap to select the Device tab and then tap Advanced Features. Tap to select Smart Capture and then slide the switch On. (Slide the switch to Off to turn off Smart Capture.) With Smart Capture activated, when you capture a screen you see a variety of options. Tap Capture More to capture the entire scrolling area of a given page rather than just the visible screen.

Set an Alarm

Your Samsung smartphone can also serve as your mobile alarm clock. The Galaxy S7 and S7 edge includes a Clock app that you can use to set your morning wake-up alarm—or any other alarms throughout the day.

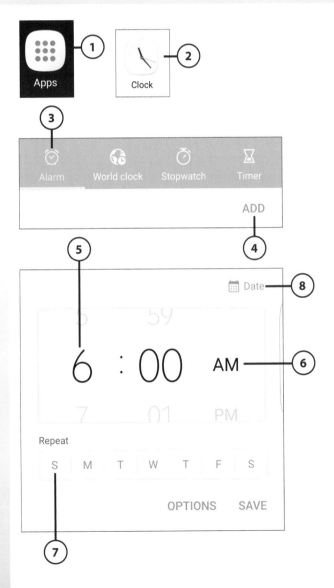

1. From your phone's Home screen, tap the Apps icon to open the Apps screen.

2. Tap the Clock icon to open the Clock app.

3. Tap to select the Alarm tab.

4. Tap Add to create a new alarm.

5. Tap the time controls to set the alarm time.

6. Tap AM or PM to set morning or afternoon.

7. Tap the days you want the alarm to repeat.

8. Tap Date to set a specific day for this alarm to sound.

9 Tap the date you want on the calendar.

10 Tap Done.

11 Tap Options to adjust the sound and snooze options.

12 By default, the alarm sounds at the selected time. To have your phone vibrate instead, or vibrate along with the sound, tap Alarm Type and make a selection.

13 Tap and drag the sound slider to adjust the volume level of the alarm sound.

14 Tap Alarm Tone to select a specific alarm sound.

15 Tap to select the alarm tone you want. When you tap a tone, you hear a preview of that sound.

16 Tap the back arrow to return to the previous screen.

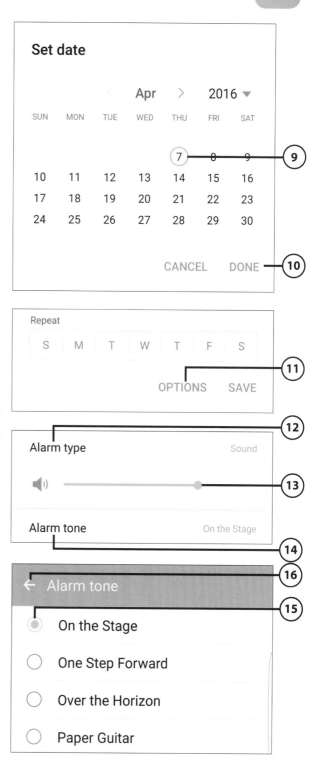

(17) By default, the alarm sounds until you tap the Snooze key, then repeats three times at five-minute intervals. If you'd rather not utilize this snooze function, or you want to choose a different interval, tap Snooze to display the Snooze screen.

(18) Tap to select the snooze interval.

(19) Tap to select how often you want the snooze to repeat.

(20) If you'd rather not utilize the Snooze function, slide the switch to Off.

(21) Tap the back arrow to return to the previous screen.

(22) Set the alarm sound to start soft and then increase in volume by sliding the Increasing Volume switch to On.

(23) Tap Alarm Name to give the alarm a name, such as "Weekday Morning" or "Saturday Afternoon."

(24) Tap Save to save this alarm.

Snooze   5 minutes, 3 times

(21) (17)

← Snooze

On   ON   **(20)**

Interval

⦿ 5 minutes ————————————— **(18)**

◯ 10 minutes

◯ 15 minutes

◯ 30 minutes

Repeat

⦿ 3 times ——————————————— **(19)**

◯ 5 times

◯ Continuously

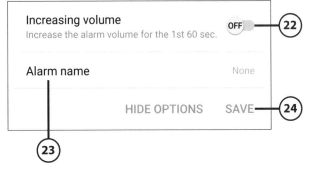

Increasing volume   OFF   **(22)**
Increase the alarm volume for the 1st 60 sec.

Alarm name   None

                        HIDE OPTIONS   SAVE   **(24)**

(23)

Set a Timer

In addition to being an alarm, the Clock app also functions as a clock (of course), stopwatch, and timer. The timer function is particularly useful when you need to keep track of something cooking or otherwise in progress.

1. From within the Clock app, tap to select the Timer tab.

2. Tap the Hours, Minutes, and Seconds controls to set the length of the timer.

3. Tap Start to begin the countdown.

Use Your Phone as a Flashlight

You may be used to turning on your phone to use its screen as a light in the dark. Well, the Galaxy S7 has a flashlight function built-in, which uses the LED flash on the back of the phone as a more powerful dedicated flashlight—great for finding things in the dark or illuminating menus in dimly lit restaurants.

1. Swipe down from the top of the screen to display the notification panel.

2. Scroll right through the icons and tap On the Flashlight icon.

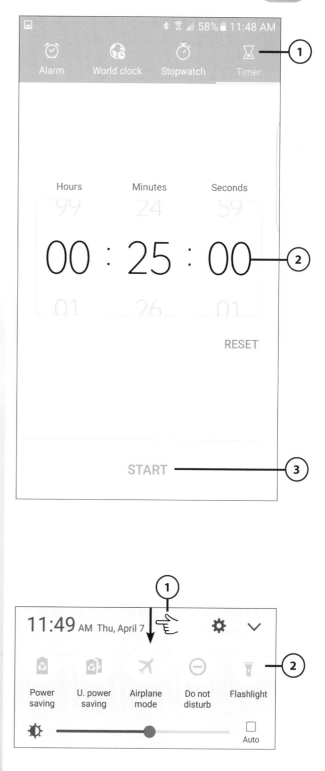

(3) When you're done using the flashlight, tap Off the Flashlight icon or tap Turn Off in the Flashlight notification.

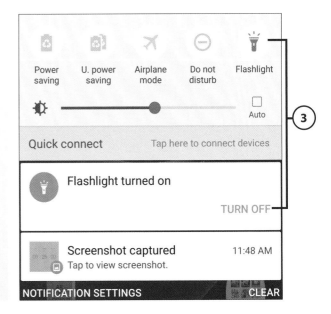

It's Not All Good

Power Drain

Extended use of the LED flashlight can quickly drain power from your phone's battery. For this reason, limit your use of the flashlight to short periods of time.

Managing Your Phone's Power

Your Galaxy S7 is a mobile device, running on power from its internal battery. This battery is rechargeable, of course; most people charge their phones overnight, so they have a full charge when they get up in the morning.

Monitor Battery Usage

The amount of charge left in your phone's battery is indicated in the status bar at the top of the screen, as a percentage. For example, if the indicator reads 40%, that means that you have 40% of a full charge left. More detailed battery usage is available, however.

1. Swipe down from the top of the screen to display the notification panel.

2. Tap Settings to display the Settings screen.

3. Tap the System tab to display the System screen.

4. Tap Battery.

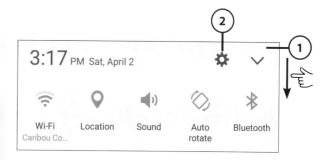

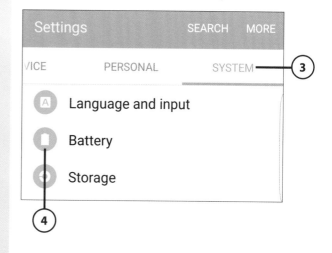

5 The Battery screen displays various configuration options for your phone's battery usage, including a detailed graph that estimates how much time the phone has left on the current charge.

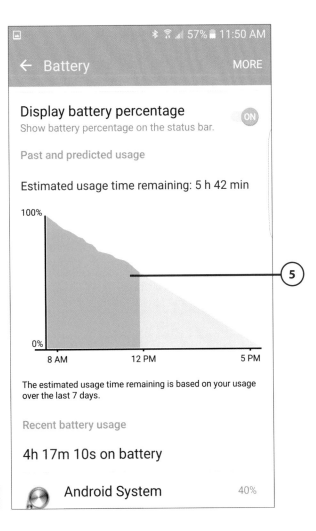

Deal with a Low Battery

Your phone notifies you when the battery is running low. At this point, the best thing to do is connect your phone to the quick charger and plug it into a power outlet to recharge. If you do not have a power outlet handy, you need to start conserving power until you can recharge.

There are many ways to conserve power on your phone. You can manually turn off power-hungry functions, such as Wi-Fi and Bluetooth. You can also enter one of two power-saving modes:

- **Power Saving Mode:** Limits maximum CPU performance, reduces screen brightness, turns off touch key lights, and turns off vibration feedback.

- **Ultra Power Saving Mode:** Switches to a grayscale display, limits the number of usable apps to only essential applications, and turns off Wi-Fi, Bluetooth, and location services.

In most instances, the normal Power Saving Mode will be enough to get you through until you can recharge your phone. Switch to Ultra Power Saving Mode when it's unlikely you'll be able to recharge within the next hour or so.

Cables

Your new Samsung phone came with one USB cable, which you use to charge your phone. Many users like to purchase additional cables; they leave one at home (for charging), but carry a second in their purse or briefcase for charging when they're on the go—and maybe even a third in the car, for charging (and connecting) when driving.

Turn On Power Saving Modes

1. Swipe down from the top of the screen to display the notification panel.

2. Tap Settings to display the Settings screen.

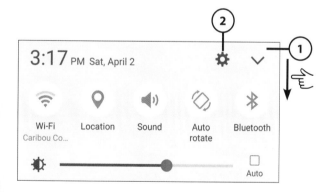

(3) Tap the System tab to display the System screen.

(4) Tap Battery.

(5) Start Power Saving Mode by tapping Power Saving Mode and then tapping On to activate.

(6) Start Ultra Power Saving Mode by tapping Ultra Power Saving Mode and then tapping On to activate.

/ICE   PERSONAL   SYSTEM —— (3)

[A] Language and input

[ ] Battery

[ ] Storage

(4)

← Battery   MORE

This screen shows the battery usage data since the device was last fully charged.

Power saving mode ———— (5)
Off

Ultra power saving mode ———— (6)
Off

>>>Go Further

EMERGENCY MODE

Your Samsung Galaxy S7 offers a special Emergency Mode for use in an emergency. This mode extends the life of your phone's battery by turning off all but essential functions. It also enables you to use your phone to dial 911, send your location to a designated contact, and even sound an alarm.

To enter Emergency Mode, press and hold the Power key and then tap Emergency Mode. Agree to the various terms and conditions and then tap Turn On.

You now see the grayscale Emergency Mode screen. To use your phone as a flashlight, tap Flashlight. To make a regular phone call, tap Phone. To dial 911, tap Emergency Call. To sound an emergency alarm, tap Emergency Alarm. To message your current location to a designated contact, tap Message Location.

When the emergency has passed, you exit Emergency Mode by tapping More, Turn Off Emergency Mode.

In this chapter, you learn how to use those features exclusive to the Samsung Galaxy S7 edge. Topics include the following:

Using the Galaxy S7 edge

The Galaxy S7 and the S7 edge share many of the same features and functionality. But the curved screen edge on the S7 edge provides for a handful of additional features, all of which use the extra screen space.

Getting to Know the Galaxy S7 edge

There are actually two versions of the Galaxy S7. There's the standard S7 and there's the S7 edge. There are some significant differences between the two.

The most obvious difference is the size. The S7 edge is slightly wider and taller than the standard S7. (Although the edge is just a smidge thinner.)

The larger size is primarily because of the edge's larger screen. The standard S7 sports a 5.1" diagonal screen, whereas the edge has a noticeably larger 5.5" screen. That makes it easier to touch and tap and type, especially if physical mobility is an issue.

The larger size also enables the edge to incorporate a slightly larger battery (3600 versus 3000 mAh). This means that the edge will last longer before draining the battery, which is a good thing.

But the feature that gives the S7 edge its name is the edge—that is, the curved edges on the left and right sides of the screen. This makes for a rather striking design (and a slightly different feel in your hand), and also provides for added functionality.

In actual use, the Edge screen on the S7 edge provides additional screen space for information and alerts. Here's what you can choose to display on the Edge screen:

- **Edge Panels:** Drag the Edge panel to the left to display different panels of options and information, including your favorite apps, tasks, and contacts, as well as the latest news and weather.

- **Edge Lighting:** The Edge screen lights up when you receive a call or notification when your phone is facing downward. (The Edge screen lights in an assigned color if you receive a call from one of your priority contacts.)

- **Edge Feeds:** Displays news, and other real-time information you select, in a scrolling ticker.

- **Night Clock:** Displays the date and time on the Edge screen.

S7 edge Only

These features are all exclusive to the Samsung Galaxy S7 edge. They are not available on the plain Galaxy S7.

Using Edge Panels

Edge panels are exclusive to the Samsung Galaxy S7 edge. There are five panels that display different types of tasks and information—Apps Edge, Tasks Edge, People Edge (contacts), News Edge, and Weather Edge.

Display the Edge Panels

Displaying and scrolling through the Edge panels is as easy as swiping your screen.

1. Drag the Edge panel handle (displayed by default on the right Edge screen) toward the center of the screen.

2. Swipe left or right to scroll through the available Edge panels.

Edit the Edge Panels

You can configure your S7 edge to display some or all of the default Edge panels. You can also download additional panels for your phone.

1. Open the Edge panel and click the Settings icon to display the Edge Settings screen.

2. To disable the Edge panel, slide the switch at the top of the screen to Off. Slide this switch to On to display the Edge panel.

3. Uncheck any panel you don't want to see. Check those you do want displayed. (Note the variety of Edge panels available but not displayed by default.)

4. Change the order of the Edge panels by tapping Reorder then tapping and dragging the top of any panel to move it to a new location.

5. Download additional Edge panels by tapping Download. This displays a list of available panels.

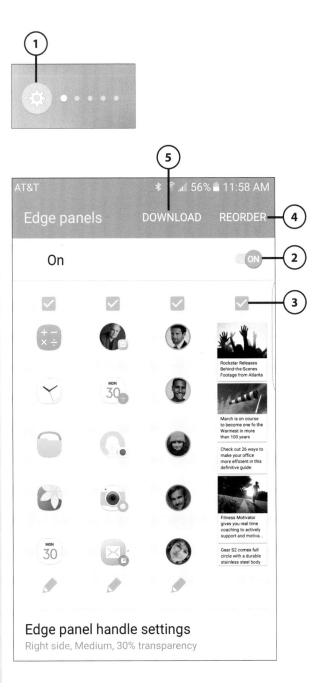

6 Tap a panel's Download button to download that item. (Some Edge panels are free; some are available for purchase.)

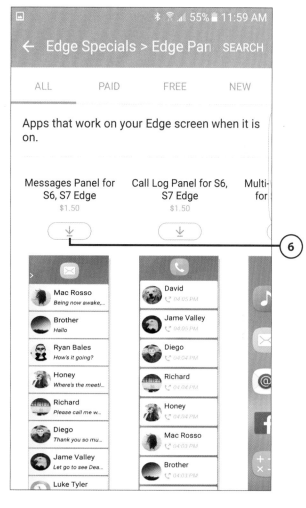

Configure the Edge Panel Handle

You can configure the S7 edge to use either the left or right edge to display various Edge-related messages and alerts. Make sure you position the phone so that you can see the side you've designated as the Edge.

1 Open the Edge panel and click the Settings icon to display the Edge Settings screen.

2 Tap Edge Panel Handle Settings.

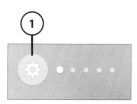

Edge panel handle settings ─ **2**
Right side, Medium, 30% transparency

(3) Tap Position and then select
either Right Side (default) or Left
Side to specify the side where the
Edge panel appears.

(4) Change the vertical position of
the handle by dragging the arrow
element up or down the side of
the screen.

(5) Tap Size and then select Small,
Medium (default), or Large to
change the size of the handle.

(6) Drag the Transparency slider left
or right to change the transparency of the handle.

(3)

← Edge panel handle settings

Drag the ⬍ handle upward or downward
to change the position of the Edge panel
handle.

Position
Right side

⬍ (4)

Size (5)
Medium

Transparency
30%

(6)

Using the Apps Edge

The Apps Edge panel can display shortcuts for up to ten of your favorite apps.
This makes it quicker and easier to open the most-used apps on your phone.

Configure Apps on the Apps Edge

You can place a shortcut for any app on
your phone on the Apps Edge panel.

(1) Open the Edge panel and scroll
to the Apps Edge panel.

(2) Add a new shortcut to the panel
by tapping a + icon. This displays
a screen with Frequently Used
and All Apps lists.

(3) Tap and drag the icon for the app you want to add to an empty slot in the Apps Edge panel.

(4) Tap and Drag any icon to a new position to change the order of shortcut icons in the Apps Edge panel.

(5) Remove a shortcut from the Apps Edge screen by tapping the – (minus sign) icon for that app.

(6) Tap the Back key on your phone to return to the Apps Edge panel.

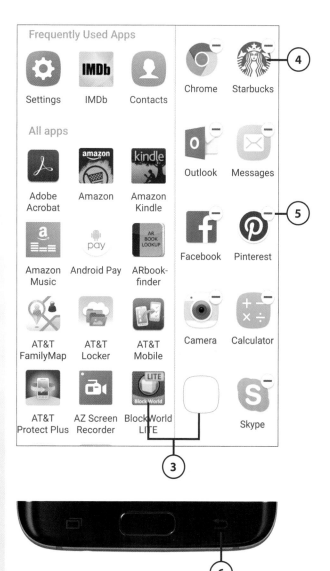

Launch an App from the Apps Edge

In many cases, launching an app from the Apps Edge panel is faster and easier than scrolling through your phone's various screens.

1. Open the Edge panel and scroll to the Apps Edge panel.

2. Tap the icon for the app you want to open.

Using the Tasks Edge

Use the Tasks Edge panel to display those tasks you perform most frequently, such as composing an email message or taking a selfie.

Configure Tasks on the Tasks Edge

You can place a shortcut for many available tasks on the Tasks Edge panel.

(1) Open the Edge panel and scroll to the Tasks Edge panel.

(2) Add a new shortcut to the panel by tapping a + icon. This displays the Tasks Edge panel along with shortcuts to common tasks, organized by app.

(3) Tap and drag the icon for the task you want to add to an empty slot in the Tasks Edge panel.

(4) Change the order of shortcut icons in the Tasks Edge panel by tapping and dragging any icon to a new position.

(5) Remove a shortcut from the Tasks Edge screen by tapping the – icon for that app.

(6) Tap the Back key on your phone to return to the Tasks Edge panel.

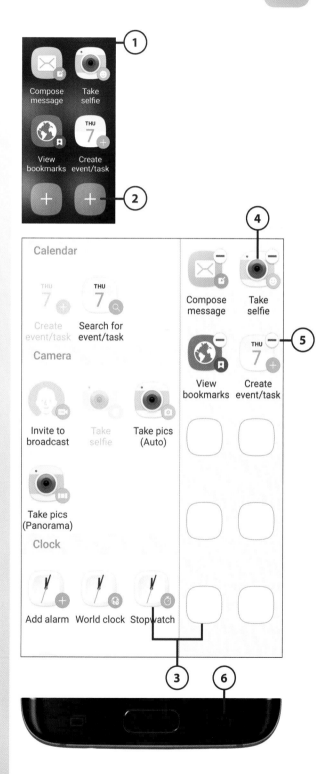

Launch a Task from the Tasks Edge

Launching a task is just like launching an app from the corresponding Edge panel.

(1) Open the Edge panel and scroll to the Tasks Edge panel.

(2) Tap the icon for the task you want to start.

Tasks edge

Create shortcuts to access specific app functions or to communicate with favorite contacts quickly and easily.

Compose message

Take selfie

View bookmarks

Create event/task

Using the People Edge

The People Edge panel lets you quickly phone, email, or text message your favorite contacts.

Add a Contact to My People

The People Edge panel displays up to five contacts you've manually added to the panel—what Samsung calls the My People list.

(1) Open the Edge panel and scroll to the People Edge panel.

(2) Tap a + icon to display your Contacts list.

Amy Lynn Elliott

Ben Elliott

Kristi Lee

Sherry Miller

(**3**) Scroll to and tap the contact you
want to add. That person is now
added to the People Edge panel.

Remove a Contact

If you want to add a new contact to the
People Edge panel but already have
five displayed, you need to remove a
contact to make space. To remove a
contact, tap and drag that contact to
the Remove (trashcan) icon at the top of
the panel.

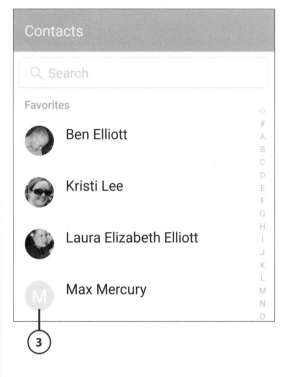

(**3**)

Change a Contact's Color

Each of your five main contacts is
assigned a unique color, which displays
when you receive a message from
that person. You can easily change the
assigned colors for these contacts.

(**1**) Open the Edge panel and scroll
to the People Edge panel.

(**2**) Tap the Settings icon to display
the Edge Panels screen.

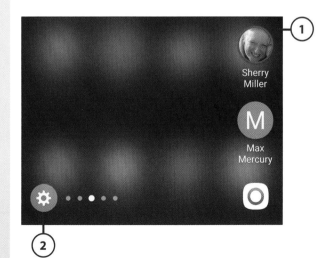

(3) Tap the Edit (pencil) icon underneath the People Edge panel.

(4) On the next screen, tap My
People.

(5) Tap the color icon next to any
contact to display the Select
Color panel.

(6) Tap the desired color.

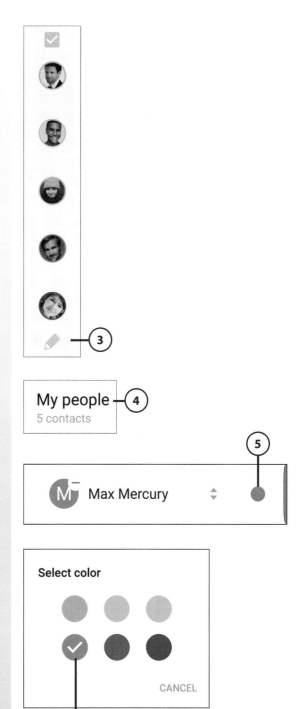

Contact a Favorite Contact

The People Edge panel makes it easy to send an email or text message to your favorite contacts—and to initiate phone calls, as well.

(1) Open the Edge panel and scroll to the People Edge panel.

(2) Tap the person you want to contact. You see the screen for that person.

(3) Tap the phone icon to call this person.

(4) Tap the message icon to send a text message to this person.

(5) Tap the email icon to send an email to this person via your default email app.

OnCircle

The S7 edge includes a feature called OnCircle that's popular among some younger users. When two users both have OnCircle enabled, they can send email, messages, pictures, live emoticons, and phone calls directly to each other. To use OnCircle, open the People Edge panel and tap the OnCircle icon at the bottom.

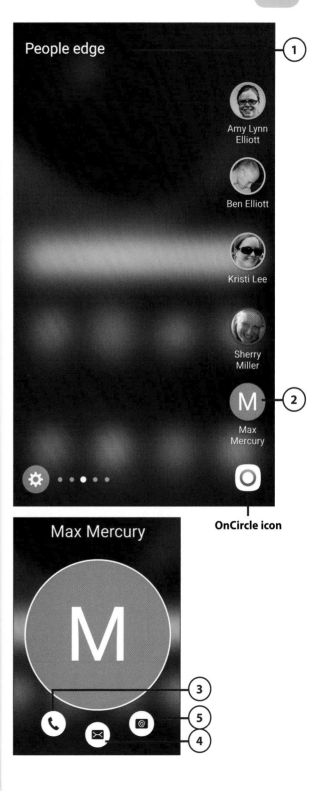

OnCircle icon

Using the News and Weather Edges

As discussed, there are many other Edge panels available for the S7. Two more are enabled by default—the News Edge and Weather Edge.

Use the News Edge Panel

The News Edge panel displays the day's top news headlines.

1. Open the Edge panel and scroll to the News Edge panel.

2. Swipe up or down to read additional news headlines.

3. Tap a news headline or picture to read that story in your web browser.

Use the Weather Edge Panel

The Weather Edge panel displays current weather conditions and the day's forecast.

1. Open the Edge panel and scroll to the Weather Edge panel.

2. Tap the Weather Edge to display more detailed weather information in the Weather app.

AccuWeather

Information displayed in the Weather Edge panel and the Weather app is provided by AccuWeather.

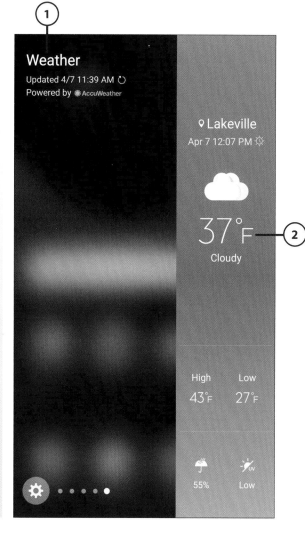

Using Edge Lighting

The S7 edge's Edge Lighting feature lights up the Edge screen when you receive a call or notification—but only when the phone is sitting facedown.

View Missed Messages

When you receive a call or text message from someone on your My People list, the entire Edge screen lights with a pulsing light in the color assigned to that person, so you can see at a glance who's calling. For example, if you assign the color green to your friend Joe, the Edge screen lights up green when Joe texts or calls you.

This light displays for only a few seconds, and then your screen goes dark and your phone relocks. When you pick up and unlock your phone, the Edge screen displays a colored bar, which lets you know you received a message from your friend.

(1) Tap and drag the colored bar to the left to display information about the messages you've received.

(2) Tap the current message icon to read a message, or to return a phone call.

(3) Tap the Phone icon to call this person.

(4) Tap the Message icon to read all text messages from this person.

(5) Tap the Email icon to read all email messages from this person.

(6) Tap the X to remove the message area from the screen.

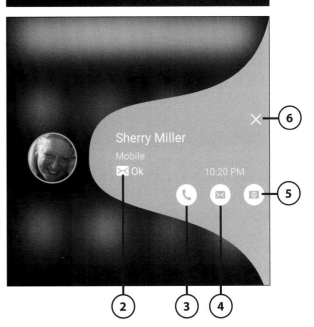

Using Edge Feeds

Edge Feeds is a series of news feeds that scroll across the Edge screen. It can display any or all of the following:

- **Briefing Feed:** Your phone's notifications
- **Yahoo! News:** Top news headlines
- **Yahoo! Finance:** Stock updates on the stocks you choose
- **Yahoo! Sports:** Scores from your favorite teams
- **S Health:** Personal fitness information gathered by the S Health app on your phone.

Activate and Configure the Information Stream

To display Edge Feeds on your Edge screen, you have to both activate and configure it for the types of information you want to receive.

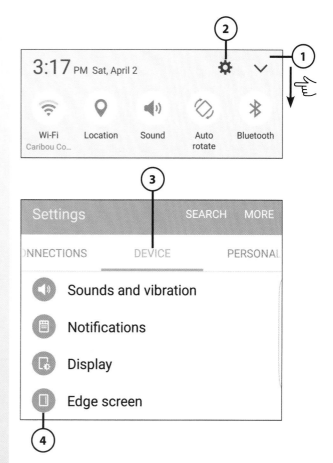

1. Swipe down from the top of the screen to display the notification panel.

2. Tap Settings to display the settings screen.

3. Tap the Device tab.

4. Tap Edge Screen.

(5) Tap Edge Feeds to display the Edge Feeds screen.

(6) To activate Edge Feeds, slide the switch at the top of the page to On.

(7) Check those feeds you want to display. Uncheck those you don't want to read.

(8) Tap Reorder to change the order of the feeds; then tap and drag the feeds into a different position.

(9) Some feeds have settings to customize what information you see. For example, you can configure which stocks to follow in the Yahoo! Finance feed, or what sports teams to follow in the Yahoo! Sports feed. Tap the Edit (pencil) icon for a given feed to customize its settings.

(10) By default, the Edge Feeds display for 30 seconds and then turn off. To change how long the Edge Feeds are visible, tap Edge Feed Timeout.

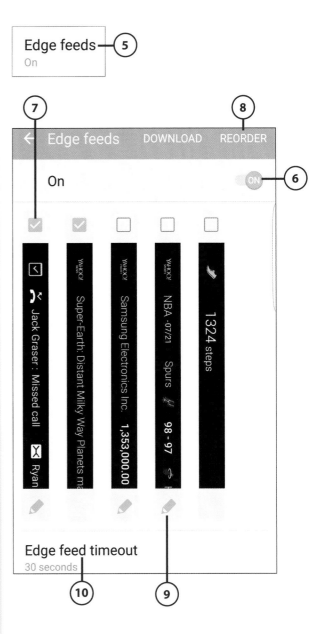

(11) Tap the amount of time you want, from 15 seconds to 10 minutes.

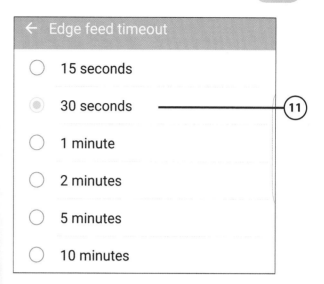

View the Edge Feeds

Edge Feeds do not appear automatically; you have to toggle them on when you want to read them.

(1) Press the Power key to turn off your phone's screen.

(2) With the phone locked, quickly slide your finger up and then down the Edge screen.

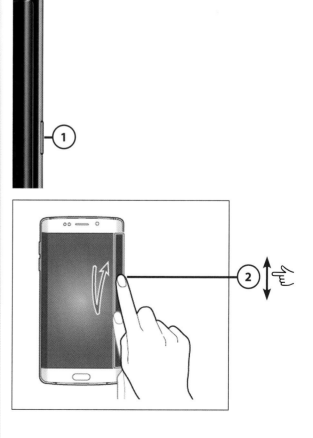

(3) The Edge Feed now displays on the Edge screen. Swipe left or right (up or down on the Information Stream) to cycle through different feeds.

(4) Tap a headline or item to view that item on your phone's main screen.

YAHOO! 4/07 10:09 AM   **Mother of Black Girl From Controversial Gap Kids Ad Has...**

(3) (4)

It's Not All Good

Difficult to Read

The Edge screen is very thin, less than a half inch tall, which limits the information that can be displayed in the Edge Feed and Night Clock. You're basically looking at a single line of information, no more than that.

The thinness also makes the information in the Edge Feed and Night Clock difficult to read, especially for those with any level of vision problems. So while these particular Edge features might sound interesting, you'll probably have to put on your glasses to read them—which might reduce their usefulness, especially in the middle of the night.

Using the Night Clock

The S7 edge's Night Clock feature turns your phone into a nighttime alarm clock and night light. With Night Clock activated, the Edge screen displays the current date and time, along with the time of the next alarm. The Edge screen itself is slightly dimmed, so it won't keep you awake all night.

Activate the Night Clock

When you activate the Night Clock, you tell your phone during what hours you want to see it. You can specify a maximum 12-hour period.

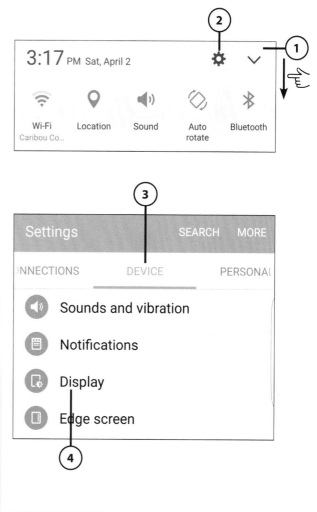

1. Swipe down from the top of the screen to display the notification panel.

2. Tap Settings to display the settings screen.

3. Tap the Device tab.

4. Tap Display.

5. Tap Night Clock to display the Night Clock screen.

6 Slide the switch at the top of the screen to On to turn on the Night Clock.

7 Tap the up and down arrows to set the Start Time. Tap the AM/PM button to switch between AM and PM.

8 Tap the up and down arrows to set the End Time. Tap the AM/PM button to switch between AM and PM.

View the Night Clock

When activated, the Night Clock appears on the Edge screen at the start time you set, and stays on until the specified end. Note that the Night Clock light is very soft, so that it won't disturb your sleep; you might have trouble viewing it in daylight.

Low Battery

The Night Clock turns off when battery power reaches the 15% level.

In this chapter, you discover various ways you can personalize your new Samsung smartphone. Topics include the following:

→ Personalizing the Screen Background
→ Personalizing Screen Settings
→ Personalizing Sounds and Notifications

Personalizing the Way Your S7 Looks and Works

Out of the box, Samsung's Galaxy S7/S7 edge is a nice-looking phone. It's easy enough to learn how to use, the screens look good, and the operations feel natural.

That doesn't mean there isn't anything that you might want to change. Maybe you want a different screen background. Maybe you don't like the sounds of the notifications. Maybe you don't like notifications at all.

Well, you're in good luck. There are lots of ways you can personalize your new Galaxy S7 or S7 edge to make the phone better fit the way you like to use it.

Personalizing the Screen Background

One of the first things that many people personalize about their phones is the screen background. On the Galaxy S7, you can set different backgrounds for the Lock screen and the Home screens. You can choose from preselected wallpaper images, or use one of your own photos as the background.

Readability

When choosing background images and colors, make sure that there's enough contrast between the background and the foreground icons and text. Don't sacrifice readability for a cool-looking background.

Change the Lock Screen Wallpaper

The Lock screen is the screen that appears when you power on or unlock your phone. You can set the Lock screen to have its own background wallpaper, or to share the background of the Home screen.

1. Swipe down from the top of the screen to display the notification panel.

2. Tap Settings to display the Settings screen.

3. Tap to select the Personal tab.

4. Tap Wallpaper.

5. Tap the down arrow at the top of the screen and select Lock Screen.

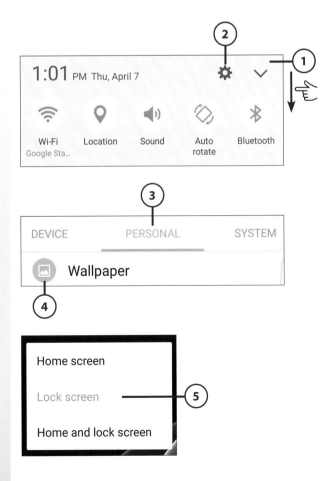

Home and Lock

To use the same image for the Lock and Home screens, tap the down arrow and select Home and Lock Screens.

6 Scroll through the available images and tap the one you want to use.

7 Tap Set as Wallpaper *or...*

8 To use a photograph as a background image, tap From Gallery. Your photo gallery opens.

9 Tap the photo you want to use.

10 Tap Done.

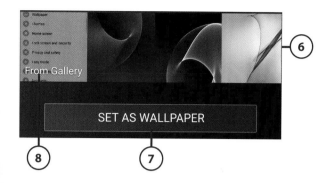

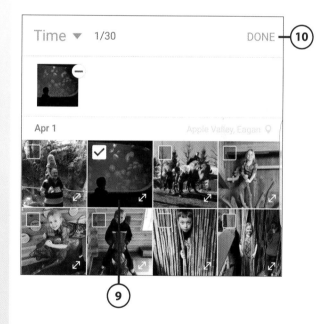

(11) Tap Set as Wallpaper to approve the image you've chosen.

1:01

.Thu, April 7

SET AS WALLPAPER (11)

>>>Go Further
PICTURES FOR WALLPAPER

Many of us like to use personal pictures—of our partners, children, or grandchildren—as background wallpaper on our phones. As you've just learned, it's easy enough to choose a photo for your background, as long as that photo is already stored on your phone, in the Gallery. So if you have a picture you'd like to use, just make sure you save it to the Gallery first.

What about pictures you might receive via email or text message? Well, you can save these to the Gallery, also, just by using the "save" function within the appropriate app. For example, to save a picture you receive in the Messages app, tap the picture to display it fullscreen, then tap the Save icon at the bottom of the screen. Once in the Gallery, you can then select that photo for your wallpaper.

Change the Home Screen Wallpaper

You can similarly change the background image on your phone's Home screens. (Actually, on both the Home and Apps screens.)

1. Swipe down from the top of the screen to display the notification panel.

2. Tap Settings to display the Settings screen.

3. Tap to select the Personal tab.

4. Tap Wallpaper.

5. Tap the down arrow at the top of the screen and select Home Screen.

6. Scroll through the available images and tap the one you want to use.

7. Tap Set as Wallpaper or…

8. To use a photograph as a background image, tap From Gallery. Your photo gallery opens.

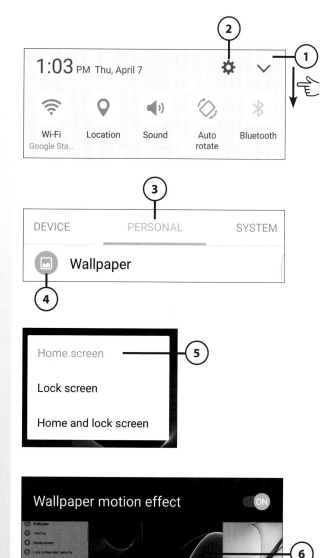

(9)   Tap the photo you want to use.

(10) Tap Set as Wallpaper to approve
        the image you've chosen.

Motion Effect

Home screen wallpaper can display a
motion effect, where the background
appears to move slightly when you tilt
the phone. To enable this effect, tap
On the Wallpaper Motion Effect switch
when you're setting the Home screen
wallpaper.

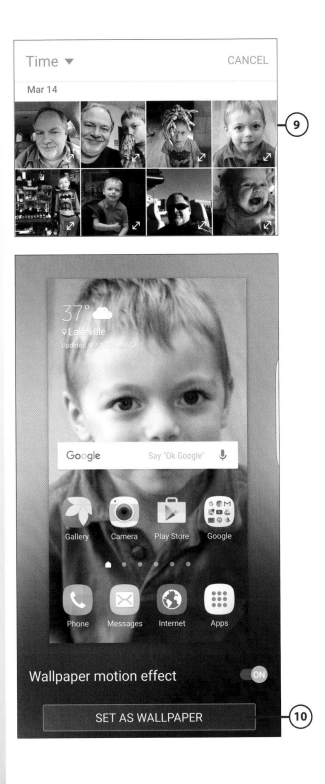

Change Your Phone's Theme

If you want a more radical change to the way your phone looks, you can change the phone's entire visual theme. A theme is a preset combination of background images, fonts, and icons that affect the look and feel of every system screen.

1. Swipe down from the top of the screen to display the notification panel.

2. Tap Settings to display the Settings screen.

3. Tap to select the Personal tab.

4. Tap Themes to display the My Themes page.

5. One or more themes may be present on your phone. (Some carriers preinstall themes; some don't.) Tap to select one of these themes.

6. Additional themes are displayed in the Recommended Themes section. Some are free; some aren't. Tap to select one of these themes.

7. Tap More Themes to view additional themes online. The Theme Store opens.

1:10 PM Thu, April 7

Wi-Fi — Google Sta...
Location
Sound
Auto rotate
Bluetooth

DEVICE PERSONAL SYSTEM

Wallpaper

Themes

45% 1:10 PM

← My themes DELETE

MORE THEMES

12:45
Sun, 1 March
Default

12:45
RainDrop

Recommended themes

12:45
Dinosaur (AOD)
Free

12:45
Jelly Hams_A...
Free

12:45
Finding Monst...
Free

8 Tap a tab to view themes by type: Categories, Featured, and All.

9 Scroll to and tap the theme you want.

10 Tap either the Download or price button.

11 Samsung now downloads the theme. When the download is complete, tap Apply.

12 When prompted, tap Apply to close all open apps and apply the new theme.

8

Theme store   MY THEMES   MORE

CATEGORIES   FEATURED   ALL

Add the Theme store icon   ✕

Top Free Themes   MORE

Red Metallic   White Sci-fi   Red Beauty
Free   Free   Free
★★★★✦   ★★★★✦   ★★★★✦

9

Wish   DOWNLOAD   **10**

DELETE   APPLY   **11**

Applying this theme may close some apps and any unsaved data may be lost.

CANCEL   APPLY

12

(13) To return to your phone's default theme, return to the Themes screen and tap Default.

(14) When prompted, tap Apply. This closes all open apps and reinstalls the original theme.

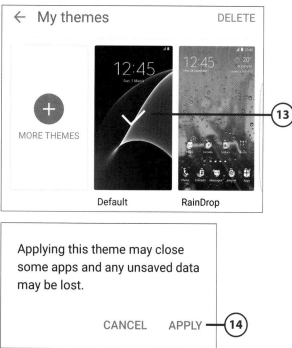

Personalizing Screen Settings

There are a number of other screen settings you can configure that help to personalize your user experience.

Screen Mode Options

There are ways to fine tune the way colors appear on your phone's screen. The Samsung S7 offers four different screen modes, each of which optimizes the color range, saturation, and sharpness of your screen in different ways, as explained in the table on the next page.

Which mode should you use? For the most accurate color rendition, Basic mode is best. If you prefer more vivid colors, however, you may like the Adaptive Display mode. For viewing movies on your phone, the AMOLED Cinema mode provides good results. And if you use your phone for editing digital photos, you'll get the best results from the AMOLED Photo mode. It all depends on what you want.

Screen Mode	Description
Adaptive Display	Dynamically adjusts images and videos depending on content. Provides higher color saturation than other modes. (This is the default mode.)
AMOLED Cinema	Optimizes display for movie playback.
AMOLED Photo	Optimizes display for photographic images. Provides calibration to the Adobe RGB standard, used in Photoshop and similar photo-editing applications.
Basic	Provides the most technically accurate color rendition—although colors may look less vivid than in other modes.

Set the Screen Mode

You set your desired screen mode from the Display and Wallpaper section of the Settings screen.

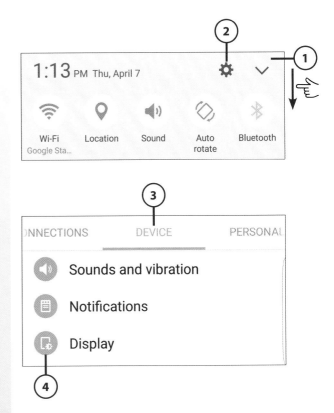

1. Swipe down from the top of the screen to display the notification panel.

2. Tap Settings to display the Settings screen.

3. Tap to select the Device tab.

4. Tap Display.

(5) Scroll down and tap Screen Mode to display the Screen Mode screen.

(6) Tap the desired screen mode. The preview picture at the top of the page changes to reflect the selected mode.

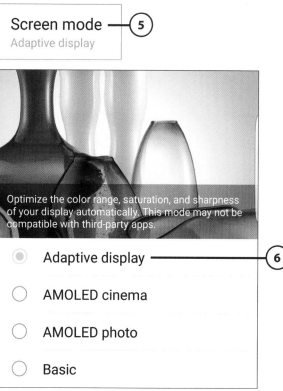

Set Screen Timeout

By default, the screen on your new smartphone turns itself off (and the phone goes into lock mode) if you haven't done anything in 30 seconds. Some people find this 30-second time-out too limiting, and want to extend the amount of time the screen stays lit.

(1) Swipe down from the top of the screen to display the notification panel.

(2) Tap Settings to display the Settings screen.

(3) Tap to select the Device tab.

(4) Tap Display.

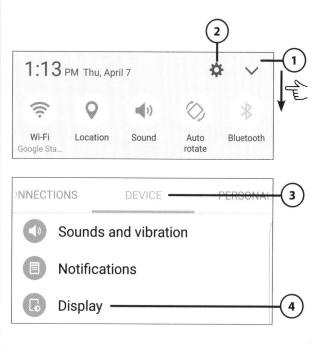

(5) Tap Screen Timeout to display the Screen Timeout screen.

(6) Select a new timeout value, from 15 seconds to 10 minutes.

Timeout and Battery Life

Leaving the screen lit for extended periods of time when you're not using the phone drains your phone's battery. Choose a shorter timeout value to conserve battery life.

Configure Smart Stay

Another way to keep the screen lit when you're using the phone is to enable the Smart Stay feature. Smart Stay prevents your phone from turning off the display as long as you're still looking at it. (It's a great feature if you use your phone to read eBooks or other onscreen content that might not require you to interact with the phone otherwise; it works by using the phone's front camera to detect your face.)

(1) Swipe down from the top of the screen to display the notification panel.

(2) Tap Settings to display the Settings screen.

(3) Tap to select the Device tab.

(4) Tap Display.

Screen timeout —— **(5)**
After 3 minutes of inactivity.

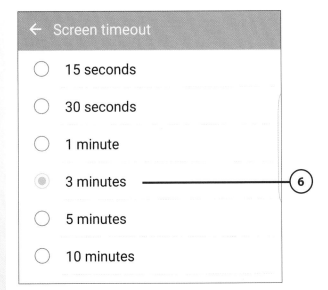

← Screen timeout

○ 15 seconds

○ 30 seconds

○ 1 minute

◉ 3 minutes —————— **(6)**

○ 5 minutes

○ 10 minutes

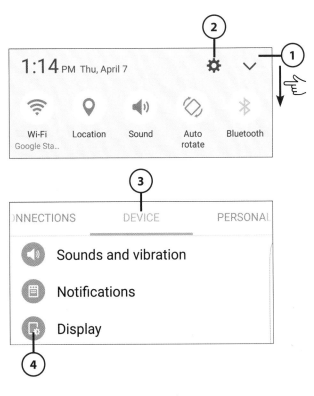

5 Tap Smart Stay to display the Smart Stay screen.

6 Tap On the switch at the top of the screen.

Stay Smart?

Many people find the Smart Stay function to be less than useful, as it tends to shut off the display when you glance away from the phone. It also has problems when the phone is placed on a flat surface. For that reason, experiment with Smart Stay before you decide to use it full time.

Prevent the Screen from Turning On Accidentally

New to the Galaxy S7 is the ability to sense when your phone is in your pocket or purse, and not turn on accidentally if you happen to hit one of the keys. It's a great way to keep from wasting battery power—or accidentally "pocket dialing" your contacts!

1 Swipe down from the top of the screen to display the notification panel.

2 Tap Settings to display the Settings screen.

3 Tap to select the Device tab.

4 Tap Display.

5 Scroll to the Keep Screen Turned Off section and tap On the switch.

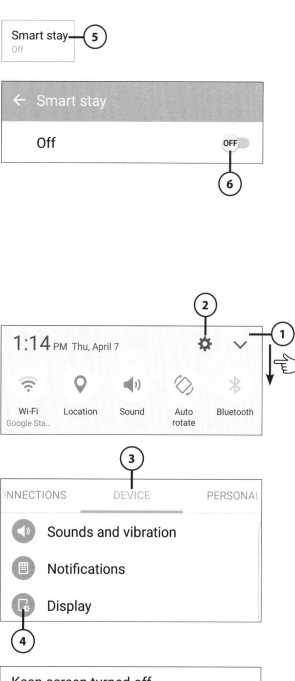

Display a Screen Saver While Charging

By default, your phone's screen turns off when you're not using it—even if the phone is plugged in and charging. If you'd rather the phone display a screensaver when charging, activate Daydream mode.

1. Swipe down from the top of the screen to display the notification panel.

2. Tap Settings to display the Settings screen.

3. Tap to select the Device tab.

4. Tap Display.

5. Tap Screensaver to display the Screensaver screen.

6. Tap On the switch at the top of the screen.

7. Tap the screensaver you want to display—Colors, Pandora, Photo Table, Photo Frame, or Google Photos. (Pandora and Google Photos only appear as options if you have those apps installed on your phone.)

Photo Screensavers

For the three photo screensavers, you can select from where the phone picks the photos to display. Just tap the Settings (gear) icon for that screensaver, and make a selection.

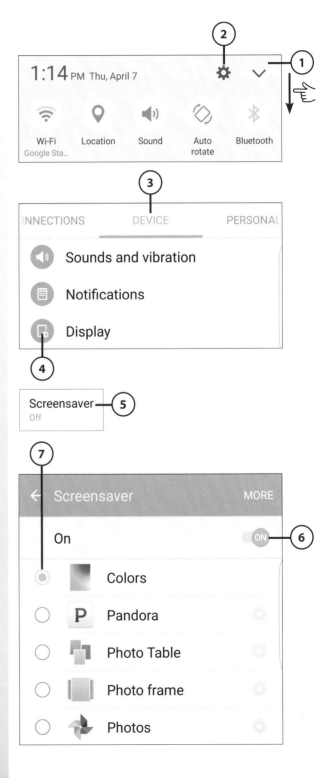

Configure the Always On Display

New to the Galaxy S7 and S7 edge is an Always On Display that displays information or an image when the screen is otherwise turned off. You can opt to display one of several clocks or calendars, or your image of choice.

1. Swipe down from the top of the screen to display the notification panel.

2. Tap Settings to display the Settings screen.

3. Tap to select the Device tab.

4. Tap Display.

5. Tap Always On Display to open the Always On Display screen.

6. To enable the Always On Display, tap On the switch at the top of the screen.

7. Tap Content to Show and select from three types of content: Clock, Calendar, or Image. Skip to step 14 if you select Calendar or step 17 if you select Image.

8. If you selected Clock, tap Clock Style to determine which type of clock displays.

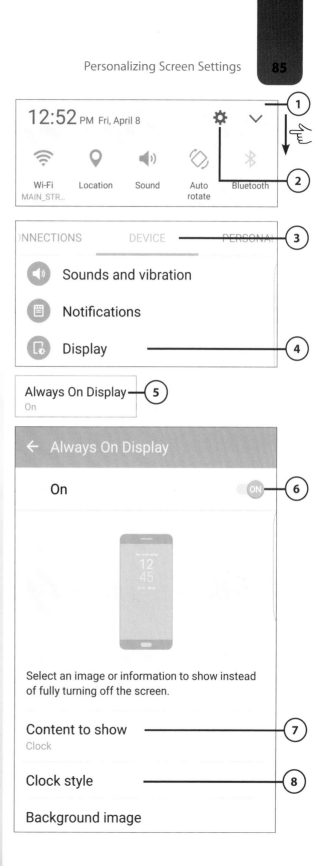

9 Tap to select the type of clock you want.

10 Tap the back arrow to return to the previous screen.

11 Tap Background Image to select a color image to display behind the clock.

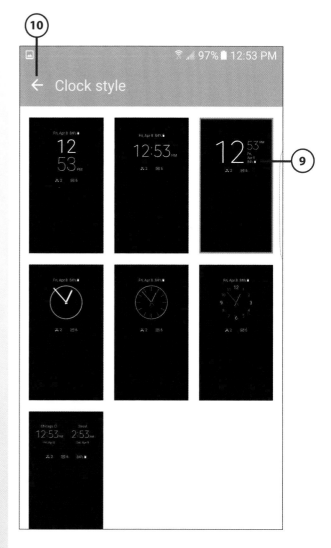

(12) Tap to select the desired background image.

(13) Tap the back arrow to return to the previous screen.

(14) If you selected Calendar, tap Calendar Style to determine which type of calendar displays.

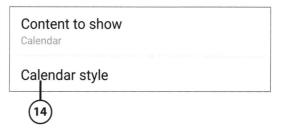

(15) Tap to select the desired calendar style.

(16) Tap the back arrow to return to the previous screen.

(17) If you selected Image, tap Image to choose the image to display.

(18) Tap to choose one of the available images.

Low Power Display

Samsung claims that, thanks to its Super AMOLED screen technology, the Always On Display uses a very small amount of battery power—less power, in fact, than constantly turning on your phone just to view the time. I like it just for that reason; it gives me an always-on clock in my pocket.

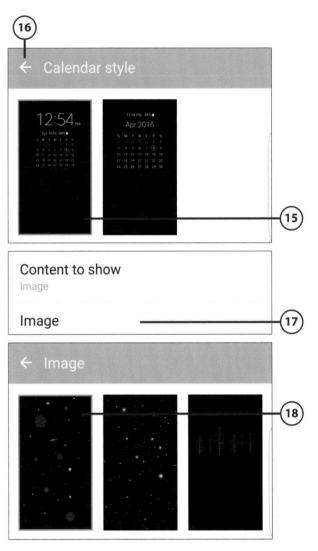

Personalizing Sounds and Notifications

Your Galaxy S7 phone can tell you a lot about what's going on. You can opt to be notified when you receive a new message or voice mail, when the phone requires some interaction from you, or when something interesting happens in a particular app.

How you choose to be notified is up to you. You can have the phone make a sound, vibrate, or display notifications on the Lock screen.

Configure Sounds and Ringtones

You can personalize your phone by choosing which sounds play for specific events:

(1) Swipe down from the top of the screen to display the notification panel.

(2) Tap Settings to display the Settings screen.

(3) Tap to select the Device tab.

(4) Tap Sounds and Vibration.

(5) Select a ringtone for when you receive incoming phone calls by tapping Ringtone.

(6) Tap to select the ringtone you want. When you tap a ringtone, you hear a preview of that sound.

(7) Tap the back arrow at the top of the screen to return to the Ringtones and Sounds screen.

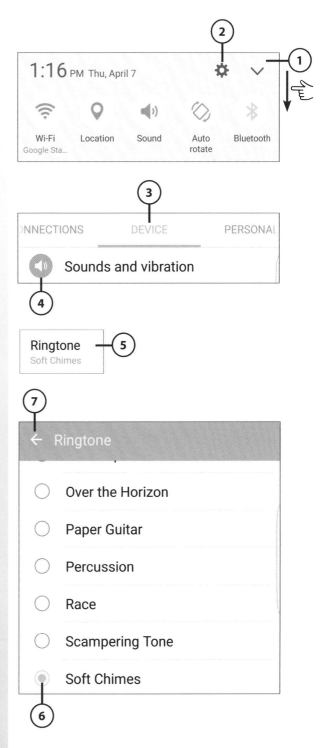

8 Change the sound that plays when you receive a notification by tapping Notification Sound.

9 Tap Default Notification Sound.

10 Tap to select the sound you want.

11 Tap the back arrow at the top of the screen to return to the Notification Sound screen.

12 Tap Messages Notifications to turn on or off message notifications.

13 By default, you receive notification of messages on your phone. To turn off message notifications, tap Off the switch at the top of the screen.

14 Tap Notification Sound and make a selection to change the sound you hear when you receive a message notification.

15 By default, your phone also vibrates when you receive a message. To turn off this vibration, tap Off the Vibrations switch.

16 Also by default, previews of new messages are displayed on your phone's Lock screen and in pop-ups when you're using the phone. To turn off these previews, tap Off the Preview Message switch.

17 Tap the back arrow at the top of the screen to return to the Notification Sound screen.

Notification sound — **8**

Set the default notification sound and notification sounds for apps such as Messages, Calendar, and Email.

Default notification sound — **9**
Pure Bell

11

← Default notification sound

○ Peanut

○ Piano

○ Pizzicato

◉ Pure Bell

10

Messages notifications — **12**
Roll

17 **14**

← Messages notifications

On   ON — **13**

Notification sound
Roll

Vibrations   ON — **15**

Preview message   ON — **16**
Show previews of new messages on the
lock screen and in pop-ups.

18 Tap Calendar Notifications to configure notifications about events on your calendar.

19 By default, you receive notification about upcoming calendar events. To turn off these notifications, tap Off the switch at the top of the screen.

20 Tap Notification Sound and make a selection to change the sound you hear when you receive a calendar notification.

21 By default, your phone also vibrates when it displays a calendar notification. To turn off this vibration, tap Off the Vibration switch.

22 Tap the back arrow at the top of the screen to return to the Notification Sound screen.

23 Tap Email Notifications to configure the notifications displayed when you receive email messages.

24 If you've set up one or more email accounts on your phone, you have the option of receiving notifications from those accounts. By default, you receive notifications when you receive email in these accounts. To turn off these notifications, tap Off the switch at the top of the screen.

25 You can set different notifications for different accounts and types of senders. Tap Priority Senders to set a sound for contacts designated priority senders.

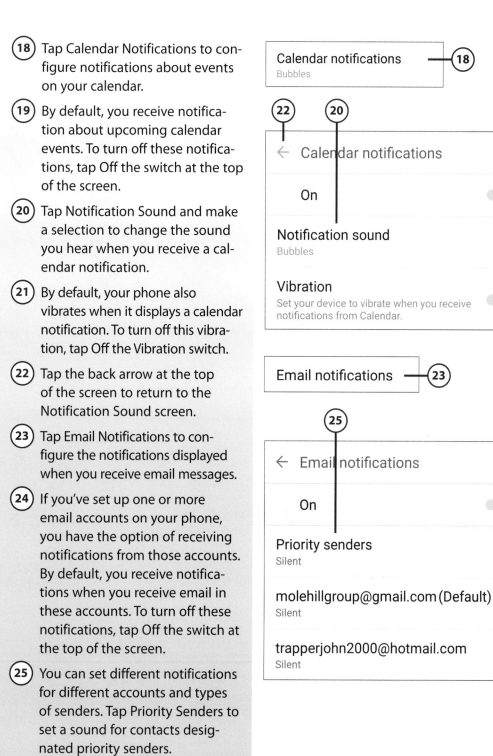

(26) Tap an account to set sounds for all messages from a given account.

(27) Tap the back arrow at the top of the screen to return to the Ringtones and Sounds screen.

Email Accounts

Learn more about setting up email accounts in Chapter 10, "Sending and Receiving Email."

(28) Tap the back arrow again to return to the Sounds and Vibration screen.

(29) Scroll down to the System section and tap Off the switch in the Touch Sounds section to turn off the sounds your phone makes when you tap the touchscreen.

(30) Tap Off the switch in the Screen Lock Sounds section to turn off the sounds your phone makes when you lock and unlock the screen.

(31) Tap off the switch in the Charging Sound section to turn off the sound your phone makes when you connect a charger.

(32) Scroll down to the Key-Tap Feedback section and tap Off the switch in the Dialing Keypad Tone section to turn off the sounds your phone makes when you tap the keypad in the Phone app.

(33) Tap Off the switch in the Keyboard Sound section to turn off the sounds your phone makes when you tap the onscreen keyboard.

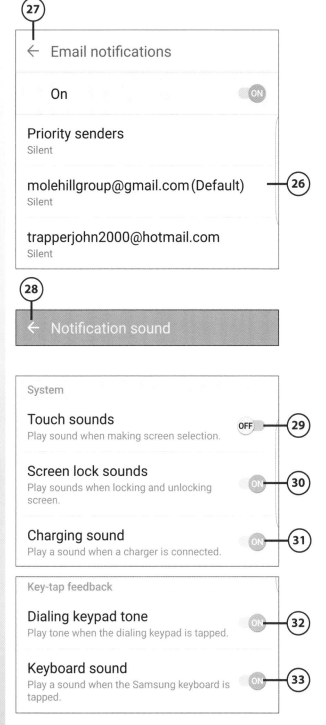

Configure Vibrations

You can also configure when and how your phone vibrates.

1. Swipe down from the top of the screen to display the notification panel.

2. Tap Settings to display the Settings screen.

3. Tap to select the Device tab.

4. Tap Sounds and Vibration to display the Sounds and Vibration screen.

5. If you don't want your phone to vibrate when ringing, tap Off the Vibrate While Ringing switch.

6. Tap Vibration Intensity to change the intensity of the phone's vibrations.

7. Adjust the sliders to the right (stronger vibration) or left (weaker vibration) for incoming calls, notifications, or overall vibration feedback.

8. Tap the back arrow at the top of the screen to return to the Sounds and Vibration screen.

9. Tap Vibration Pattern to change the pattern of the vibration.

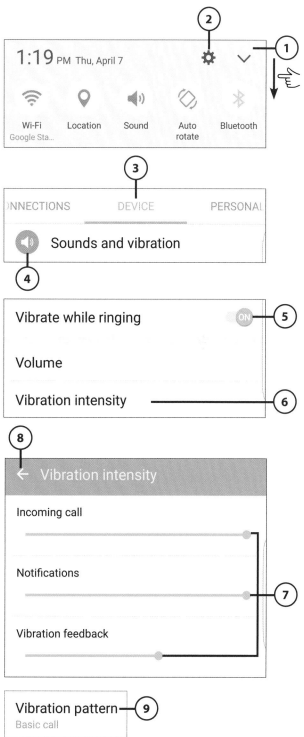

(10) Tap the vibration pattern you want—Heartbeat, Ticktock, and so forth. When you select a pattern, you feel a preview of that vibration.

(11) Tap the back arrow at the top of the screen to return to the Sounds and Vibration screen.

(12) By default, the phone vibrates slightly when you tap certain onscreen "soft keys." To turn off these vibrations, scroll to the System section and tap Off the Vibration Feedback switch.

(13) By default, you'll feel a slight vibration when you tap the onscreen keyboard. To turn off this vibration, scroll to the Key-Tap Feedback section and tap Off the Keyboard Vibration switch.

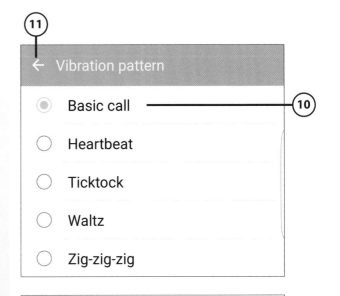

Configure Notifications

Your Galaxy S7 displays a lot of notifications. Fortunately, you have some control over the notifications you receive.

(1) Swipe down from the top of the screen to display the notification panel.

(2) Tap Settings to display the Settings screen.

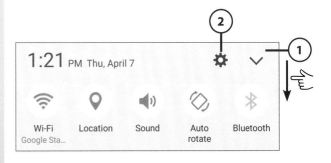

(3) Tap to select the Personal tab.

(4) Tap Lock Screen and Security.

(5) By default, notifications are displayed on the Lock screen. To hide these notifications, tap Notifications on Lock Screen.

(6) Tap Content on Lock Screen and then select to Show Content (displays detailed information), Hide Content (displays basic information), or Do Not Show Notifications (hides all notifications).

(7) By default, your phone displays notifications from all apps. If you want to show notifications only from selected apps, tap Off the All Apps switch.

(8) You can now configure notifications from each app individually. Tap On those apps from which you want to receive notifications; tap Off those apps from which you don't want to see notifications. (If the On/Off switch is shaded for a given app, you can't change its notification setting.)

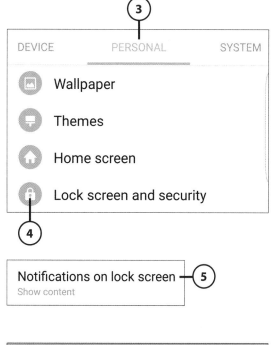

Configure the LED Light

By default, the LED indicator on the front of your phone lights when charging or when you've received incoming messages or notifications. You can opt to turn this light off if you want.

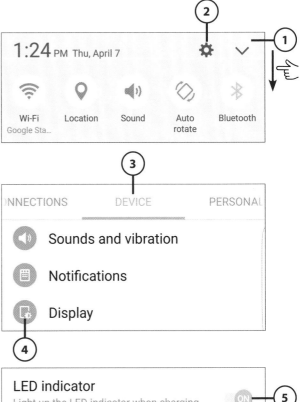

(1) Swipe down from the top of the screen to display the notification panel.

(2) Tap Settings to display the Settings screen.

(3) Tap to select the Device tab.

(4) Tap Display.

(5) Scroll down and tap Off the LED Indicator switch.

Turn on Do Not Disturb

The S7's Do Not Disturb mode silences all calls and alerts during the time period you specify. This is good for keeping your phone silent while you're sleeping or during important meetings.

(1) Swipe down from the top of the screen to display the notification panel.

(2) Tap Settings to display the Settings screen.

(3) Tap to select the Device tab.

(4) Tap Sounds and Vibration.

(5) Tap Do Not Disturb to display the Do Not Disturb screen.

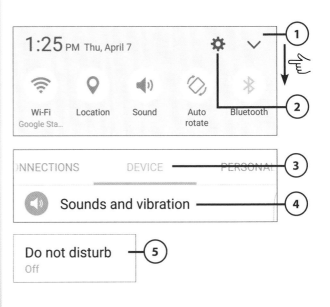

6 Tap On the Turn On Now switch to immediately activate Do Not Disturb mode.

7 Tap On the Turn On as Scheduled mode to activate Do Not Disturb according to a preset schedule.

8 Tap Days and select which days of the week you don't want to be disturbed.

9 Tap Start Time to set the time of day that Do Not Disturb is activated.

10 Tap End Time to set when Do Not Disturb ends.

11 Tap Allow Exceptions to set exceptions to the rule by selecting what things you want to be disturbed by.

12 By default, Do Not Disturb mutes all calls and alerts. Tap Alarms Only to allow alarms to sound during Do Not Disturb time.

13 Tap Custom to set custom exceptions to Do Not Disturb.

← **Do not disturb**

Silence all calls and alerts. You can allow exceptions.

Turn on now   ON — **6**

Turn on as scheduled   ON — **7**
Turn Do not disturb on and off automatically at scheduled times.

Days ———————————————— **8**
Mon, Tue, Wed, Thu, Fri, Sat, Sun

Start time ——————————————— **9**
10:00 PM

End time ——————————————— **10**
7:00 AM next day

Allow exceptions ———————————— **11**
No exceptions

← **Allow exceptions**

◉ **No exceptions**
Mute all calls and alerts.

○ **Alarms only** ——————————— **12**
Allow only alarms to sound or vibrate while Do not disturb is turned on.

○ **Custom** ——————————————— **13**
Set custom exceptions that can sound or vibrate while Do not disturb is turned on.

Making the Galaxy S7 More Accessible

Let's face it. As we get older, it often becomes more difficult to read fine print and sometimes to perform fine motor functions. And your phone packs a lot of things into its relatively small package. The result is that we sometimes have trouble seeing what's onscreen, or tapping where we need to tap.

Fortunately, there are several settings on the Galaxy S7/S7 edge that can make life easier for us. These include accessibility options as well as a special Easy Mode that simplifies the phone's operation.

Working with Easy Mode

Today's smartphones can do so many things that it's easy to get confused. With so many options available, just what things should you tap—and which should you ignore?

If you have difficulty operating your phone, or if you find that the default screen icons are just too small to see or use comfortably, consider switching to Easy Mode. This mode presents a different screen layout and experience than the default mode.

Switch to Easy Mode

You can easily switch back and forth between Easy Mode and your phone's default mode.

1. Swipe down from the top of the screen to display the notification panel.

2. Tap Settings to display the Settings screen.

3. Tap to select the Personal tab.

4. Tap Easy Mode to display the Easy Mode screen.

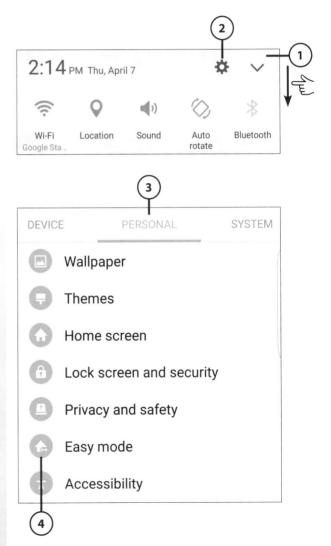

5 Tap to select Easy Mode.

6 Scroll down to the Easy Applications section and tap On each of the apps you want to display in Easy Mode. You can choose to display the Camera, Email, Gallery, Internet, Messages, Phone, and Calendar. Select only those you think you'll use regularly.

7 Tap Done. Your phone resets itself in Easy Mode.

Back to Normal
To switch back to standard mode, select Settings, Personal, Easy Mode and then tap to select Standard Mode.

○ Standard mode

◉ Easy mode

5   **7**

CANCEL   DONE

Use your device more easily with a simpler Home screen layout and straightforward app interactions. Select apps below to view in simpler layouts. The large font size will be applied throughout the device.

Easy applications

Camera   ON

@ Email   ON

Gallery   ON

Internet   ON   **6**

Messages   ON

Phone   ON

THU
7 Calendar   ON

Use Easy Mode

Easy Mode displays fewer icons per screen, but the icons are larger. You see icons only for those apps you selected during the configuration process. In addition, all the onscreen text is larger, which makes it easier to see for anyone with vision difficulties.

1. Swipe left or right to view additional screens.

2. Tap any icon to launch that application.

3. Remove an application from the screen by tapping Edit.

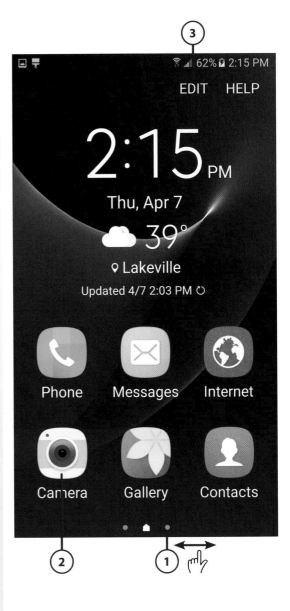

4 Tap the minus sign to hide that app from the Easy Mode screen.

5 Tap Done when you're done hiding icons.

6 View all the apps installed on your phone, even if they're hidden in Easy Mode, by tapping More Apps.

7 Add an icon for another app to the Easy Mode screen by tapping one of the + icons.

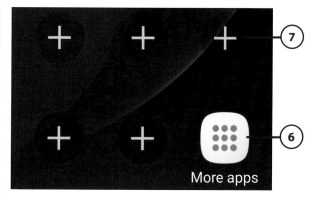

(8) Tap the app you want to add and an icon for that app is added to the Easy Mode screen.

Changing Screen Fonts and Sizes

If you find the onscreen text on your Galaxy S7 or S7 edge difficult to read, you can change it. Samsung enables you to change both the font and the font size displayed for icon labels, screen headings, and the like.

Select Screen Fonts and Sizes

(1) Swipe down from the top of the screen to display the notification panel.

(2) Tap Settings to display the Settings screen.

(3) Tap to select the Device tab.

(4) Tap Display to display the Display screen.

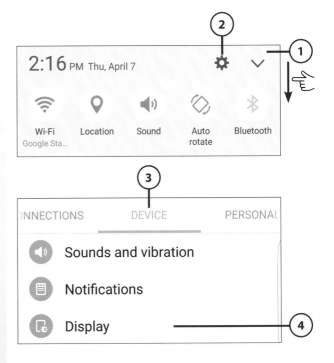

5 Tap Font.

6 Drag the Font Size slider to the left (smaller) or right (larger) to change the font size.

7 In the Font Style section, tap the name of a font to switch to that font.

8 Tap Default to return to Samsung's default font.

9 Tap Done.

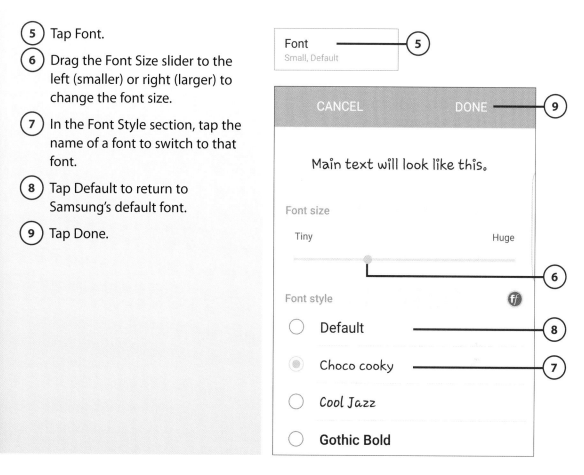

Font
Small, Default — **5**

CANCEL   DONE — **9**

Main text will look like this.

Font size

Tiny   Huge

— **6**

Font style

○ Default — **8**

◉ Choco cooky — **7**

○ Cool Jazz

○ Gothic Bold

Using Voice Feedback

If you have trouble seeing what's on the screen, you can enable Samsung's Voice Assistant, which provides voice feedback when you're using your phone.

Enable the Voice Assistant

The S7's Voice Assistant feature reads aloud whatever is selected on the phone's screen. When activated, your phone reads whatever is under your finger when you tap.

1. Swipe down from the top of the screen to display the notification panel.

2. Tap Settings to display the Settings screen.

3. Tap to select the Personal tab.

4. Tap Accessibility to display the Accessibility screen.

5. Tap Vision to display the Vision screen.

6. Tap Voice Assistant.

7. Tap On the switch at the top of the screen.

Tutorial

The first time you activate the Voice Assistant, you're prompted to okay its operation and then you're led through an interactive tutorial on how to use the feature.

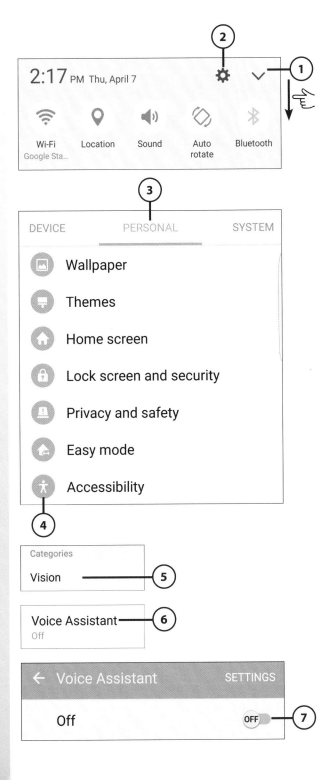

Use the Voice Assistant

With the Voice Assistant is activated, any item you tap onscreen generates a voice telling you what that item is—and, in some instances, information about that item. For example, if you tap the Email icon when you have new messages waiting, the Voice Assistant tells you how many new messages you have. You can also tap an open item to have the Voice Assistant read the content of a message or document.

Because tapping an item tells you about it, with Voice Assistant activated you have to double-tap apps to open them or perform specific operations. In fact, most touch gestures change when you're using the Voice Assistant, as indicated in the following table.

Gesture	Action
Tap	Reads aloud the item under your finger.
Double-tap	Opens the selected item.
Double-tap and hold	Moves an item across the screen or accesses an available option.
Swipe left	Moves to previous item.
Swipe right	Moves to next item.
Swipe up or down	Uses the most recent menu item or changes its settings. In text selection mode, moves the cursor backward or forward to select text.
Swipe left then right (in one motion)	Scrolls up the screen.
Swipe right then left (in one motion)	Scrolls down the screen.
Swipe up then down (in one motion)	Move to the first item on the screen.
Swipe down then up (in one motion)	Move to the last item on the screen.

Explore the Screen

To explore the items on the screen in Voice Assistant mode, simply place your finger on the screen and then move it around.

Configuring Visibility Options

In addition to the Voice Assistant, there are several other options you can configure to make it easier to operate your phone if you have vision problems. These are detailed in the following table.

Option	Description
Text-to-Speech Options	Adjusts the speed of Samsung's text-to-speech engine.
Accessibility Shortcut	Displays accessibility options when you hold down the Power key or tap and hold the screen with two fingers.
Voice Label	Record voice labels you can place on various items around your house, and have your phone read them back to you.
Font Size	Changes the size of onscreen fonts from Tiny to Huge.
High Contrast Fonts	Adjusts the color and outline of fonts to provide more contrast with the background.
High Contrast Keyboard	Adjusts the size and changes the color of the onscreen keyboard.
Show Button Shapes	Displays a shaded background around onscreen buttons to make them more visible.
Magnifier Window	Displays a small window that magnifies the selected area of the screen. (Tap and drag to move the magnification window around the screen.)
Magnification Gestures	Zooms into or out of areas of the screen when you triple-tap the screen.
Grayscale	Changes the phone's display from color to grayscale.
Negative Colors	Reverses the onscreen colors. (White background changes to black; black text changes to white.)
Color Adjustment	Enables adjustment of onscreen colors for better viewing.

Voice Label

The Voice Label feature works in conjunction with special labels you can purchase from Samsung. You use your phone to record your voice saying what the label is affixed to; then you place the label on that item. Later, you can hover your phone over the item and its label to use your phone's NFC technology to "read" the label to you. It's a great way for people with vision impairment to better get around—and locate items in—their homes.

Enable Visibility Options

All visibility options are accessed via the Visibility screen.

1. Swipe down from the top of the screen to display the notification panel.

2. Tap Settings to display the Settings screen.

3. Tap to select the Personal tab.

4. Tap Accessibility.

5. Tap Vision to display the Vision screen.

2:18 PM Thu, April 7

Wi-Fi   Location   Sound   Auto   Bluetooth
Google Sta...   rotate

DEVICE   PERSONAL   SYSTEM

Wallpaper

Themes

Home screen

Lock screen and security

Privacy and safety

Easy mode

Accessibility

Categories

Vision

Enable those options you want to use.

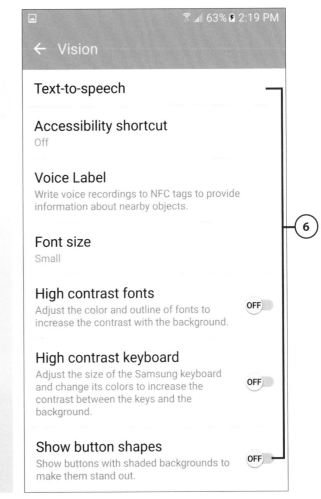

Configuring Hearing Options

Your Samsung S7 or S7 edge offers several options of use if you have impaired hearing. These are detailed in the following table.

Option	Description
Sound Detectors	Vibrates the phone when a baby cries or the doorbell rings.
Flash Notification	Flashes the camera's LED flash when you receive notifications or alarms.
Turn Off All Sounds	Turns off all of the phone's sounds.

Option	Description
Hearing Aids	Adjusts the phone's sound quality to work better with hearing aids.
Samsung Subtitles	Enables and configures Samsung's subtitle function.
Google Subtitles	Enables and configures Google's subtitle function, built into the Android operating system.
Left and Right Sound Balance	Adjusts the left and right audio balance.
Mono Audio	Switch from stereo to mono audio for when you are using a single earphone.

Enable Hearing Options

All hearing options are configured on the Hearing screen.

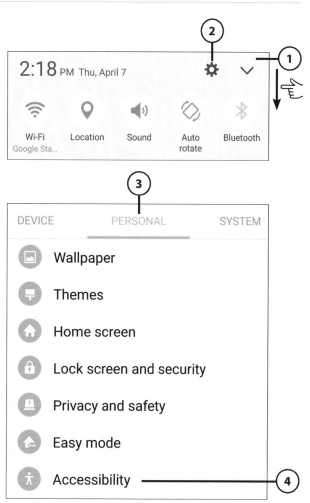

(1) Swipe down from the top of the screen to display the notification panel.

(2) Tap Settings to display the Settings screen.

(3) Tap to select Personal.

(4) Tap Accessibility.

5 Tap Hearing to display the Hearing screen.

6 Tap to enable or configure the options you want.

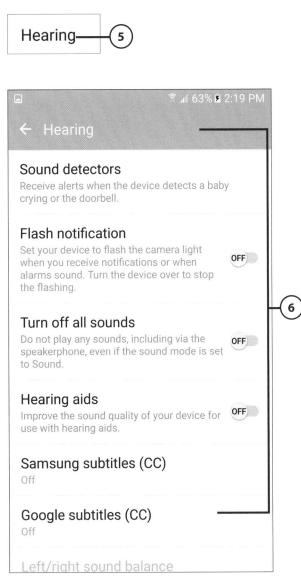

Option	Description
Universal Switch	Create custom switches to interact with your phone and select onscreen items.
Assistant Menu	Display an Assistant icon that provides one-handed access to important system operations. (Discussed later in this chapter.)
Easy Screen Turn On	Enables you to wake up your phone by moving your hand above the screen.
Press and Hold Delay	Adjusts the delay for when you press and hold the screen.
Interaction Control	Customizes the way you interact with apps and settings, by blocking or unblocking areas of the screen, turning off auto rotate, and only showing app notifications on the notification panel and status bar.

Accidental Activation

If you find yourself accidentally activating onscreen items because you press the screen too long, set the Press and Hold Delay to Long instead of the default Medium.

Enable Dexterity and Interaction Options

All of these options are enabled on the Dexterity and Interaction screen.

1. Swipe down from the top of the screen to display the notification panel.

2. Tap Settings to display the Settings screen.

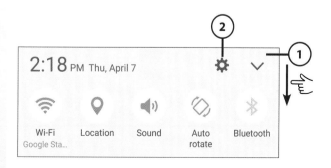

(**3**) Tap to select the Personal tab.

(**4**) Tap Accessibility.

(**5**) Tap Dexterity and Interaction to display the Dexterity and Interaction screen.

(**6**) Tap to enable or configure the options you want (not shown).

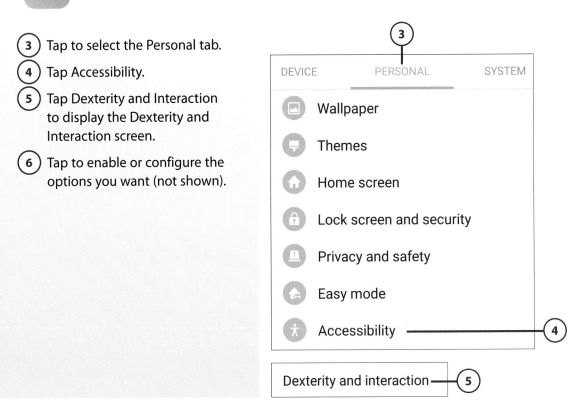

Working with the Assistant Menu

Your Samsung S7 or S7 edge can be configured to display an Assistant menu, in the form of a round button that floats at the bottom right of every screen. When tapped, this button displays large icon shortcuts to key phone operations. The Assistant menu enables you to operate your phone with one hand.

Enable the Assistant Menu

The Assistant menu is disabled by default. When you enable the menu, there are several settings you can configure.

(**1**) Swipe down from the top of the screen to display the notification panel.

(**2**) Tap Settings to display the Settings screen.

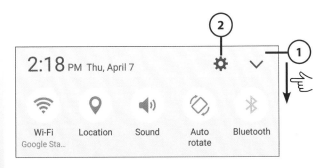

(3) Tap to select the Personal tab.

(4) Tap Accessibility.

(5) Tap Dexterity and Interaction to display the Dexterity and Interaction screen.

(6) Tap Assistant Menu to display the Assistant Menu screen.

(7) Tap On the switch at the top of the screen.

(8) By default, the Assistant icon appears at the bottom right of the screen. To switch it to the left side, tap Dominant Hand and then select Left.

(9) To change or rearrange the items on the Assistant menu, tap Edit and then make your changes.

(10) To include contextual menu options for selected applications in the Assistant menu, tap Assistant Plus and then toggle on those apps you want.

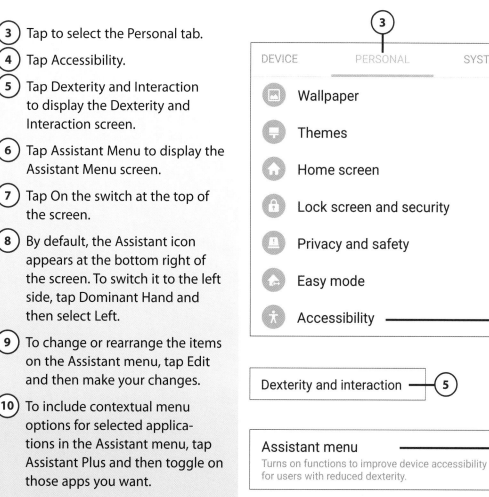

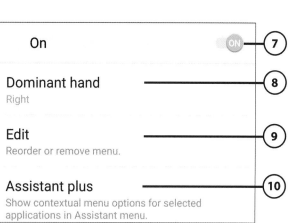

Use the Assistant Menu

When activated, the Assistant icon appears at one side at the bottom of your phone's screen.

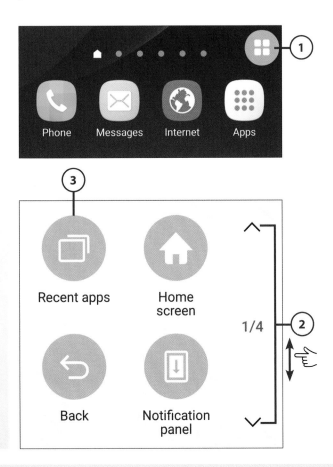

1. Tap the Assistant icon to display the Assistant panel.

2. Swipe up or down to see more items.

3. Tap to launch an item.

>>>Go Further

ONE-HANDED OPERATION

Given the large screen of the Galaxy S7 (and even larger screen of the S7 edge), you may have trouble operating the phone with one hand. If you like to hold the phone in the palm of your hand and then tap onscreen elements with your thumb, the screen may simply be too large to do this comfortably or accurately.

Fortunately, you can configure the S7/S7 edge for better one-handed operation by effectively shrinking the screen. To do this, display the Settings screen, select the Device tab, and tap Advanced Features. From the Advanced Features screen, tap One-Handed Operation. You can now select to Reduce Screen Size (when you tap the Home key three times) and/or reduce the size of the onscreen keyboard for One-Handed Input. These two settings can make your phone much more usable!

This chapter shows you how to connect your Samsung smartphone to the Internet. Topics include the following:

→ How Your Galaxy S7 Connects
→ Connecting to the Internet via Wi-Fi
→ Connecting to the Internet via Cellular
→ Monitoring and Managing Your Data Usage
→ Turning Your Phone into a Mobile Hotspot

Connecting to the Internet and Cellular Networks

Without an Internet connection, your smartphone is just an expensive phone. You need to connect to the Internet to play streaming music and videos, browse Facebook and other social networks, send and receive email, participate in video chats, and use many apps and games.

How Your Galaxy S7 Connects

Your Samsung S7 or S7 edge can connect to the Internet in two different ways. If there's a Wi-Fi network or hotspot handy, it can connect via Wi-Fi. If there's no Wi-Fi network nearby (such as when you're driving down the interstate), it can connect to the Internet via the same cellular network you use for voice calls and text messages.

By default, your phone attempts to connect via Wi-Fi if a Wi-Fi network or hotspot is available; that's because you incur no data charges when using Wi-Fi. If there's no Wi-Fi connection, your phone uses your cellular network to connect to the Internet—but it switches back to Wi-Fi when a network becomes available.

Cellular Networks

Your phone is always connected to your carrier's cellular network, which handles all your voice calls and text messages—the one you pay AT&T, Sprint, T-Mobile, Verizon, or other carrier each month to use.

Chances are that your carrier charges you in two or more stages. First, you pay for the basic voice service, typically a flat dollar amount per month. Some carriers include text messaging in this fee; others charge separately for a limited or unlimited number of texts.

Then there's what your carrier calls the data plan. This refers to digital data downloaded from the Internet to your phone via the cellular network. (It also includes data you upload to the Internet, in the form of email messages and files you send.)

Most U.S. carriers sell you a certain amount of data (measured in gigabytes, or GB) per month, for a set fee. If you use more than the set amount of data, you're charged extra—sometimes a lot extra. For this reason, you want to limit the amount of Internet usage over your cellular network. When given the choice, you should always opt to connect to the Internet over Wi-Fi instead of cellular, because your phone carrier doesn't have anything to do with what you do when you're connected to Wi-Fi.

Wi-Fi Networks

A Wi-Fi network is much different from a cellular network. Wi-Fi is a type of wireless protocol designed to carry digital data only, not voice calls, and most Wi-Fi networks operate over a limited distance. Thus you might have a Wi-Fi network that covers all the rooms in your house, but doesn't stretch to your neighbor's house. In a larger building, such as a hotel or office building, the network size is bigger thanks to the use of multiple wireless routers that are linked together.

Wi-Fi

Wi-Fi (short for *Wireless Fidelity*) is the consumer-friendly name for the IEEE 802.11 wireless networking standard. Most of today's wireless networks are Wi-Fi networks and use Wi-Fi-certified products.

Wi-Fi networks use a hub-and-spoke configuration where each Wi-Fi-enabled device connects to a central hub or router. Devices do not connect directly to each other; the signal from a given device goes to the router first, and is then routed to other connected devices.

The Wi-Fi router is also connected to the Internet, and routes the Internet signal to all devices connected to the network. So when your smartphone connects to the Internet over your home network, it's actually connecting to your Wi-Fi router first, which in turn connects to the Internet.

(Public Wi-Fi hotspots work the same way. Your phone connects to the hotspot's router and the router connects to the Internet.)

The nice thing about connecting to the Internet via Wi-Fi (instead of cellular) is you don't pay for the data transmitted. Many public Wi-Fi hotspots, like you find at Starbucks and McDonald's, are free. Those that do charge (like you find at some hotels) typically charge you a flat rate, no matter how much data you use. And, of course, it doesn't cost anything to connect to your home Wi-Fi network— save for the monthly bill you pay to your Internet service provider.

Connecting to the Internet via Wi-Fi

If you have a Wi-Fi network or hotspot available, this is how you want to connect to the Internet. This could be the Wi-Fi network in your home or office, or a Wi-Fi hotspot at a local retailer, hotel, or restaurant.

Disable and Re-Enable Wi-Fi

Your phone's Wi-Fi functionality is turned on by default. You can manually turn off Wi-Fi (to conserve battery power) and turn it back on.

1. Swipe down from the top of the screen to display the Notification panel.

2. Tap off the Wi-Fi icon. This disables your phone's Wi-Fi functionality. (The icon dims when off, and lights when on.)

3. Re-enable Wi-Fi functionality by tapping the icon again.

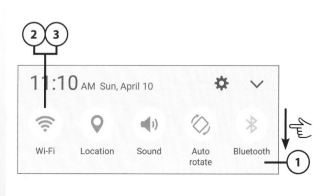

Connect to a New Wi-Fi Network

When your phone is near an active Wi-Fi network or hotspot, you see a "not connected" icon in the status bar. (And if you're on the Lock screen, you see a notification about "Wi-Fi networks available.") You choose which Wi-Fi network to connect to, and then you connect to it.

1. Swipe down from the top of the screen to display the notification panel.

2. Tap the Wi-Fi Networks Available notification *or…*

3. Tap and hold the Wi-Fi icon.

4. You now see the Wi-Fi screen, with available Wi-Fi networks listed in descending order of signal strength. Open networks (those that don't require a password) have a basic icon, whereas private networks that do require a password have a lock on the icon. Tap the network to which you want to connect.

5. If you're connecting to a public network, you see a connection panel for that network, along with information about security on that network. Tap Connect to connect to the network.

6. If you're connecting to a private network, you see a panel for that network and the onscreen keyboard appears. Use the onscreen keyboard to enter the network's password into the Password box. (Tap Show Password if you want to see the actual characters as you type; otherwise, you just see dots.)

7. Tap Connect. You're now connected to the network and can start using the Internet.

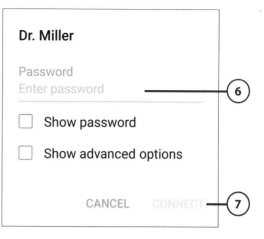

Switching Networks

If multiple Wi-Fi networks are nearby, you may accidentally connect to the wrong one. To switch from one wireless network to another, open the Wi-Fi screen and then tap a different network to connect.

>>>Go Further
SIGNING IN

Private Wi-Fi networks are like the one you have in your home. Private networks require you to enter a password (sometimes called an SSID, for Service Set Identifier) to access the network. This password is typically created when you first set up your wireless router, or provided by the network host if you're connecting to an office network.

Public Wi-Fi networks do not require a password to connect. However, some public hotspots do require you to manually sign in. In most instances, your phone automatically displays a sign-in screen for that network. In other cases, you have to manually launch the web browser and try to open any web page; the host's sign in page is then displayed instead of the normal web page, and you can sign in from there.

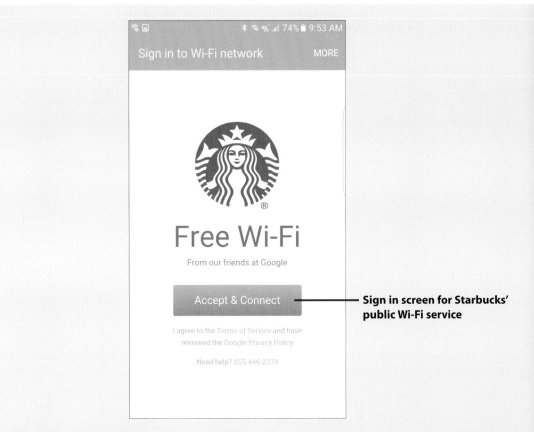

Sign in screen for Starbucks' public Wi-Fi service

Some sign-in pages ask you to agree to the host's terms of service as to how you'll use the connection. Others just want you to click the "sign in" button. Whatever the case, do what's asked of you so you can sign in and get started on the Internet.

Connect to a Wi-Fi Network You've Used Before

When you're in range of a Wi-Fi network that you've connected to before, there's nothing you have to do. Because your phone remembers the networks you've connected to, your phone automatically connects to this familiar network.

Wi-Fi Direct

Your Galaxy S7 enables you to connect directly to other devices that feature Wi-Fi Direct functionality, such as other Samsung smartphones and some wireless storage devices. To connect directly to another device in this fashion, open the Wi-Fi page, tap Wi-Fi Connect and then follow the on-screen instructions to locate and connect to the other device.

It's Not All Good

Connection Problems

Not all Internet connections are always good. Sometimes the Wi-Fi network or hotspot you connect to has problems, which can keep you from connecting to the Internet.

For example, the Wi-Fi hotspot I use at one of my local coffeehouses has a tendency to go missing every few hours. That is, I'll be connected one minute and the next minute find that I'm not connected—and that the hotspot itself is no longer visible on my phone. Normally I wait a minute or two, the hotspot reappears, and my phone reconnects. The best I can figure is that the coffeehouse's Wi-Fi router has rebooted, for some reason, which kicks everyone using it off until it powers back on.

You can also run into similar connection problems with your home Wi-Fi network. In many cases, the problem corrects itself automatically within a few minutes. If the problem persists, try turning off your phone's Wi-Fi and then turning it back on. This forces your phone to establish a new connection to the wireless network or hotspot, which often fixes the problem.

>>>Go Further

ACTIVATING AIRPLANE MODE

If you fly, you know the drill about turning off all your devices during takeoff and landing. After you're in the air, most airlines let you connect to their in-flight Wi-Fi service—often for a cost. But you can also use your phone during flight with all connectivity turned off. This way you can still listen to downloaded music, watch downloaded videos, or read downloaded eBooks while you're in-flight.

The best and easiest way to do this is to enable your phone's Airplane mode. To switch to Airplane mode, swipe down from the top of the screen, swipe to the right and tap to activate Airplane Mode. When prompted, tap Turn On. This turns off all connectivity for voice calls, texts, and data/Internet. You can turn off Airplane mode when you land to resume normal operation.

Connecting to the Internet via Cellular

Your Samsung smartphone automatically connects to the cellular network of your mobile phone carrier. (When you have a network connection available, of course.) AT&T has its own cellular network, as do Sprint, T-Mobile, Verizon, and other carriers. The networks are not interchangeable; if you're a Verizon user, for example, you can't connect your phone to AT&T's network. (Verizon users can, of course, make phone calls to AT&T subscribers; you just can't connect to their network.)

When you purchased your new Galaxy S7 or S7 edge, your mobile carrier or retailer programmed your phone to connect to your carrier's network. This involved registering your phone number and other technical stuff. The end result is that you were handed a working phone, capable of making and receiving phone calls right out of the box.

As part of the purchase process, you had to sign up for your mobile service, and probably for some sort of data plan. It's the data plan that lets you connect to the Internet through your mobile carrier. If you didn't sign up for a data plan, you can't connect to the Internet via AT&T or T-Mobile or whomever; instead, you can only connect via Wi-Fi.

While connecting to the Internet via your mobile carrier can be costly (you only pay for a certain amount of data use; anything beyond that costs extra), it's necessary if you want to access the Internet when there are no Wi-Fi networks or hotspots nearby. If you're driving down the interstate in your car, for example, you need to connect to the Internet via your mobile carrier. If you're out in a park or field or in the middle of a lake, far away from any big buildings, you need to connect to the Internet via your mobile carrier. If you're visiting a friend and don't want to or can't connect to their home wireless network, you need to connect to the Internet via your mobile carrier.

The speed of your Internet connection depends on the type of data service offered by your mobile carrier. Older second generation (2G) networks, sometimes called EDGE networks, are extremely slow, much like old-fashioned dial-up phone connections—not nearly fast enough to transmit streaming video or audio. Third-generation (3G) networks are considerably faster, fast enough for streaming audio and video, but they still feel sluggish at times. Newer fourth-generation (4G) networks, sometimes dubbed LTE networks, are much, much faster—ideal for anything you need to stream or send over the Internet. (The following table details typical connection speeds for each type of mobile network.)

Type of Network	Typical Download Speed (in megabits per second)
1G (AMPS)	Up to 14.4 kbps
2G (EDGE)	Up to 0.2 Mbps
3G (HSPA)	Up to 14.4 Mbps
4G (LTE)	100 Mbps to 300 Mbps

Different mobile carriers offer different data networks in different parts of the country. If you live in a big city, chances are your carrier offers 4G coverage. If you're in a smaller town or in the suburbs, you might have 4G coverage or you may be in a 3G zone. If you're out in the sticks, it's possible your carrier only offers 2G networking. Check your carrier's coverage maps to see where you stand.

The type of network you're connected to is displayed in the S7's status bar at the top of the screen. If you see you're connected to a slower 2G network, you might want to refrain from doing any data-intensive tasks, such as watching movies or listening to Pandora. (Personally, I find 2G networks too slow to even download radar weather maps!)

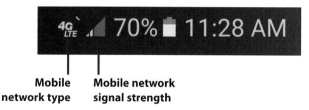

Mobile network type   **Mobile network signal strength**

You don't have to do anything to connect your phone to your carrier's mobile network; it connects automatically whenever you're in range of a signal. However, your Galaxy S7 is designed by default to use Wi-Fi to connect to the Internet. So if there's a Wi-Fi network nearby your phone attempts to connect to it for Internet usage, even if it's already connected to your mobile carrier for voice calls.

Manually Connect to a Data Network

If, for whatever reason, you want to use your mobile carrier for Internet even when there are Wi-Fi networks available, you have to manually turn off your phone's Wi-Fi.

1. Swipe down from the top of the screen to display the notification panel.

2. Tap off the Wi-Fi icon. Your phone now turns off its Wi-Fi (and thus disconnects from any Wi-Fi networks) and switches to your carrier's mobile data network.

3. To re-enable Wi-Fi, tap on the Wi-Fi icon.

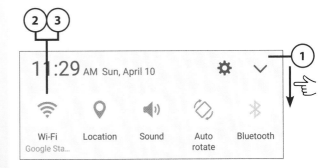

Enable Smart Network Switching

Sometimes you can be connected to a Wi-Fi network that has a poor or unstable connection to the Internet. In this instance, you're better off disconnecting from that Wi-Fi network and using your mobile carrier's data network until the connection improves. You can do this automatically by enabling your phone's smart network switching.

1. Swipe down from the top of the screen to display the notification panel.

2. Tap and hold the Wi-Fi icon. This displays the Wi-Fi screen.

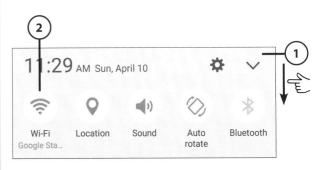

3 Tap More at the top of the screen.

4 Tap Smart Network Switch to display the Smart Network Switch panel.

5 Tap On. Your phone automatically switches to your carrier's data network when it senses a poor Internet connection via Wi-Fi.

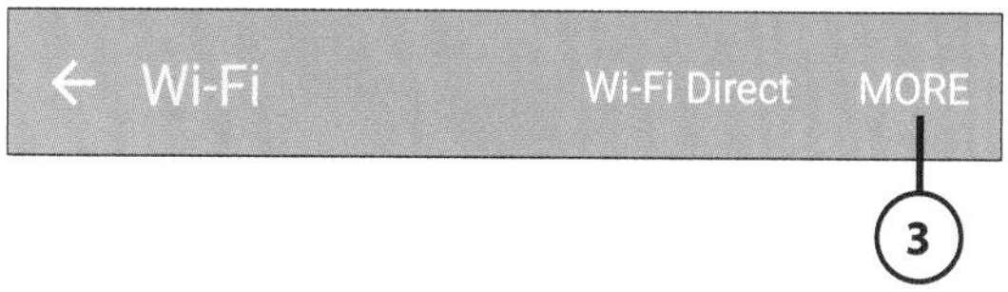

← Wi-Fi   Wi-Fi Direct   MORE

3

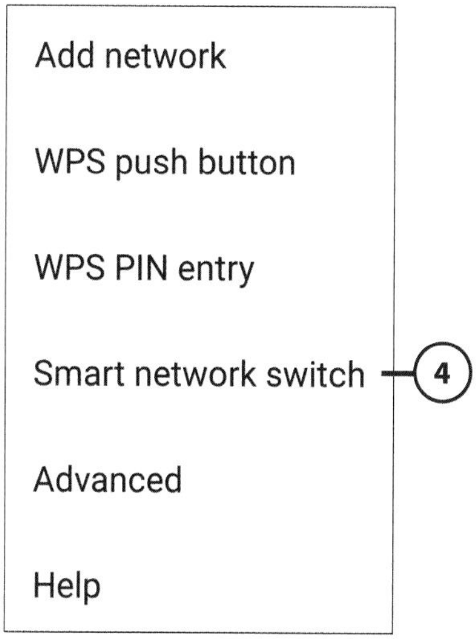

Add network

WPS push button

WPS PIN entry

Smart network switch ─ **4**

Advanced

Help

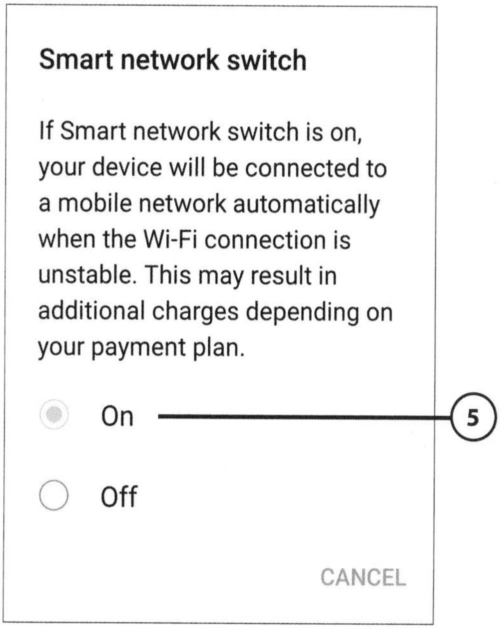

Smart network switch

If Smart network switch is on, your device will be connected to a mobile network automatically when the Wi-Fi connection is unstable. This may result in additional charges depending on your payment plan.

◉ On ──────────── **5**

○ Off

CANCEL

Monitoring and Managing Your Data Usage

Given the restrictions most carriers place on their mobile data plans, it pays to keep track of just how much data you're using each month. This way you'll know when you're nearing your plan limits, and can adjust your usage accordingly.

Monitor How Much Data You've Used

Your phone keeps track of how much data you upload and download via your mobile carrier.

1. Swipe down from the top of the screen to display the notification panel.

2. Tap Settings to display the Settings page.

3. Tap to select the Connections tab.

4. Tap Data Usage.

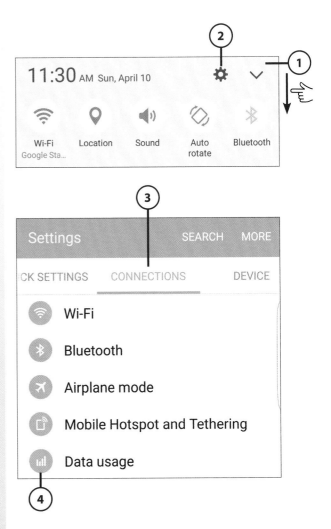

5 The graph on this page displays data usage by day. Your total data usage for this month's plan is displayed above the graph.

6 Scroll down the screen to see data usage by application. This shows you which apps are using the most data bandwidth.

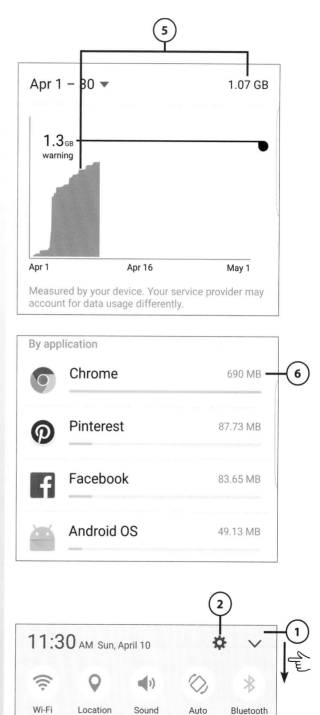

5

Apr 1 – 30 ▼   1.07 GB

1.3 GB
warning

Apr 1   Apr 16   May 1

Measured by your device. Your service provider may account for data usage differently.

By application

Chrome   690 MB — **6**

Pinterest   87.73 MB

Facebook   83.65 MB

Android OS   49.13 MB

Set Data Usage Alert Level

To avoid going over your data plan limits, you might want to set an alert that notifies you when your usage reaches a level you select.

1 Swipe down from the top of the screen to display the notification panel.

2 Tap Settings to display the Settings page.

11:30 AM Sun, April 10   ✿   ∨   **1**

2

Wi-Fi   Location   Sound   Auto   Bluetooth
Google Sta...   rotate

3 Tap to select the Connections tab.

4 Tap Data Usage.

5 Tap to drag the usage level line to a specific level. You will now receive an alert when your data usage reaches this level.

3

CK SETTINGS	CONNECTIONS	DEVICE

Wi-Fi

Bluetooth

Airplane mode

Mobile Hotspot and Tethering

Data usage

4

7.5 GB
warning   **5**

Apr 1   Apr 16   May 1

Limit Data Usage

If warning you about your usage level isn't enough, you can configure your Galaxy S7 to turn off data usage when you reach your plan's limit. With the Limit Data Usage option turned on, your phone disables mobile data functionality when a preset level (typically the top end of your data usage plan) is reached.

1 Swipe down from the top of the screen to display the notification panel.

2 Tap Settings to display the Settings page.

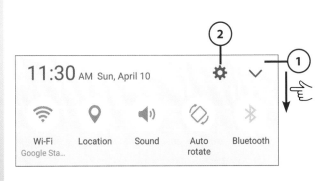

2

1

11:30 AM Sun, April 10

Wi-Fi   Location   Sound   Auto rotate   Bluetooth
Google Sta...

3 Tap to select the Connections panel.

4 Tap Data Usage.

5 Tap On the Set Mobile Data Limit switch.

6 Tap to drag the red limit line to a specific level. Your phone's data functionality is disabled when your usage reaches this level.

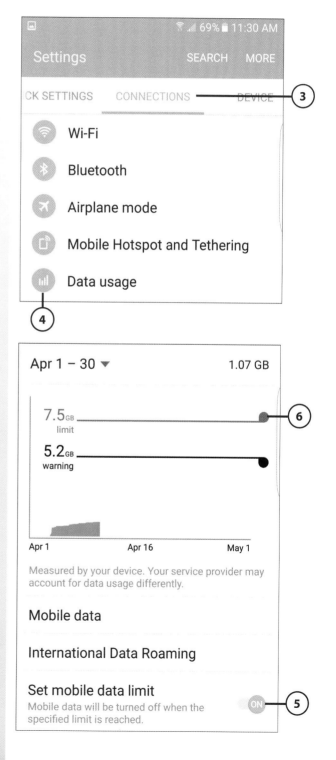

Turning Your Phone into a Mobile Hotspot

Sometimes you're in a location where there is no Wi-Fi available, but you want to connect your computer or tablet to the Internet. Well, if you have your Samsung S7 or S7 edge with you, and you have a strong connection to your mobile data network, you can connect your computer or tablet to your phone, wirelessly, to share that data connection.

In effect, this turns your phone into a mobile Wi-Fi hotspot. Your phone connects to the Internet via your mobile data network, then your other devices connect to your phone via Wi-Fi.

It's Not All Good

Data Tethering Concerns

To share your phone's data connection, your carrier's data plan needs to include what they call *data tethering*. Some carriers let you do this at no charge, as part of the basic plan; others charge extra for tethering functionality. Make sure you can use tethering on your phone before you try to use this feature.

Also, know that when you use your smartphone as a mobile Wi-Fi hotspot for other devices, you typically end up using a lot of data bandwidth. All that data counts against the limits on your data plan. You should avoid heavy-duty operations with your computer or tablet, such as watching movies or downloading big files, when you're using your phone in this fashion.

Enable a Mobile Hotspot

Before you turn your phone into a mobile hotspot, make sure you have a strong mobile signal. (A 4G connection is preferable to 3G; 2G is probably not usable in this situation.) You can then enable the mobile hotspot function.

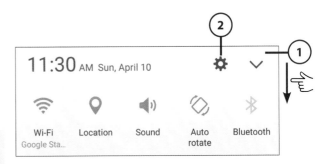

1. Swipe down from the top of the screen to display the notification panel.

2. Tap Settings to display the Settings screen.

(3) Tap to select the Connections tab.

(4) Tap Mobile Hotspot and Tethering.

(5) Tap Mobile Hotspot to display the Mobile Hotspot screen.

(6) Tap On the switch at the top of the screen.

(7) The Mobile Hotspot screen displays the name of and password for the new network. Keep this screen open or write down the name and password; you'll need them to log onto the mobile hotspot from another device.

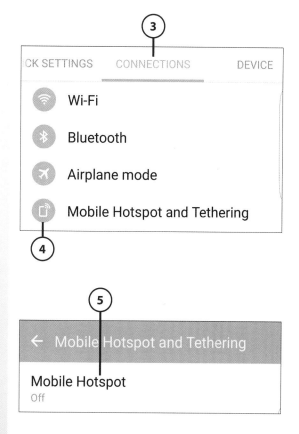

(3)

CK SETTINGS   CONNECTIONS   DEVICE

Wi-Fi

Bluetooth

Airplane mode

Mobile Hotspot and Tethering

(4)

(5)

← Mobile Hotspot and Tethering

Mobile Hotspot
Off

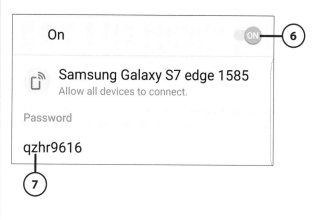

On   ON — (6)

Samsung Galaxy S7 edge 1585
Allow all devices to connect.

Password

qzhr9616

(7)

Connect Another Device to Your Phone via Wi-Fi

You can connect your computer or tablet to your phone via Wi-Fi.

1. On your other device, make sure that Wi-Fi is enabled and then display the list of available networks.

2. Select your smartphone from the list of devices. (The device name for your phone was displayed on the Mobile Hotspot screen.)

3. When prompted to enter the network security key or password, enter the password displayed on your phone's Mobile Hotspot screen. You should now be connected and using your phone's data connection.

Tether Another Device to Your Phone

You can also connect your computer or tablet to your phone via USB to share your phone's Internet connection. Samsung calls this *data tethering*. (Yes, that's the same phrase your carrier uses for any sharing of mobile data.)

1. Swipe down from the top of the screen to display the notification panel.

2. Tap Settings to display the Settings screen.

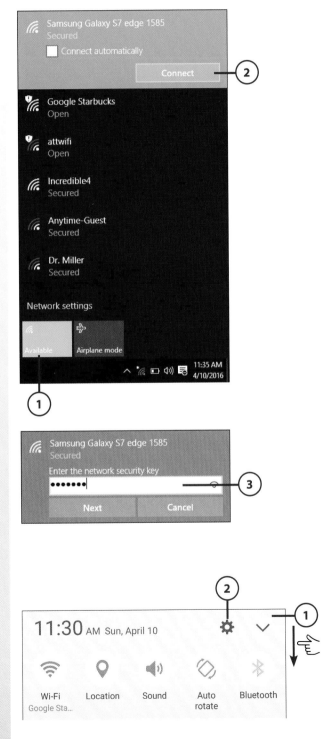

(3) Tap to select the Connections tab.

(4) Tap Mobile Hotspot and Tethering.

(5) Connect the other device to your phone via USB cable and then tap On the USB Tethering switch.

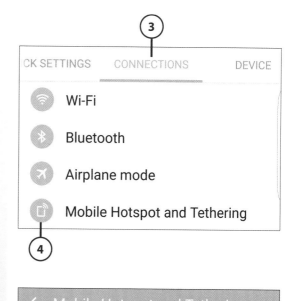

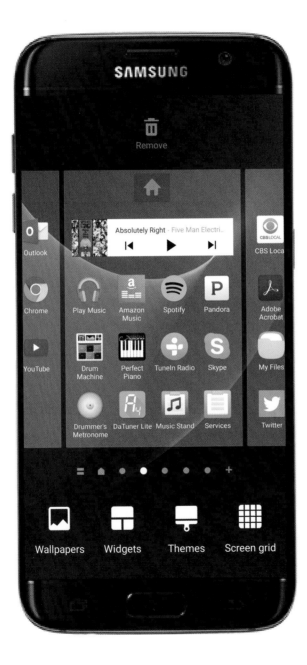

In this chapter, you learn how to find, install, use, and manage apps on your Galaxy S7 or S7 edge. Topics include the following:

→ Using Apps
→ Managing Installed Apps
→ Downloading New Apps from the Google Play Store

Installing and Using Apps

Most of what you do on your Galaxy S7 or S7 edge you do via applications, or apps. An app is a self-contained program designed to perform a particular task or serve a specific purpose. There are apps for news and weather, apps for email and text messaging, apps for Facebook and Pinterest, even apps for listening to music and watching videos. The camera function on your phone is actually an app, as is the phone dialer. Whatever you want to do on your Galaxy S7 or S7 edge, there's probably an app for it.

Your new phone came with more than a dozen apps preinstalled, but these aren't the only apps you can use. There are tens of thousands of additional apps available, most for free or low cost, in the Google Play Store. It's easy to find new apps and install them on your phone—and then use them every day.

Using Apps

Your apps are displayed in two different places on your phone. All of your apps are listed on the Apps screen, which you access by tapping the Apps icon at the bottom of any Home screen. Shortcuts to your favorite apps are displayed on the Home screens; you have to manually add these shortcuts from the complete list of apps on the Apps screen.

View All Your Apps on the Apps Screen

Shortcuts to the apps you use most often are displayed on the Home screen, which you access by pressing the Home key on the front of your phone. When you want to view or access all the apps installed on your phone, you need to display the Apps screen. The Apps screen is also where you create shortcuts to place on your Home screen, as well as uninstall apps you no longer use.

1. From any Home screen, tap the Apps icon.

2. Swipe left or right to view additional Apps screens.

3. To view your apps in alphabetical order, tap A-Z at the top of the screen.

4. To search for a specific app, tap Search.

(5) Use the onscreen keyboard to enter the name of the app you want into the search box.

(6) As you type, matching apps appear onscreen.

(7) Press the Home key to return to the Home screen.

Open an App

You can open an app from the Apps screen or from the Home screen. The process is identical.

(1) Navigate to the screen that displays the icon for the app you want to open.

(2) Tap the icon to open the app.

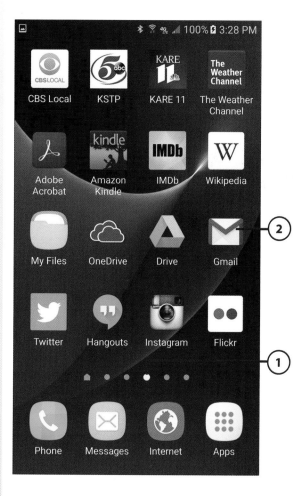

Close an App

Apps remain open until you manually close them. When you're not using an app, it remains paused in the background, but it doesn't consume system resources. Because of this, you don't have to close an app when you're done with it—although you can if you want.

(1) Tap the Recents key to display a stack of recently opened apps.

(2) Tap the X for the app you want to close, or just tap and drag the app off to one side until it disappears.

(3) Tap Close All to close all open apps.

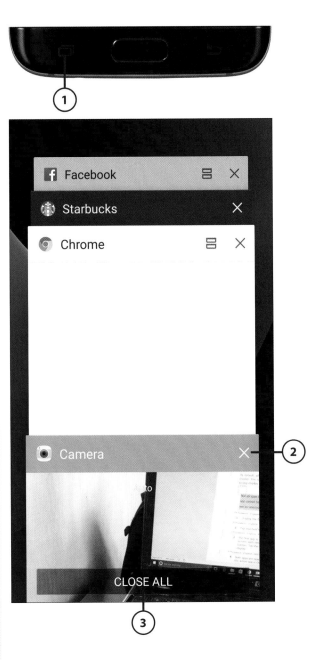

Switch Between Open Apps

When you have more than one app open, how do you switch from one app to another? By using the same app-switcher functionality you use to close apps.

(**1**) Tap the Recents key to display a stack of recently opened apps.

(**2**) Swipe up or down to scroll through all the apps.

(**3**) Tap the app you want to switch to.

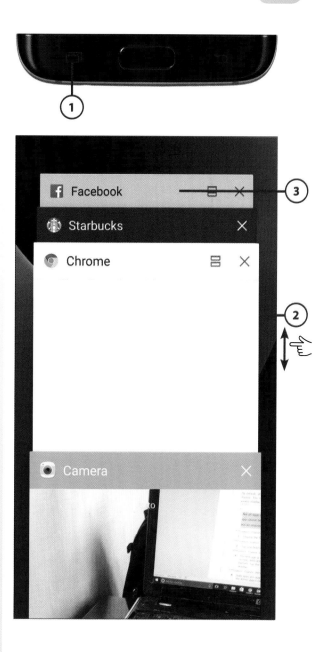

Use Multi Window

By default, all apps run full-screen on your phone's display. You can, however, display two apps in a split-screen display that Samsung calls Multi Window.

Compatibility

Not all apps support Multi Window display. If an app cannot be displayed in the split screen, you'll see an onscreen notification to that effect.

(1) Display the first app you want to view.

(2) Tap and *hold* the Recents key.

(3) The first app is now displayed at the top of the split screen, with other app icons displayed at the bottom. Tap the icon for the other app you want to display.

(4) Both apps are now displayed onscreen together; the active app is the one with the blue border. To resize the windows, select one of the application windows to display the border button in the middle of the window border; then tap and drag the border up or down, accordingly.

(5) Tap the border button to display additional window controls.

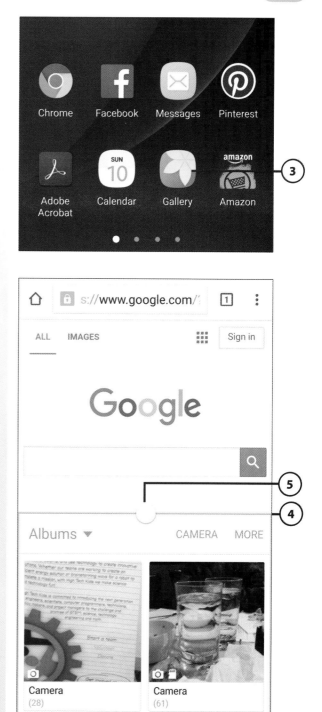

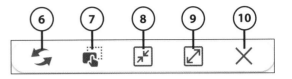

6 Tap the Switch Windows button to switch the top and bottom app positions.

7 Tap the Drag and Drop button to move content from one app to the other.

8 Tap the Minimize Window button to minimize the selected app window.

9 Tap the Maximize Window button to view the selected app in full-screen view.

10 Tap the Close App (X) button to close the selected app.

>>>Go Further

POP UP WINDOW

Multi Window view also lets you display the current app as a pop-up window. Tap and drag the top-left corner of the current app down and to the right; this places the app in its own onscreen window. To move the window around the screen, tap the border button and drag the window to a new position. You can also, of course, tap and hold the border button to display the normal Multi Window controls.

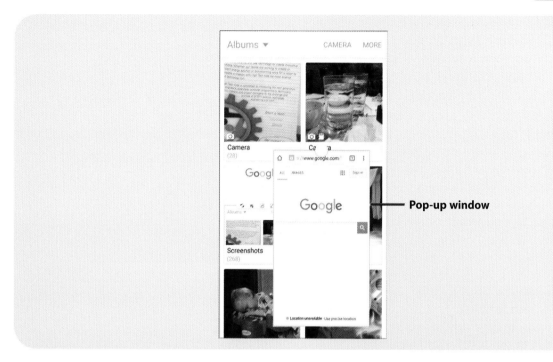

Pop-up window

Managing Installed Apps

You can easily personalize which apps appear on your phone's Home screens, and where they appear. You can also organize apps into folders and uninstall those apps you don't use.

Add App Shortcuts to the Home Screen

You add app shortcuts to the Home screen from the Apps screen.

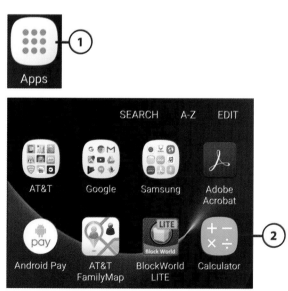

1. Tap the Apps icon to display the Apps screen.

2. Tap and hold the icon for the app you want to add. The display changes to show the Home screens on your device.

3 Drag the icon to the desired Home screen and then release. The shortcut icon is now displayed on that screen.

Favorite Apps

You can add new app shortcuts to any Home screen or to the Favorite Apps area that appears at the bottom of all Home screens. By default, the Favorite Apps area holds four app icons (Phone, Messages, Internet, or Apps), although you can add a fifth icon to this area if you like. You can also remove any of the default icons and replace them with other app icons of your choosing. Just drag and drop icons to and from this area as you would anywhere else on the screen.

Rearrange Apps on the Home Screens

One of the easiest ways to personalize your Galaxy S7 or S7 edge is to rearrange app shortcuts on the Home screens.

1 Tap and drag the app icon to a new position on the current screen or...

2 Tap and drag the icon to a different Home screen.

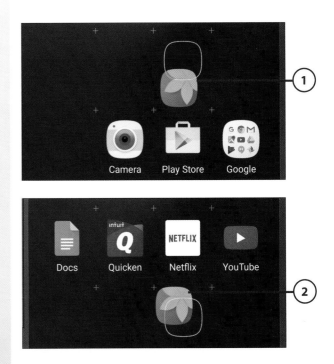

Remove an App Shortcut from the Home Screen

If you find that you're not using a specific app all that much, you may want to free up space by removing that app's shortcut from the Home screen.

1 From a Home screen, tap and hold the icon for the app you want to remove.

2 Drag the app's icon up and then drop it onto the Remove (trash can) icon above the screen.

② **①**

Remove   Move apps

53° ☀

♀Lakeville
Updated 4/10 2:41 PM ↻

Remove, Not Uninstall

Removing a shortcut from the Home screen does not remove that app from your phone. The app remains and is still accessible from the Apps screen. To remove the app from your phone, you have to uninstall the app, as discussed next.

Uninstall an App

You can uninstall or disable and hide from view apps that you have downloaded onto your phone. However, some apps that were preloaded onto your phone cannot be uninstalled or disabled.

1 Tap the Apps icon to display the Apps screen.

Apps   **①**

2 Tap Edit. Apps that can be uninstalled or disabled display with a minus (–) icon.

SEARCH   A-Z   EDIT   **②**

3 Tap the minus (–) icon for the app you want to remove and then follow the onscreen instructions to either uninstall or disable the app.

4 Tap Done when done.

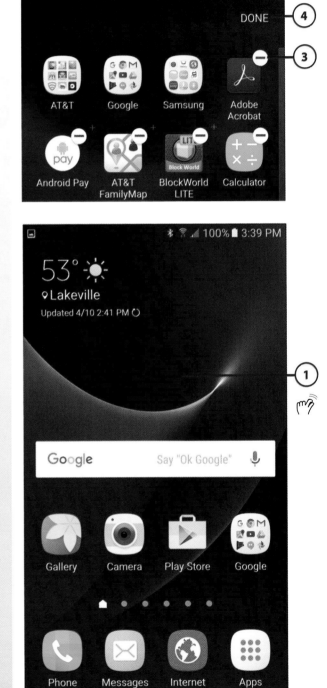

Manage the Screens on the Home Screen

The Home screen is actually a series of screens, each holding 16 shortcut icons plus the favorites row at the bottom of the screen. If you have more shortcut icons than you presently have Home screens to hold them, you can add new screens to the Home screen—and rearrange the Home screens in any order.

1 Pinch any Home screen to display the Home screens in editing mode.

(2) Remove a screen by tapping and dragging it to the Remove (trash can) icon at the top of the screen.

(3) Tap the Home icon at the top of a screen to make that screen the main Home screen that displays when you tap the Home key.

(4) Change the order of the screens by tapping and dragging a screen left or right to a new position.

(5) Add a new blank screen by scrolling to the last Home screen and tapping +.

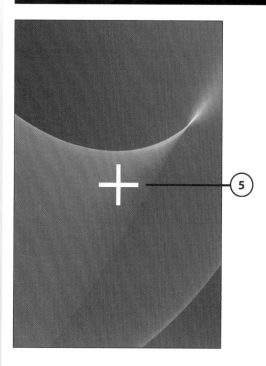

6 Press the Home key to exit screen editing mode.

Editing Mode

You can also enter editing mode from the Settings screen; select the Personal tab and then tap Home Screen.

Change the Icon Grid

By default, your Galaxy S7 displays icons in a 4 × 4 grid—4 icons across and 4 icons tall. You can opt to display more icons on the screen, in either a 4 × 5 or 5 × 5 grid, although the icons will be smaller.

1 Pinch any Home screen to enter editing mode.

2 Tap the Screen Grid icon.

(**3**) Select which grid you want; you can see the results in the screens above.

(**4**) Tap Apply.

Add a Widget to the Home Screen

In addition to app shortcut icons, you can also place widgets on the Home screens. A widget is a self-contained application that runs on the screen itself. Out of the box, your Galaxy S7 came with two such widgets, both on the first Home screen—the Weather widget and the Google Search widget. (Many widgets, like the weather widget, have transparent backgrounds so they appear seamlessly against the screen background.)

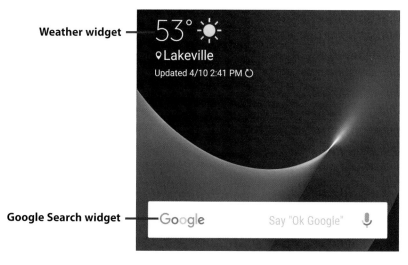

Beyond these two widgets, your Galaxy S7 includes a number of other widgets that you can add to your Home screens. You can find even more widgets in the Google Play Store, as described later in this chapter.

In addition, many apps have their own widgets that display specific information on the Home screen. Some apps, like the Music app, let you operate them via widgets. Other widgets display news headlines, messages, and the like.

Space

Most widgets are a specific size, and can only fit on screens that have that same-sized space available. For example, a 4 × 1 widget takes up 4 icons wide by 1 icon tall; a 4 × 2 widget is 4 icons wide by 2 icons tall. Make sure you have adequate empty space for the widgets you want.

(1) Pinch any Home screen to display the Home screens in editing mode.

(2) Tap Widgets at the bottom of the screen. This displays all the widgets installed on your phone.

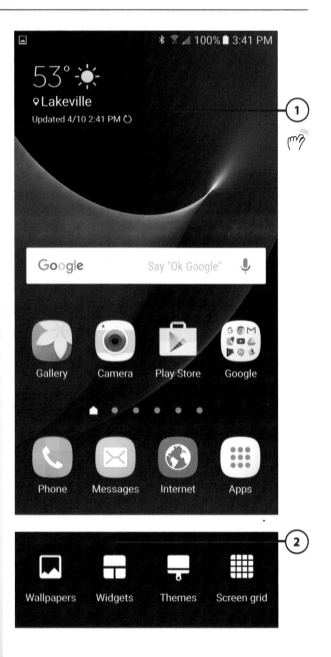

3 Touch and drag the widget you want to the desired Home screen.

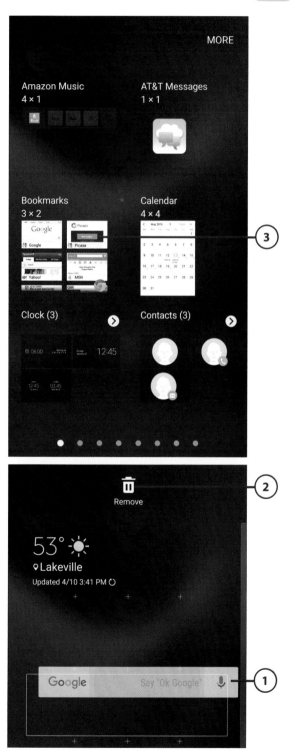

Remove a Widget from the Home Screen

You remove a widget from the Home screen much as you remove shortcut icons.

1 From a Home screen, tap and hold the widget you want to remove.

2 Drag the widget up and then drop it onto the Remove (trash can) icon above the screen.

Organize Apps into Folders

If you have a lot of similar apps on your phone, you might want to organize those app shortcuts into folders on your Home screen. A folder can contain several screens worth of apps and help you minimize the screen real estate devoted to app shortcuts.

(1) From any screen, tap and drag the icon for the first app onto the icon for the second app you want in the folder.

(2) This creates the folder, with the first two apps inside.

(3) Tap Enter Folder Name and enter the name for this folder.

(4) To add another app shortcut to the folder, tap the + icon.

(5) Tap outside the folder to return to the Home screen.

Open and Close a Folder

After you've organized your apps into folders, it's easy to access those apps.

(1) Tap the folder you want to open.

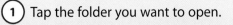

(**2**) The folder opens, displaying the apps inside. Tap an app to open it.

(**3**) Tap outside the folder to close it and return to the Home screen.

Removing a Folder

You remove a folder from the Home screen the same way you remove a normal app icon, by dragging it onto the Remove icon above the screen. When you delete a folder, the apps themselves are not deleted and remain available on the Apps screen. You can also remove an app from a folder, by opening the folder and dragging the app icon back to the Home screen. If there is only a single app remaining, the folder itself disappears and the remaining app is transferred to the Home screen.

Videos

NETFLIX
Netflix   YouTube

Set Default Applications for Common Operations

There are a lot of applications out there, many of which perform similar operations. For example, there are tons of music player apps for playing music on your phone, and most manufacturers preinstall at least two text messaging apps (the default Android one and one from your mobile carrier) on the Galaxy S7. You'll also want to set a default web browser from between either Samsung's built-in browser (dubbed Samsung Internet) or Google Chrome.

Let's start by setting the default application for three common system operations: web browsing, calling, and text messaging.

1. Swipe down from the top of the screen to display the notification panel.

2. Tap Settings to display the Settings screen.

3. Tap to select the Device tab.

4. Tap Applications to display the Applications screen.

5. Tap Default Applications.

6. Tap Browser App.

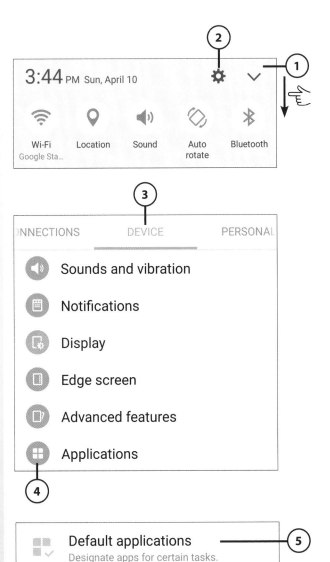

7 Tap the browser you want to use: Internet (Samsung's built-in browser) or Chrome (Google's popular browser).

8 Tap the back arrow to return to the Default Applications screen.

9 Tap Calling App.

10 Tap to select the calling app you want to use. (There might be only one option.)

11 Tap the back arrow to return to the Default Applications screen.

12 Tap Messaging App.

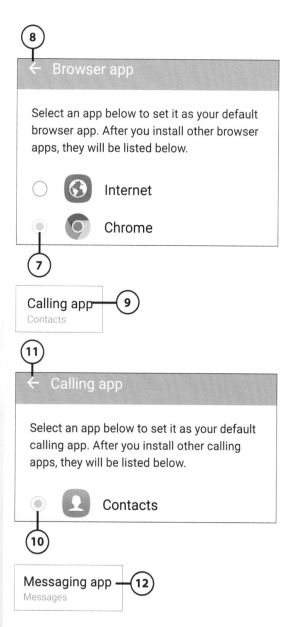

(13) Tap to select the messaging app you want to use.

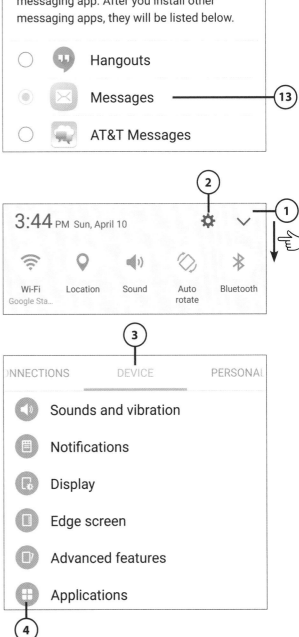

Set Other Default Applications

You can also set other apps as the default for various operations. For example, you can set Adobe Acrobat as the default reader for PDF files or Google Docs as the default app for opening word processing files.

(1) Swipe down from the top of the screen to display the notification panel.

(2) Tap Settings to display the Settings screen.

(3) Tap to select the Device tab.

(4) Tap Applications to display the Applications screen.

5 Tap Default Applications.

6 Tap Set as Default to display a list of installed apps.

7 Tap the icon for a given app.

8 Tap Go to Supported URLs.

9 Tap Via This App. (Or, if you'd prefer to always make a manual selection when opening links of this type, tap Always Ask.)

Default applications — **5**
Designate apps for certain tasks.

Set as default — **6**

Adobe Acrobat — **7**
Set as default

Amazon
None set as default

Amazon Music
None set as default

Android Pay
None set as default

Adobe Acrobat ⓘ

This app is set to open by default for some actions.

CLEAR DEFAULTS

App links

Select whether to open this app instead of your browser app when you go to supported web addresses.

Go to supported URLs — **8**
Always ask

Via this app — **9**

Always ask

In other app

Use the Application Manager

Your Samsung smartphone includes an Application Manager you can use to view information about any installed app, including what resources are being used by that app. You can also use Application Manager to stop an app that may be taking up too many resources or causing other problems.

1. Swipe down from the top of the screen to display the notification panel.

2. Tap Settings to display the Settings screen.

3. Tap to select the Device tab.

4. Tap Applications to display the Applications screen.

5. Tap Application Manager to open the Application Manager.

6. Tap the icon for a specific app. You now see information pertaining to that app, including how much storage space and data have been used.

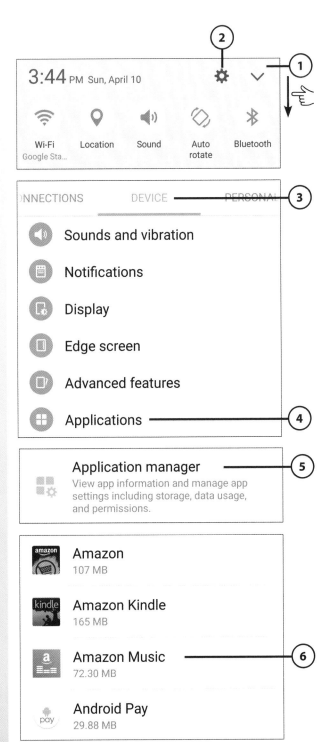

(**7**) Force the app to stop by tapping the Force Stop button.

(**8**) Uninstall this app by tapping the Uninstall button.

(**9**) Some apps (such as system apps) cannot be uninstalled, but can be disabled; in this instance, tap the Disable button.

It's Not All Good

Stop with Caution

It's safe enough to stop most apps from running. Be cautious, however, about stopping any system processes, such as the Android System itself. Stopping a key process can cause your phone to freeze up or otherwise behave badly. (If this happens, power off your phone and then restart it.)

Downloading New Apps from the Google Play Store

Where do you find new apps to use on your smartphone? There's one central source that offers apps from multiple developers—the Google Play Store.

Browse and Search the Google Play Store

The Google Play Store is an online store that offers apps, music, videos, and eBooks for Android phones. Most apps in the Google Play Store are free or relatively low cost. It's easy to find new apps by either browsing or searching.

1. Tap the Play Store icon to open the Google Play Store.

2. Tap Apps & Games to display available apps. (And games!)

3. Tap in the Search box at the top of the screen and enter the name or type of app you're looking for or...

4. Tap the Categories tab to browse for apps by category.

5. Tap the category you're interested in to display apps of that type.

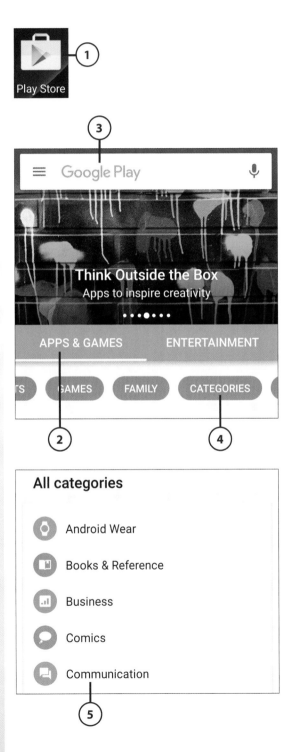

6 Tap the app in which you're interested.

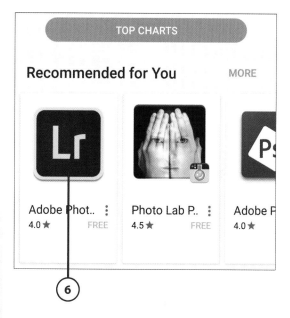

Purchase and Download Apps

Many apps in the Google Play Store are free. Others you have to pay for.

1 Download a free app by tapping the Install button.

2 Tap Accept on the permissions panel. The app is downloaded to and installed on your phone.

3 Purchase a paid app by tapping the price button.

4 Tap Accept on the permissions panel. The purchase panel displays.

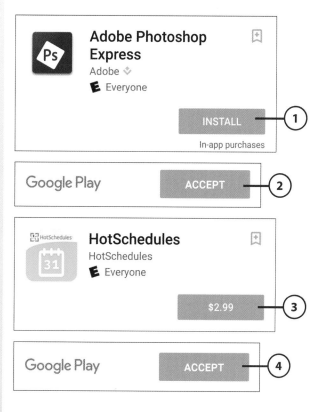

5 Tap the payment area to enlarge the panel, then tap Payment Methods.

6 Select a payment option.

7 If you have not yet set up a payment method, tap either Add Credit or Debit Card or Add PayPal and then follow the onscreen instructions to add your payment information.

8 Tap the Buy button to complete the transaction and download the app.

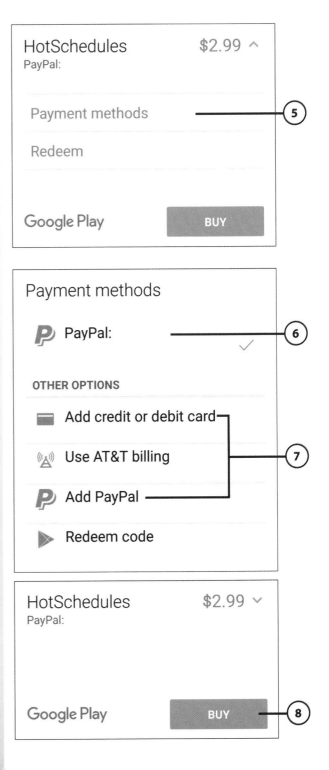

>>>Go Further

UPDATING APPS

Apps are software programs, and like any software program, are occasionally updated to include new features, bug fixes, and the like. Most apps update automatically when updates are available, and you'll see a notification of this on the Lock screen and notification panel.

Some app updates need your approval to proceed. If you receive a notification to this effect, tap the notification and you'll be transferred to the Google Play Store. Tap the Update or Update All (if there are multiple apps that need updating) button to proceed.

By the way, if you'd rather manually approve every single app update, you can turn off the auto update feature. Launch the Google Play Store app, tap the Options (three-line) button, and select Settings. Go the General section and tap Auto-Update Apps. On the next panel, tap Do Not Auto-Update Apps.

The other options are to update only when you're connected via Wi-Fi and to auto-update apps at any time, over any type of network. That last option isn't recommended, as updating large apps can eat up a ton of your mobile data usage—and cost you money in data charges.

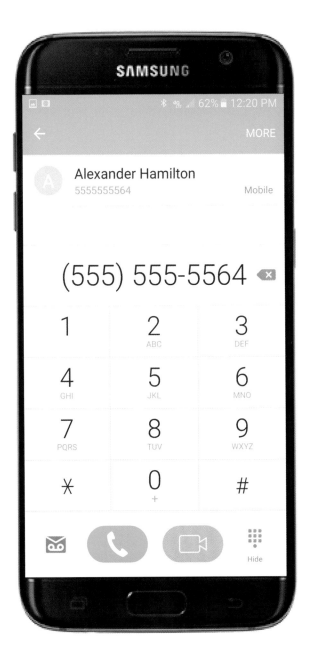

In this chapter, you learn how to make and receive mobile phone calls on your Samsung Galaxy S7 or S7 edge. Topics include the following:

→ Calling on Your Galaxy S7
→ Using Speed Dial
→ Handling Multiple Calls and Activities
→ Managing Your Call Log
→ Using Voice Mail
→ Configuring Call Settings
→ Connecting via Headset or Car Speaker

Making Phone Calls

Even though there's a lot of focus on web connectivity, app downloads, and other bells and whistles, your new Galaxy S7 or S7 edge smartphone is, first and foremost, a mobile telephone. This chapter shows you how to use the phone features of your new smartphone, as well as how to manage your voice mail and call logs.

Calling on Your Galaxy S7

Of all the things that your new Samsung smartphone can do, the one that it does first and best is send and receive mobile phone calls. Making a call is as simple as dialing a number—as long as you have a strong signal from your carrier, of course!

When you talk on your Galaxy S7 or S7 edge, hold it to the side of your face as you would an old-school telephone handset. Your new smartphone may look like a high-tech, shiny, glass-and-metal rectangle, but it works just like a traditional phone. You'll hear the other person from a tiny speaker at the top of the phone, and speak into a tiny microphone at the bottom. Speak loud enough for the other person to hear you, and you should hear her just fine, as well.

Dial a Number

There are many ways to make a call from your Samsung Galaxy S7. The simplest is to just dial the number.

Phone

(**1**) From the Home screen, tap the Phone icon to open the Phone app.

(**2**) If the keypad is not visible, tap the green Keypad icon.

(**3**) Tap the number you want to dial into the onscreen keypad.

(**4**) Tap the green Dial (phone) icon to dial the number. When the other party answers, hold the phone to the side of your head to listen to and speak with that person.

Area Codes

When dialing from a mobile phone, you always need to enter the area code in front of the standard seven-digit number, like this: 555-555-5555. You do not need to enter a "1" before the area code.

From the Lock Screen

If you don't have your lock screen protected by a PIN or password, you can dial directly from the Lock screen without first unlocking your phone. Just drag the Phone icon up to display the call screen, and proceed from there.

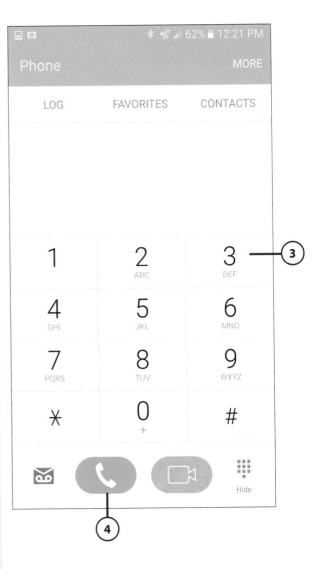

Quick-Dial from Your Contacts List

Your Samsung phone includes a Contacts app that lets you store information about the people you know—including their phone numbers. After you've entered a contact's information, it's a lot easier to dial that person from within your contacts list than try to remember the person's full phone number.

Contacts

1. From the Home screen, tap the Contacts icon to open the Contacts app *or*...

2. From within the Phone app, tap the Contacts tab.

3. Scroll to and tap the name of the contact you want to call.

4. Tap the green phone icon next to this person's phone number. If a contact has more than one phone number listed (home, mobile, and work, for example), tap the appropriate phone number. The person is now called.

Contacts

Learn more about your contacts and contacts list in Chapter 8, "Managing Your Contacts List."

Dial a Favorite Contact

In the Contacts app, you can specify any number of people as favorites. This makes it easier for you to find and dial these contacts' numbers.

 From within the Phone app, tap the Favorites tab.

 Tap the name of the favorite you want to call.

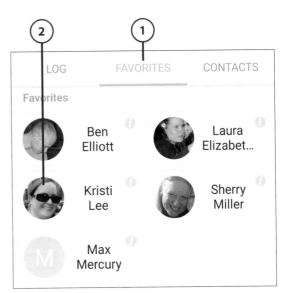

Dial a Recent Number

Your phone keeps track of calls you've made and received. If you want to redial someone you've recently talked to, you can easily do so.

1. From within the Phone app, tap the Log tab.

2. Tap the name or number of the recent call you want to revisit. You see a list of recent calls to/from this person.

3. Tap the green Dial (phone) icon to redial this person.

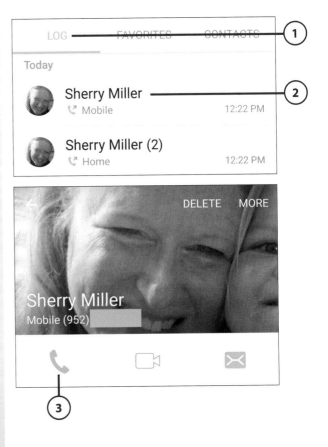

Answer a Call

Dialing out is easy enough. What do you do when someone calls you?

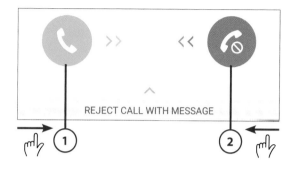

REJECT CALL WITH MESSAGE

(1) Touch and drag the green Answer icon to the right to answer the call.

(2) If you don't want to answer this call, you can reject it and send it automatically to voice mail. To do this, tap and drag the red Reject icon to the left.

Answering When Active
If you're on the Home screen or your phone is currently locked when you receive a call, you see the screens shown with this task. If, on the other hand, you're using another app when the call comes in, you see the Answer and Reject icons in a pop-up window.

Options During a Call

When you're talking to someone on your phone, you have several options available to you.

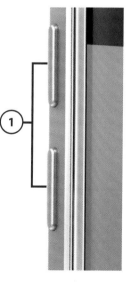

(1) To change the volume level of the caller, press the Up or Down Volume keys on the left side of the phone.

(2) Tap Speaker to start using the speakerphone. Tap this button again to switch back to normal phone use.

(3) Mute the call so that the other person can't hear what you're saying by tapping Mute. Tap Mute again to unmute the call.

(4) To input any numbers during a call (if you're calling your bank, for example), tap Keypad to redisplay the onscreen keyboard.

(5) Tap the red End icon to disconnect the call.

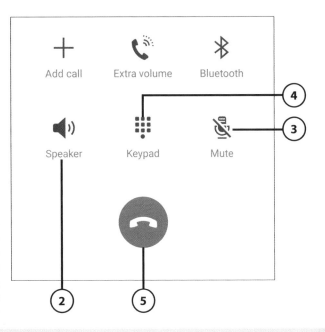

>>>Go Further

WHAT'S MY NUMBER?

In this era where every phone number is stored in your phone, and all you have to do is tap an icon to call someone, there's little incentive to memorize a person's phone number. If you're like me, this means that you don't remember anyone's phone number anymore. We rely on our smartphones to do the remembering for us.

It also means, if you're also like me, that you probably don't even remember your own phone number. You don't have to give it out to people; they see your number on their own smartphones when you call, and add it to their own contacts list.

So, what is your phone number? The easiest way to find out is to open the Contacts app. There, at the very top of the Contacts list, is the My Profile section, with a single contact listed—you! Tap your name and you see your profile picture and your mobile number. Voila!

By the way, if you have any emergency medical information that others might need to know, it can be displayed here, too. Just tap the Emergency Medical Information section and enter information about your medical conditions, allergies, current medications, blood type, and such.

Using Speed Dial

Your new Samsung phone lets you store up to 100 numbers in a Speed Dial list. With Speed Dial, phoning a person is as easy as tapping one or more number keys.

Create a Speed Dial Entry

You add numbers to Speed Dial from within the Phone app.

(1) From the Phone app's dialing screen, tap More.

(2) Tap Speed Dial to display the Speed Dial screen.

(3) Tap the + icon next to the first open Speed Dial position.

(4) Tap the name of the contact you want to add. The person is now added to your Speed Dial list.

Voice Mail

By default, voice mail is assigned to the first Speed Dial position.

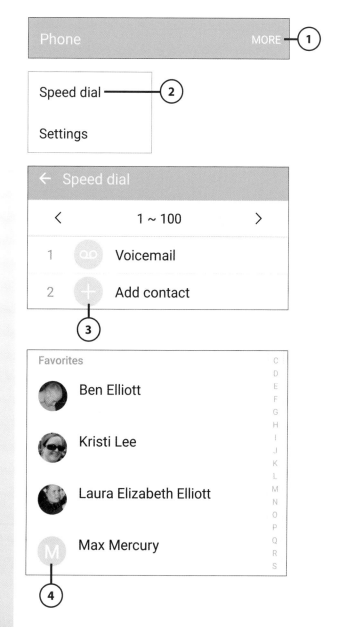

Remove a Person from Speed Dial

Samsung makes it easy to edit your Speed Dial List.

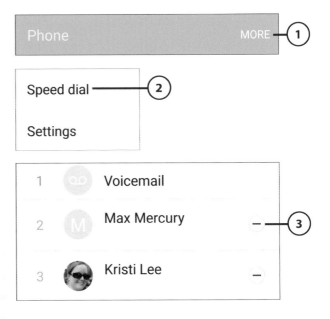

(1) From the Phone app's dialing screen, tap More.

(2) Tap Speed Dial to display the Speed Dial screen.

(3) Tap the minus (–) icon next to the person you want to remove from Speed Dial.

Make a Call with Speed Dial

The joy of Speed Dial is being able to call someone with just a tap or two on your phone's screen.

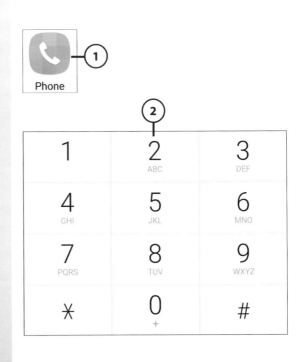

(1) From the Home screen, tap Phone to open the Phone app.

(2) Enter the Speed Dial number assigned to this person. When entering, tap and *hold* the last number. For example, if this person is in Speed Dial slot number 2, tap and hold **2**. If this person is in Speed Dial slot 14, tap **1** then tap and hold **4**.

Handling Multiple Calls and Activities

Most mobile carriers let you handle two calls at once. This means answering an incoming call while you're on another, or placing a new call when you're already on the phone. You can even continue using your other smartphone functions—including Internet browsing—while talking.

Make a New Call While on Another

If your carrier supports this feature, you can make a new call while you're currently on an existing one.

(**1**) While you're on a call, tap +
Add Call to display the numeric keypad.

(**2**) Tap the new number into the keypad.

(**3**) Tap the green Dial icon.

(**4**) Tap Merge if you want to conference both callers into a single call. You will hear both callers at once—and they will hear each other, too.

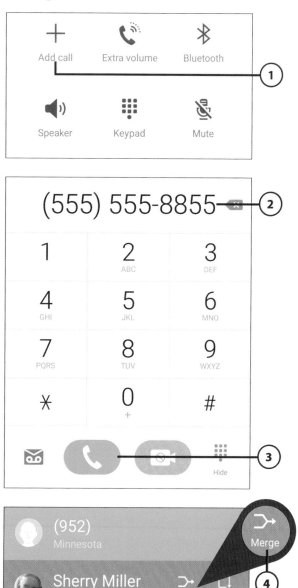

Receive a New Call While on Another

Thanks to Call Waiting (supported by most carriers), you can answer an incoming call while you're on another call.

(1) Slide the green Answer icon to the right to answer the new call.

(2) When prompted, opt to answer the call and put the other caller on hold; merge the new call with the existing call; or end the previous call to take the new call.

(3) If you opted to place the original caller on hold, tap Swap to switch from the new call back to the original call.

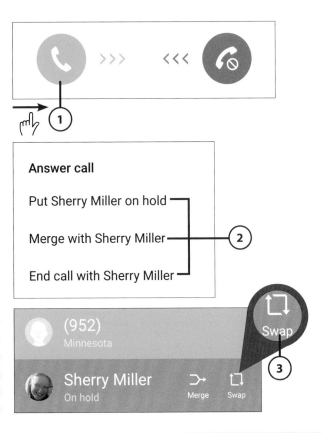

>>>*Go Further*

USING OTHER SMARTPHONE FUNCTIONS DURING A CALL

Most carriers enable you to use other functions on your Samsung phone while you're engaging in a phone call. This multitasking can be quite useful; for example, you can look something up on Google to answer a question posed during the voice call.

To multitask in this fashion, simply press the Home key to return to the Home screen while you're talking. The voice call continues, and you can then tap any app icon to open and use that app.

In addition, your phone has several preset app options built into the Phone app. From within the call screen, swipe to the right and then tap the icon for Email, Message, Browser, Contacts, Calendar, or Memo.

To return to the call screen, swipe down from the top of the screen to display the notification panel and then tap Call Notification. To end the call from the notification panel, tap End Call.

Managing Your Call Log

All the calls you make and receive are recorded in your phone's call log, so you can easily review your call history. The call log even logs those calls you've missed.

View Recent Calls

You view your call log from within the Phone app.

(1) From within the Phone app, tap the Log tab to display the call log, in reverse chronological order (newest first).

(2) Outbound calls are indicated with an upward arrow on the phone icon—green if answered, red if not answered. Incoming calls are indicated with a downward arrow on the phone icon—also green if answered, red if not answered. Calls you've rejected are indicated with a circle with a line through it. If the call was to or from someone on your contact list, you see that person's name. Tap a call to view more information.

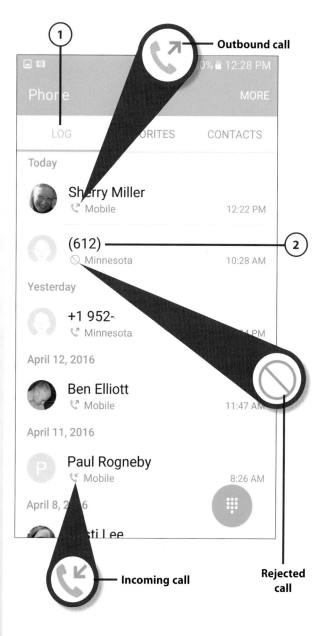

Outbound call

Incoming call

Rejected call

(3) Recent calls to/from this number are displayed. Tap the green Dial (phone) icon to redial this person.

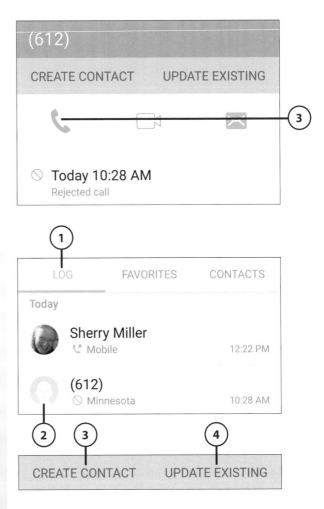

Save a Recent Caller to Your Contact List

If someone calls you, or if you call someone else, you can add that person's information to your contact list from within the call log.

(1) From within the Phone app, tap the Log tab to display the call log.

(2) Tap a call to view more information about that call.

(3) Tap Create Contact to add this number to your contact list.

(4) Tap Update Existing to update an existing contact with this new number.

Delete a Call from Your Call Log

On occasion you'll receive calls from numbers you don't want to remember. (Or don't want anyone snooping through your phone to see.) Fortunately, you can delete any call from the call log.

(1) From within the Phone app, tap the Log tab to display the call log.

(2) Tap More at the top of the screen.

(3) Tap Delete.

(4) Tap to check the call(s) you want to delete.

(5) Tap Delete.

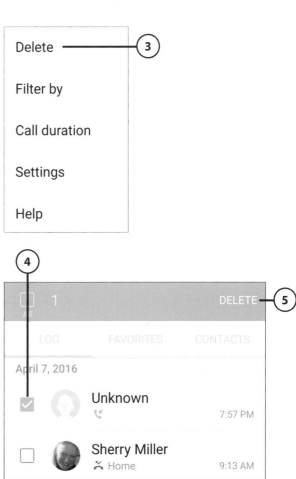

Delete ——— (3)

Filter by

Call duration

Settings

Help

(4)

| ☐ 1 | | | DELETE —— (5) |

LOG   FAVORITES   CONTACTS

April 7, 2016

☑   Unknown
                                    7:57 PM

☐   Sherry Miller
              Home   9:13 AM

Reject Future Calls from a Given Number

It happens. Some telemarketer or scammer or debt collector gets hold of your mobile number, and you don't want that person to keep calling you. Fortunately, you can add any number to a Block List, so if you receive a call from that number, it's automatically rejected without you having to answer it.

(1) From within the Phone app, tap the Log tab to display the call log.

(2) Tap a call from the number you want to reject.

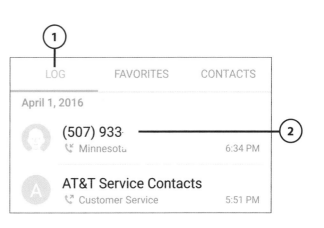

(1)

LOG   FAVORITES   CONTACTS

April 1, 2016

(507) 933· ———————— (2)
Minnesota   6:34 PM

AT&T Service Contacts
Customer Service   5:51 PM

③ Tap More.

④ Tap Block/Unblock Number.

⑤ Tap On the Call Block switch to block all phone calls from this number.

⑥ Tap On the Message Block switch to block all text messages from this number.

⑦ Tap OK. You'll never hear from this number again.

Rejecting Mistakes

If you accidentally add a number to the Block List, you can remove it from that list at a later time. From within the Phone app, tap More and then tap Settings. On the Call Settings screen, tap Call Blocking and then tap Block List. Find the number you rejected by mistake and tap the minus (–) sign.

Block Unknown Numbers

If you find yourself getting a lot of calls from unknown numbers (probably telemarketers), you can configure your phone to block all calls from numbers you don't know.

① From within the Phone app, tap More.

② Tap Settings to display the Call Settings screen.

③ Tap Call Blocking.

④ Tap Block List to display the Block List screen.

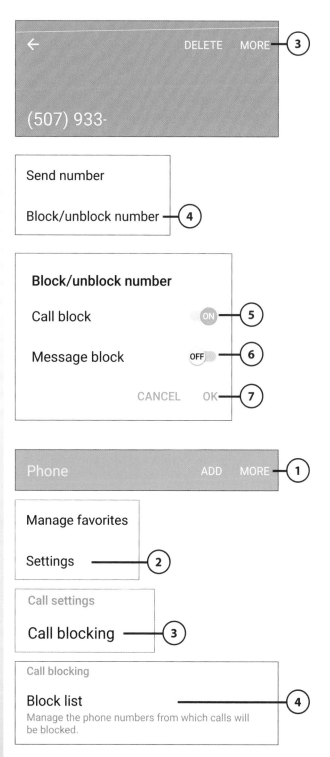

⑤ Tap On the Block Anonymous Calls switch.

Block anonymous calls	ON

Using Voice Mail

Your mobile carrier provides voice mail service in addition to your normal voice calling. Voice mail is like a digital version of a traditional answering machine; it lets callers leave you messages when you don't answer the phone.

Your voice mail is not stored on your phone; it's on your mobile carrier's system. For this reason, you actually have to dial into your voice mail to hear your messages.

Set Up Your Voice Mail

When you first sign up with a mobile carrier, you need to set up your voice mail account. This voice mail account follows you from phone to phone (it's specific to your mobile phone number and account), so if your new Samsung Galaxy S7 phone was added to an existing carrier account, there's nothing new to set up.

If you're a new customer with a mobile carrier, however, you do need to set up your voice mail. The process is different with different carriers, but works more or less like this.

① From within the Phone app, tap and hold **1** to access voice mail via Speed Dial.

② When connected, follow the voice prompts to create your password, record your name announcement, and record your voice greeting.

1	2 ABC	3 DEF
4 GHI	5 JKL	6 MNO
7 PQRS	8 TUV	9 WXYZ
*	0 +	#

Check Voice Mail Messages

When you purchased your new Samsung Galaxy S7, your carrier should have set up your phone with the correct voice mail number. When you receive a new voice mail message, you'll see a notification to that effect; you can then dial into your voice mail account to listen to the message.

(1) Tap the notification to call your voice mail number *or…*

(2) From within the Phone app, tap and hold **1** to access voice mail via Speed Dial.

(3) When connected, follow the voice prompts to listen to or delete messages.

Voice Mail Apps

Some carriers launch their own voice mail app for managing voice mail messages. For example, AT&T offers the Visual Voicemail app for just this purpose. If your carrier offers such a voice mail app, follow that app's instructions to play your messages.

Configuring Call Settings

There are numerous things you can configure from within the Phone app. In addition, you can easily set different ringtones for your incoming calls.

Set Your Default Ringtone

You can choose from a number of different tones to ring when you receive incoming calls.

(**1**) From within the Phone app, tap More.

(**2**) Tap Settings to display the Call Settings screen.

(**3**) Tap Ringtones and Keypad Tones.

(**4**) Tap Ringtones to display available ringtones.

(**5**) Tap to select the ringtone you want. When you tap a ringtone, you hear a preview of that sound.

Other Ringtones

To use a ringtone other than those built into your phone, scroll to the bottom of the Ringtones list and tap Add Ringtone. You can then choose any sound file stored on your phone.

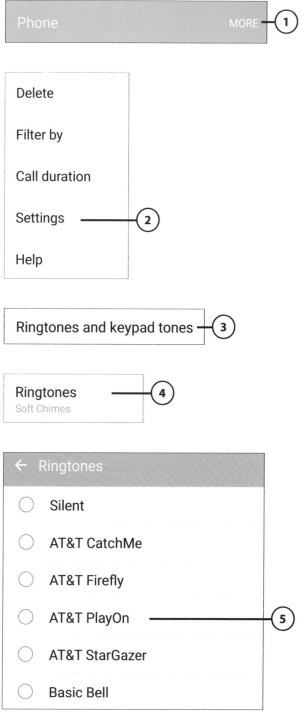

Configure Other Call Settings

Your Samsung smartphone has a number of settings you can configure to personalize the calling experience. All are accessible from the Call Settings screen.

(1) From within the Phone app, tap More.

(2) Tap Settings to display the Call Settings screen.

(3) Tap On the Swipe to Call or Send Messages switch to be able to initiate a call or message by swiping across a person's contact screen.

(4) By default, your phone shows contacts with phone numbers and hides contacts without numbers. To show all contacts, tap Off the Contacts with Numbers switch.

(5) Tap Answering and Ending Calls to answer calls by pressing the Home key, automatically answer the phone after two seconds when using a Bluetooth device, or end calls by pressing the Power key.

(6) Tap Call Alerts to have your phone vibrate or sound a tone when a call is answered or ends, or not sound or display system notifications when a call is in progress.

(7) Tap More Settings to configure Call Forwarding, Call Waiting, and other options.

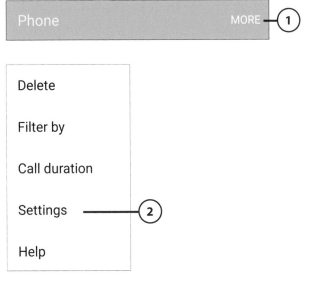

Phone   MORE — (1)

Delete

Filter by

Call duration

Settings — (2)

Help

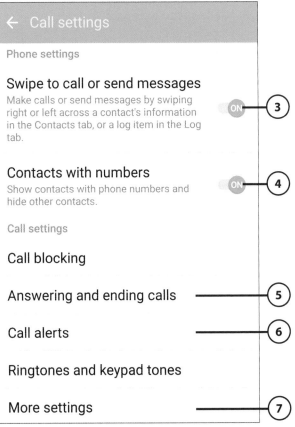

← Call settings

Phone settings

Swipe to call or send messages
Make calls or send messages by swiping right or left across a contact's information in the Contacts tab, or a log item in the Log tab.   ON — (3)

Contacts with numbers
Show contacts with phone numbers and hide other contacts.   ON — (4)

Call settings

Call blocking

Answering and ending calls — (5)

Call alerts — (6)

Ringtones and keypad tones

More settings — (7)

Hearing Aids

To improve the sound quality of your phone when using a hearing aid, open the Settings screen, tap More Settings, and then then tap On the Hearing Aids switch.

Connecting via Headset or Car Speaker

If you do a lot of talking on the phone, you might find it more convenient to use a wired or wireless headset instead of holding your Galaxy S7 to your ear. In addition, if your automobile offers Bluetooth functionality, you can do your calling over your car's audio system.

Connect a Wired Headset

Connecting a wired headset is as easy as plugging it in. You can connect either phone headsets for making and receiving calls, or earbuds or headphones for listening to music.

(**1**) Plug your headset/earplugs/headphones into the headset jack on the bottom of the phone.

(**2**) For headset operation, consult the directions that came with your headset.

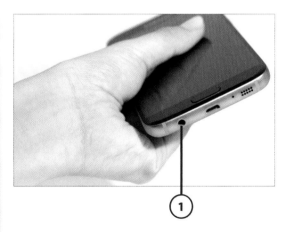

Connect a Bluetooth Headset

Many people prefer to use wireless headsets, which not only eliminate the connecting wires but also let you walk a short distance away from your phone, if you want. Wireless headsets connect via Bluetooth technology, which is built into your Galaxy S7 phone.

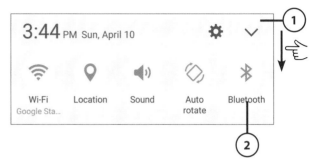

(1) Swipe down from the top of the screen to display the notification panel.

(2) Tap and hold the Bluetooth icon to display the Bluetooth screen.

(3) If Bluetooth is turned off, tap On the switch at the top of the screen.

(4) Make sure that your Bluetooth headset is turned on and placed in discoverable mode. (Consult your headset directions on how to do this.) It should appear, along with any other nearby Bluetooth devices, in the Available Devices section. If not, tap Scan at the top of the Bluetooth screen.

(5) Tap the name of your wireless headset. Your phone now attempts to pair with this device. When prompted to confirm the pairing request, tap OK. If automatic pairing is unsuccessful, enter the passcode supplied by the wireless headset.

Connect to Your Car via Bluetooth

If your car includes Bluetooth functionality, you can connect your phone to your car's audio system via Bluetooth. You can then make and receive phone calls over your car's audio system and microphone.

1. Swipe down from the top of the screen to display the notification panel.

2. Tap and hold the Bluetooth icon to display the Bluetooth screen.

3. If Bluetooth is turned off, tap On the switch at the top of the screen. This makes your phone discoverable by your car.

4. In your car, follow the manufacturer's instructions to begin the Bluetooth pairing process. In most instances, your car recognizes your phone and asks you to enter a passcode on your phone. Enter this code as instructed.

5. Your phone attempts to pair with your automobile. When pairing is successful, you may be prompted to share your phone's contacts with your car. If so, tap Allow.

Bluetooth Audio

Many cars also let you listen to music stored on your phone over the car's audio system, via the same Bluetooth connection. Learn more in Chapter 18, "Listening to Music."

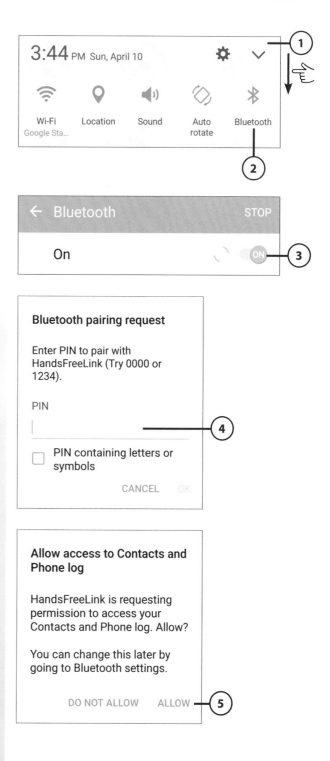

3:44 PM Sun, April 10

Wi-Fi   Location   Sound   Auto rotate   Bluetooth
Google Sta...

← Bluetooth   STOP

On   ON

Bluetooth pairing request

Enter PIN to pair with HandsFreeLink (Try 0000 or 1234).

PIN

☐ PIN containing letters or symbols

CANCEL   OK

Allow access to Contacts and Phone log

HandsFreeLink is requesting permission to access your Contacts and Phone log. Allow?

You can change this later by going to Bluetooth settings.

DO NOT ALLOW   ALLOW

Call from Your Car

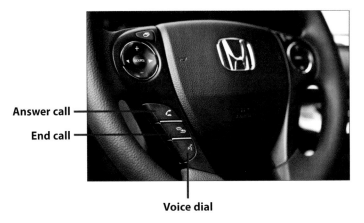

Answer call —

End call —

Voice dial

When your Galaxy S7 is connected to your car via Bluetooth, you can initiate a call in one of two ways.

First, you can simply start the call on your phone. You should be able to hear the sound over your car's audio system; if not, from the Galaxy S7's Phone app, tap Speaker to switch to car audio.

Second, you can initiate the call from your car. Each manufacturer has its own unique call functionality, but you should be able to press a button on your car's steering wheel or in-dash display and then use voice commands to dial your favorite contacts. You need to set up these voice commands in advance, of course; consult your car's instruction manual for more details.

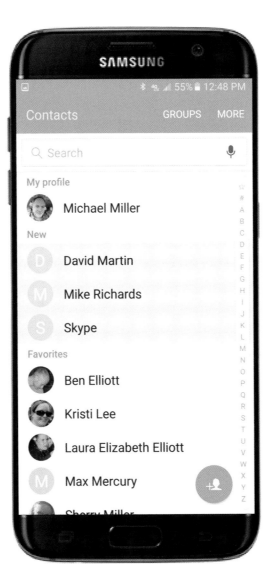

Managing Your Contacts List

Although you can enter phone numbers manually each time you want to make a call or send a text, it's a lot easier to store the numbers of your friends and family in a contacts list and access that list when you want to reach out to your contacts. Samsung's Contacts app lets you store all sorts of useful information in addition to names and phone numbers. You can also store a person's street address and email address, as well as link to that person's profile on Facebook, Twitter, and other social networks.

Adding and Editing Contacts

All of your contacts are stored in your phone's Contacts app. This app is accessible from the favorites section at the bottom of every Home screen.

Add a New Contact

You can add new contacts manually or when you receive a phone call from a new person.

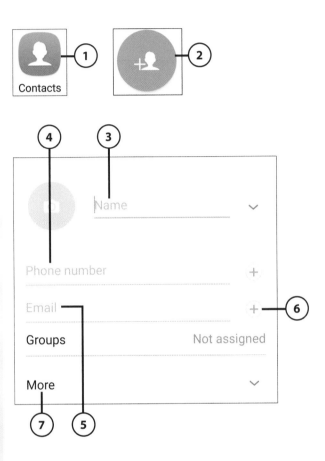

1. Tap Contacts on any Home screen to open the Contacts app.

2. Tap the round Add icon at the bottom of the screen.

3. Enter the contact's name (first and last) into the Name box.

4. Enter the contact's phone number into the Phone Number box. (By default, this is listed as a mobile number; to identify it as a home, work, or other type of number, tap Mobile next to the phone number and then make another selection.)

5. If you want, enter the person's email address into the Email box. (By default, this is listed as a home email address; to identify it as a work or other type of email address, tap Home next to the address and then make another selection.)

6. Add secondary phone numbers or email addresses by tapping the + next to that section and then entering the necessary information.

7. Tap More to add other types of information for this contact.

8 Tap the type of field you want to add—Organization, Address, Web Address, and so forth.

9 Enter the appropriate information for that field.

10 Tap Save when you're done entering information.

Add a New Contact from a Call

As discussed in the previous chapter, if you receive a phone call from someone new, you can quickly add that person to your contacts list. From the Phone app, tap to select the Log tab and then tap the call from the person you want to add. From the next screen, tap Create Contact and a new contact is created.

Edit Contact Information

You can, at any point, edit the information for any person in your contact list.

1 From within the Contacts app, navigate to and tap the name of the contact you want to edit.

2 Tap Edit on the person's contact screen.

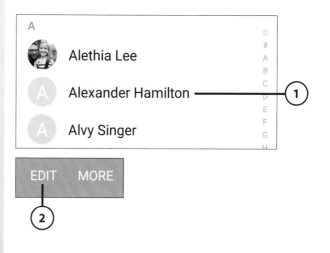

(3) Tap the field you want to edit and make your changes.

(4) Tap Save when done.

CANCEL   SAVE — (4)

Alexander ⌄

Hamilton

Phone number +

555-555-5564   Mobile —

Email +

alex@buybigco.com —

(3)

Star Favorite Contacts

You can designate the people you call or email the most as favorite contacts. All contacts marked as a favorite display together in the Favorites section at the top of your contacts list.

(1) From within the Contacts app, navigate to and tap the name of the contact you want to mark as a favorite.

(2) When the person's contact screen appears, tap the star icon, which turns gold. This contact is now favorited.

A   ☆
                                         #
Alethia Lee   A
                                         B
Alexander Hamilton   C
                                         D
                                         E
Alvy Singer ———————— (1)   F
                                         G
                                         H

Alvy Singer ★

(2)

People Edge and Contact Colors

If you have a Galaxy S7 edge (not the regular S7), you can activate the People Edge feature to display your priority contacts in color on the Edge screen. Learn more about this in Chapter 2, "Using the Galaxy S7 edge."

Assign a Unique Ringtone to a Contact

If you often get calls from a specific contact and want to be alerted when this person is calling, you can assign a unique ringtone to that person.

(1) Open the person's contact screen and tap Edit.

(2) Tap More.

(3) Scroll down the screen and tap Ringtone.

(4) Tap to select the ringtone you want for this person.

Add a Photo to a Contact

You can also add a person's picture to their contact information. This way you see the person's picture onscreen when they call you.

(1) From the person's contact screen, tap Edit.

(2) Tap the camera icon next to the person's name. (If the person already had a contact photo, click that photo to change it.)

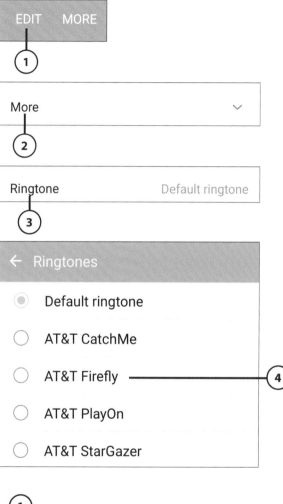

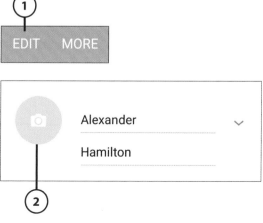

(3) Tap the Camera button to take a picture of this person (assuming he or she is right in front of you) *or…*

(4) Tap the Picture icon to upload a picture of this person that's stored on your phone. Your photo gallery opens.

(5) Scroll to and tap the picture you want to use.

(3)   (4)

6 Use your fingers to move, pinch, or spread the photo to better fit within the circle.

7 Tap Done.

8 If you want to touch up the photo, tap the Edit (magic wand) icon, select a filter, then tap Apply.

9 Tap Save to add this photo to the contact.

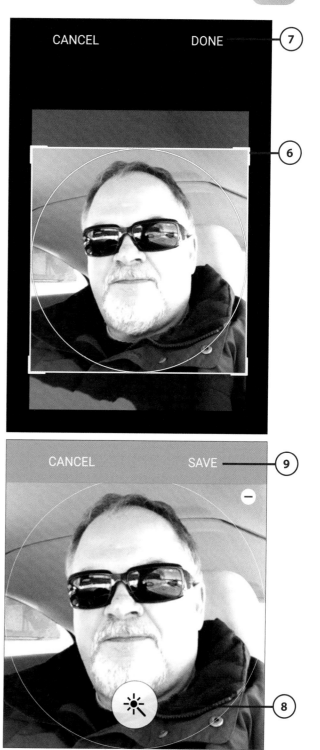

Delete a Contact

Sometimes you find you no longer communicate with a given person, and don't need (or want!) them in your contacts list. Fortunately, it's easy to delete contacts from your list.

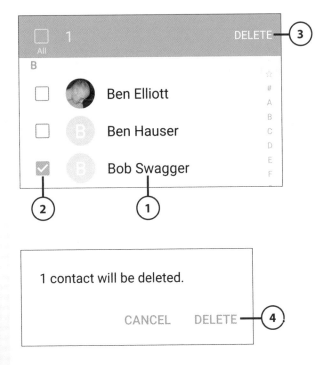

1. From within the Contacts app, tap and hold the name of the contact you want to delete.

2. The screen changes to display check boxes beside each contact, with the current contact selected. Tap to select any other contacts you want to delete.

3. Tap Delete at the top of the screen.

4. Tap Delete in the prompt box.

Using the Contacts App

After you've added your contacts to the Contacts app, there's a lot you can do with them—including making phone calls and sending texts and emails directly from a person's contact page.

Sort Contacts

By default, the contacts in your contacts list are organized into sections: My Profile (your contact information), New, and Favorites. Beneath that, all contacts are sorted alphabetically by first name. You can, however, choose to sort your contacts by last name instead.

1. From within the Contacts app, tap More.

2 Tap Settings to display the Settings screen.

3 Tap Sort By.

4 Tap First Name to sort by first name.

5 Tap Last Name to sort by last name.

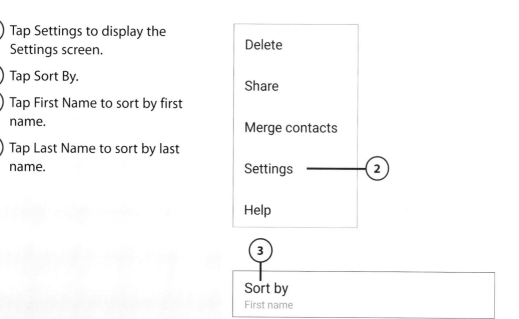

Delete

Share

Merge contacts

Settings —— **2**

Help

3

Sort by
First name

First name —— **4**

Last name —— **5**

Change the Display Format

By default, the Contacts app displays your contacts in the First, Last name format. You can, if you like, switch to the Last, First name format.

1 From within the Contacts app, tap More.

2 Tap Settings to display the Settings screen.

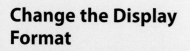

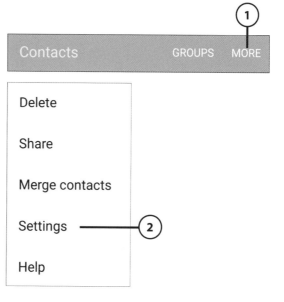

Contacts   GROUPS   MORE   **1**

Delete

Share

Merge contacts

Settings —— **2**

Help

(**3**) Tap Name Format.

(**4**) Tap Last, First to display last name first.

(**5**) Tap First, Last to display first name first.

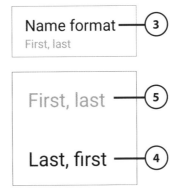

Search for Contacts

If you have a lot of contacts in your list, it might become cumbersome to scroll down until you find them. If this is a problem for you, you can use the Contact app's search function to search for specific contacts.

(**1**) At the top of the contacts list, enter a person's partial or entire name into the search box. Matching contacts display underneath the search box.

(**2**) Tap a contact to view that person's contact screen.

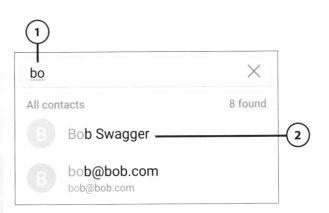

Contact a Contact

You can call, text, or email a contact directly from his or her contact screen.

(**1**) In the Contacts app, tap the name of the person you want to contact.

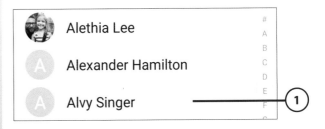

(2) Tap the Phone icon to initiate a voice call with this person.

(3) Tap the Video icon to open a video call with this person (if this person has a video camera activated).

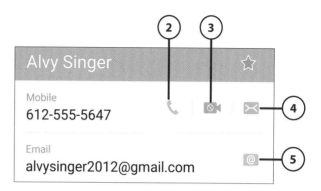

(4) Tap the Message icon to send a text message to this person.

(5) Tap the Email icon to send an email to this person.

It's Not All Good

No Icons

You'll only see the Phone, Video, and Message icons if you have information of that type entered for a contact. If you have not entered a person's email address, for example, you won't see an Email icon and won't be able to email this person from within the Contacts app.

Linking to Other Contacts

By default, the Contacts app contains only those contacts you've manually added to your phone. However, you can add contacts from other email accounts to your Galaxy S7, and your friends from those social networks are automatically added to your contacts list.

Add a New Account

When you first started using your Samsung Galaxy S7, you were prompted to enter your Google Account information. This makes it easier to use various Google and Android-related functions. It also adds your Gmail contacts (if you have a Gmail account) to your main contacts list.

You can connect your other email and messaging accounts to your contacts list. This way all your contacts are housed and accessed from the same app.

1. From within the Contacts app, tap More.

2. Tap Settings to display the Settings screen.

3. Tap Accounts to display the Accounts page. You should see settings for all accounts you've previously connected.

4. Tap Add Account.

5. Tap the type of account you want to add.

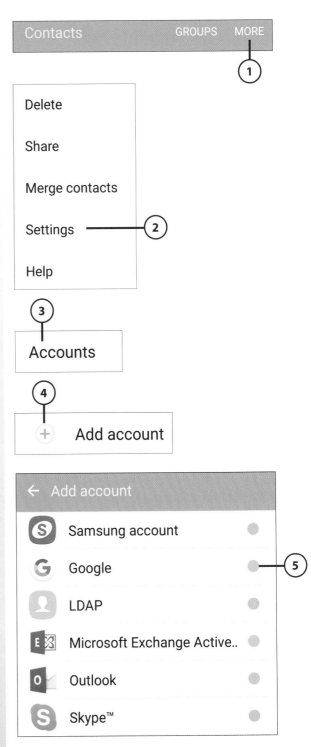

(6) If prompted to sign into the account, do so and then follow any additional onscreen instructions.

Merge Contacts from Different Accounts

If you have the same friends on different social networks, or on different email lists, you might end up having multiple contacts for them in the Contacts app. If this happens, you can merge multiple contacts for the same person into a single contact.

(1) From within the Contacts app, tap More.

(2) Tap Merge Contacts.

(3) Tap to select two or more contacts that you know are for the same person.

(4) Tap Merge. The selected contacts are merged into a single contact.

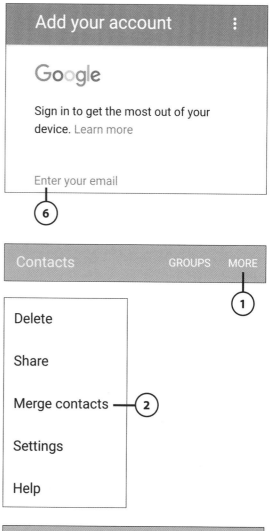

Delete Accounts

You might find that you don't actually want all the contacts from your various accounts synced into a single contacts list; too many contacts can sometimes be overwhelming. If this is the case, you can opt to disconnect a given account from your phone.

1. From within the Contacts app, tap More.

2. Tap Settings to display the Settings screen.

3. Tap Accounts to display the Accounts page.

4. Tap to select the account you want to delete.

5. Tap More.

6. Tap Remove Account.

7. Tap Remove Account in the prompt box.

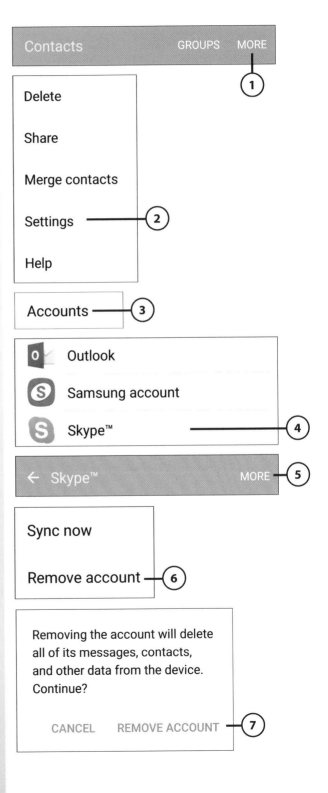

Working with Groups

There's one more thing you can do from the Contacts app. If you regularly send emails or texts to a group of people—members of a golf league, say, or friends in a book club—you can create a contacts group. You can then send messages or emails to everyone in the group with a single action; you don't have to enter every single name separately.

Create a Group

You create new groups from within the Contacts app. In fact, the app comes with several common groups preloaded.

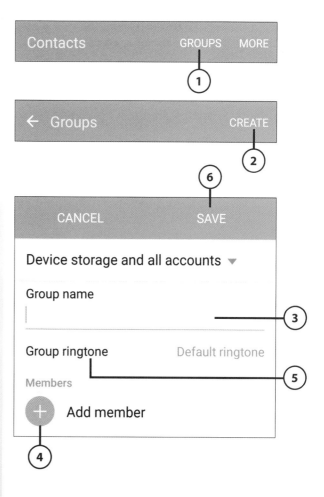

1. From within the Contacts app, tap Groups to display the Groups screen. You see a list of existing groups.

2. Tap Create to add a new group.

3. Type a name for the group into the Group Name box.

4. If you want to add members now, tap Add Member. (See the "Add Contacts to a Group" section for more information.)

5. Tap Group Ringtone and make a selection to set a default ringtone for messages from members of this group.

6. Tap Save.

Add Contacts to a Group

You add new members to a group from your main contacts list.

1. From within the Contacts app, tap Groups to display the Groups screen.

2. Tap the group you want to add members to.

3. Tap Edit.

4. Tap Add Member to display your contacts list.

5. Tap to select those contacts you want to add.

6. Tap Done. The selected contacts are now added to the group.

Send Group Messages

You can send group messages via text or email. From within your messaging or email app, simply enter the name of the group as the recipient. Compose your message and tap send, and the message will be sent to all members of that group.

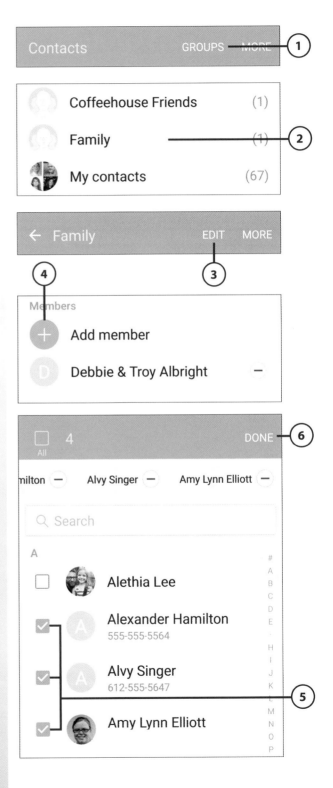

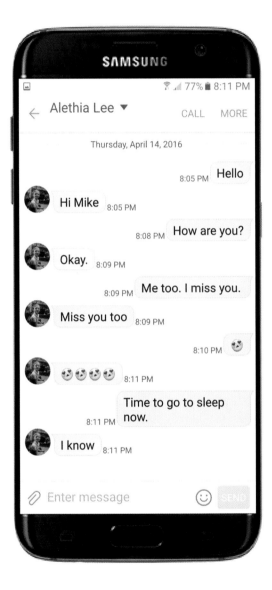

In this chapter, you see how to send and receive text and multimedia messages on your phone. Topics include the following:

→ Sending and Receiving Text Messages
→ Sending and Receiving Multimedia Messages
→ Working with Priority Senders
→ Configuring the Messages App

Texting Friends and Family

These days, an increasing number of people use their phones less for voice calls and more for text messaging—what we colloquially call texting. It's easy to pop off a short text message while you're in the middle of doing something else; you can even participate in multiple text sessions with different people at the same time.

Of course, to be a proficient texter you need nimble fingers, proficiency with your phone's onscreen keyboard, and a decent messaging app. Although this book can't help you with your fingers, it does examine the most popular text messaging app and how to get the most out of it.

Sending and Receiving Text Messages

Text messages are sent over your mobile carrier's network. You might have to subscribe to a separate service or level to send and receive messages. Some plans offer a set number of messages for a flat price; others offer unlimited messaging. If your plan limits the number of messages you can send or receive, take care not to go over this limit, or you'll incur excess messaging charges.

Fortunately, sending and receiving text messages is easy. (If it wasn't so easy, people wouldn't text so much!) And although it's likely that your children and grandchildren do a lot more texting than you ever will, you need to know how to text if you want to keep in touch.

Choosing a Messaging App

There are lots of messaging apps available for your phone. Every Samsung smart-phone comes with Samsung's Messages app preinstalled. You may also have a messaging app from your phone carrier installed, and you can find still more messaging apps for download from the Google Play Store. We'll work with the Messages app in this chapter; if you need to make this app your default, open the Settings screen, select the Device tab, and tap Applications. From the next screen, tap Default Applications, then tap Messaging App and select Messages.

Send a Text Message

A text message is nothing more than a line or two of text—or even just a single word!

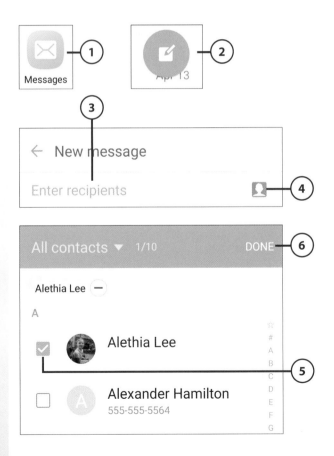

(1) From your phone's Home screen, tap the Messages icon to launch the Messages app.

(2) Tap the Compose button to display the New Message screen and onscreen keyboard.

(3) Type the name of the person you want to text into the Enter Recipients box. Separate multiple names with semicolons (;) or...

(4) Tap the Add Recipient icon to display your contacts list.

(5) Tap to select one or more recipients for this text. The recipients' names appear at the top of the screen.

(6) Tap Done to return to the New Message screen.

(7) Tap in the Enter Message area and use the onscreen keyboard to type your message.

(8) Tap Send to send the message.

Exit Before Sending

If you exit the Messages app before sending a message, that message will be saved as a draft you can send at a later time.

Read and Reply to a Message

When someone sends you a text, you receive a notification to that effect. (You also see a new message icon in your phone's status bar.) You can read and respond to the text from the notification or from the Messages app.

(1) From the notification, tap View or…

(2) Swipe from the top of the screen to view the notification panel and then tap the message or…

(3) From the main screen of the Messages app, tap the message you want to read.

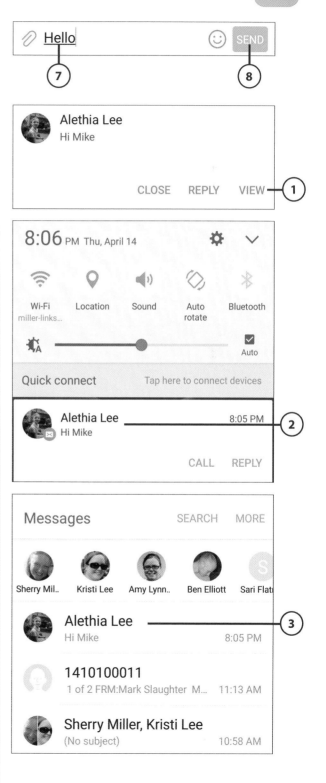

4 You now see all recent messages to and from this person or group of people. (This is called a *conversation*.) Your messages appear on the right side of the screen; messages from other participants appear on the left.

5 Reply to this message by tapping in the Enter Message area and, when the onscreen keyboard appears, typing your message.

6 Tap Send.

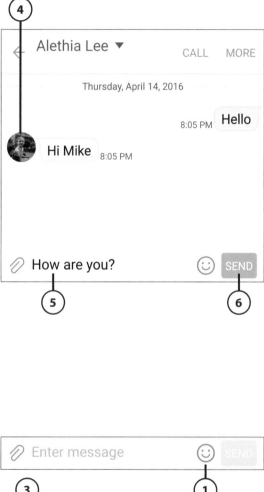

Use Emoji

Some people like to enhance their messages with little icons called emoji. As mentioned in Chapter 1, "Getting Started with Your Samsung Galaxy S7," an emoji is a small picture or icon used to express an emotion or idea. For example, if you like a person's text, you might reply with a smiley face or thumbs-up emoji instead of (or in addition to) a text message. If there's something you don't like, respond with a frowning face or thumbs-down emoji. You get the idea.

1 From within a message or conversation, tap the Emoji icon in the Enter Message area. This displays a collection of emoji.

2 Tap the appropriate tab to view a certain type of emoji.

3 Tap the emoji you want to send.

4 Tap ABC to return to the alphanumeric keyboard.

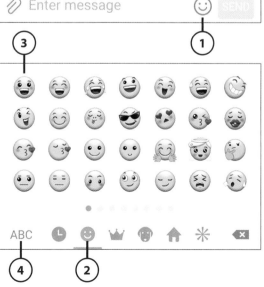

Delete Conversations

All your conversations are displayed on the main Messages screen. If you want to clean up this screen a bit, you can delete older conversations. (In fact, it's a good idea to delete your older conversations periodically, especially those that include videos or photos, to free up storage space on your phone.)

(1) From the main Messages screen, tap More.

(2) Tap Delete.

(3) Tap to select those conversations you want to delete.

(4) Tap Delete.

(5) When prompted to delete the conversation, tap Delete.

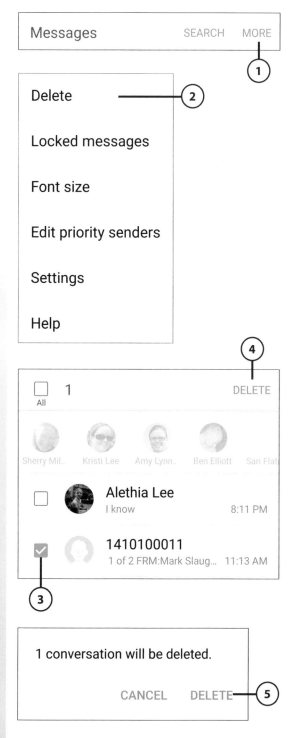

>>>Go Further

TEXTING ETIQUETTE

Just what should you text—and how? There is some very real etiquette involved in texting.

First, you don't have to use complete sentences. You don't have to use proper punctuation. You don't even have to use correct spelling. Texting is all about quickness and immediacy, and sometimes that means sending a single word or typing without capitalizing any letters. In the world of texting, it's better to be fast than to be precise. It's okay to make mistakes.

Second, don't write long-winded texts. Texts are short messages, with the emphasis on *short*. You don't have to write in complete paragraphs and sentences. Write enough words to get your point across, then tap the Send button. That's enough.

Third, about that fast thing. When somebody texts you, they expect an immediate response. If they didn't want an immediate response, they would email you instead. Think of texting as carrying on a conversation, but by typing instead of talking. You don't want to leave unnecessary gaps in the conversation.

Fourth, don't bombard your friends with too many texts. Yes, the kids text all the time about nothing much in particular, but you're not a kid and you're not texting other kids. (Unless you're texting your own kids or grandkids, of course, then all bets are off.) Text your friends and family when there's something important to share. Otherwise, don't.

Fifth and finally, don't text and drive. In many states it's against the law. In every state, it's just plain dangerous. Texting in the car requires you to take your eyes off the road, even if just for a second or two—and that's long enough for bad things to happen that you won't have time to respond to. Ignore the dinging of those incoming texts and keep focused on your driving. You can answer any text you receive at your next stop.

Sending and Receiving Multimedia Messages

The Messages app lets you send both text and multimedia messages. This lets you send photos and videos to your friends and family.

SMS and MMS

Text messages are technically called *SMS* messages. SMS stands for Short Messaging Service, and it lets you send and receive text messages to and from other mobile phones. When you send and receive pictures or videos via messaging, you're using a similar protocol dubbed *MMS* (short for Multimedia Messaging Services). This enables non-text attachments to be sent along with text messages.

Attach a Photo or Video File

It's easy to send a photo or video along with your normal text messages. Recipients can then view these files when they read your texts.

1. From within an existing or new conversation, tap the File icon to display the Attach panel beneath the message.

2. Tap to select the Gallery tab.

3. Tap to select the image or video you want to send. The file is added to the current message. (You can add additional photos or videos to this message, if you want.)

4. Enter any accompanying text (optional).

5. Tap Send to send the message with the photo or video attached.

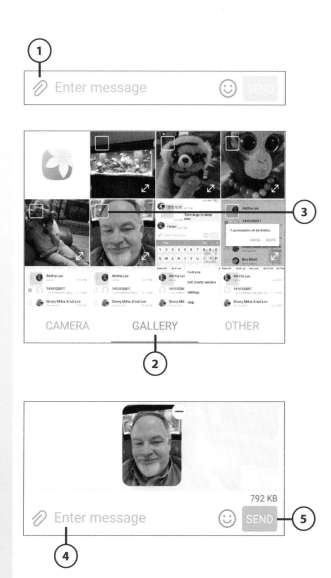

Shoot and Send a Photo or Video

You're not limited to sending photos or videos stored in your phone's gallery. You can also shoot a new photo or video on the spot to send with your text.

(1) From within an existing or new conversation, tap the File icon to display the Attach panel beneath the message.

(2) Tap to select the Camera tab.

(3) Take a photo by aiming at your subject and then tapping the Camera button.

(4) Take a video by aiming at your subject and then tapping the red Record button. When you're done recording, press the Stop button.

(5) The picture or video is now added to the current message. Enter any accompanying text, as you like.

(6) Tap Send to send the message with the photo or video attached.

View Photos and Videos You Receive

What do you do if someone sends you a photo or video via text? Look at them, of course!

(1) Tap a picture to view it fullscreen.

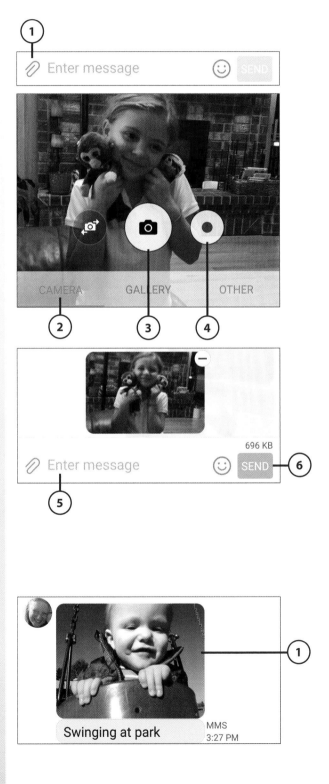

(2) Tap a video to watch it fullscreen.

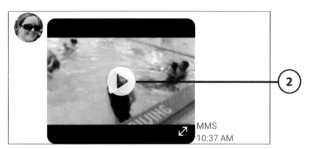

MMS
10:37 AM

Working with Priority Senders

If you find yourself texting with the same people over and over, you set those folks as *priority senders*, which makes it easier to send messages to them.

Set Priority Senders

You can designate any person in your contacts list as a priority sender—and have multiple priority senders in your Messages app.

(1) All of your priority senders are displayed in a scrolling list at the top of the main Messages screen. Scroll to the right and tap the + icon to add a new priority sender.

(2) Tap to select any person or group you've recently messaged. *Or...*

(3) Tap Contacts to display your contacts list.

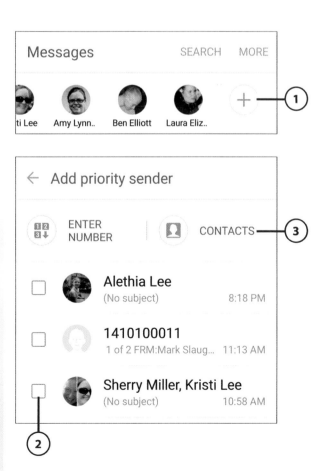

(4) Tap to select a contact you want
to set as a priority sender.

(5) Tap Done.

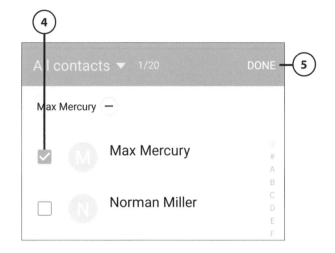

Text to Priority Senders

Priority senders appear at the top of
the Messages screen. You can add
other priority senders by tapping the +
button.

(1) From the main screen in the
Messages app, tap the priority
sender you want to text.

(2) If you've previously texted this
person, you see your past conversation. Otherwise, you see the
New Message screen. Enter your
text as normal.

(3) Tap Send.

Configuring the Messages App

There are several settings in the Messages app you can configure to personalize
your texting experience. In particular, you can personalize the display and font
size to make your texts easier to read.

Personalize the Display

The first thing you can configure is the text display itself—the backgrounds and bubbles you see on the main Messages screen.

(1) From the main screen in the Messages app, tap More.

(2) Tap Settings to display the Settings screen.

(3) Tap Backgrounds.

(4) Tap the desired background at the bottom of the screen.

Messages	SEARCH	MORE

(1)

Settings	(2)

Backgrounds	(3)

🔋 71% 8:28 PM

← Backgrounds

8:28 PM **Hi**

Hello! 8:28 PM

(4)

Change Font Size

You might find that the default font size in the Messages app is too small to read comfortably. Fortunately, it's easy to increase the size of the font to make it easier to read.

(1) From the main screen in the Messages app, tap More.

(2) Tap Font Size to display the Font Size panel.

(3) Tap Off the Use Device Font Sizes switch.

(4) Tap to select the size you want, from Tiny to Extra Huge.

(5) Tap Done.

Resizing on the Fly

You can also resize message text when you're reading a message. Just pinch or stretch the screen with your fingers to make the text smaller or larger.

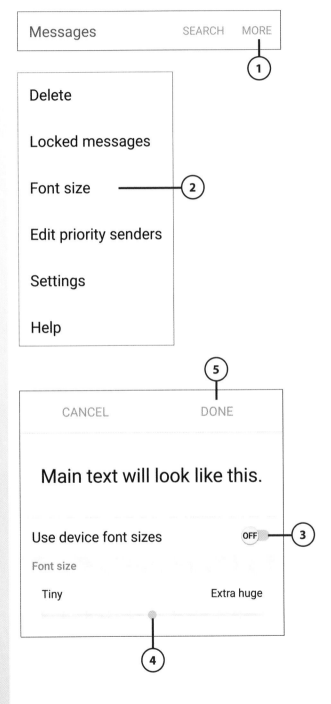

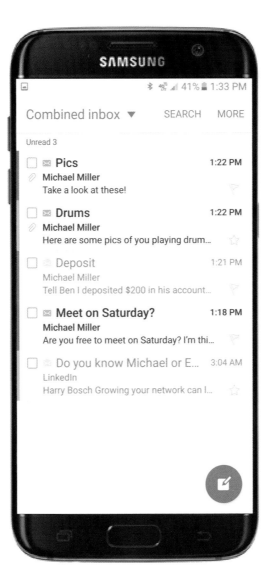

In this chapter, you learn how to send and receive email on your new Samsung Galaxy S7 or S7 edge. Topics include the following:

→ Setting Up the Email App
→ Receiving and Sending Messages

Sending and Receiving Email

Email is an essential part of most people's lives. It's how we communicate with friends and families, as well as with co-workers and organizations we work with. Because your new Samsung smartphone connects to the Internet, you can use it to send and receive email messages.

Setting Up the Email App

The default email app for Samsung smartphones is called, simply, Email. You can configure the Email app to work with AOL Mail, Gmail, Microsoft Exchange, Outlook.com, Yahoo! Mail, and IMAP/POP3 email services.

Add a New Account

Before you can use the Email app, you need to configure it to work with your various email accounts. In most instances, all you need to know to do this is your email address and password.

1. From your phone's Home screen tap the Email icon to open the Email app.

2. The first time you use the Email app, you'll be prompted to set up your email account. On subsequent uses, tap More to add additional accounts.

3. Tap Settings to display the Settings screen.

4. Tap + Add Account.

5. Enter your email address into the Email Address box.

6. Enter your email password into the Password box.

7. If you want this to be your primary email account when sending emails from your phone, select the Set as the Default Account for Sending Email option.

8. Tap Sign In. Follow the onscreen instructions to finish adding this new account to the app.

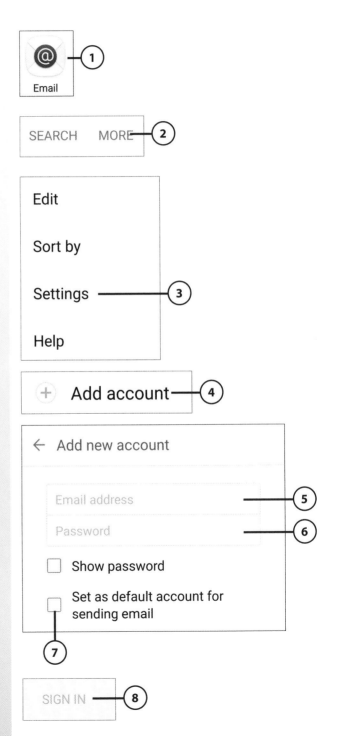

Other Email Apps

There are several other email apps you can use on your Galaxy S7. Most web-based email services, such as Gmail, Outlook, and Yahoo! Mail, offer their own apps—or you can configure Samsung's Email app to access those accounts.

Switch Between Accounts

If you have the Email app configured for more than one account, you can display the inbox for each account, or for all accounts combined.

Combined inbox ▼ ──①

③ ②

Mailbox   SETTINGS   MORE

Combined view

✉ Combined inbox ③

✉ | molehillgroup@gmail.com ①

✉ | trapperjohn2000@hotmai... ②

✉ | trapperjohn2000@gmail.com

✉ Unread ③

👤 Priority senders ──────④

① From the Email app's main screen, tap the Inbox down arrow.

② Tap a specific account to view that account's inbox.

③ Tap Combined Inbox to view messages from all your accounts in a single inbox, identified by color.

④ Tap Priority Senders to view messages from your designated priority senders.

Receiving and Sending Messages

You can use the Email app to read, reply to, and compose new email messages from your Galaxy S7 phone.

Read and Reply to Messages

Email messages you receive from other users are stored in your inbox. From there you can read and reply to these messages.

1. Open the Email app, tap the Inbox down arrow, and select a specific account or your combined inbox.

2. All incoming messages in the selected account are displayed, the newest first. (If you're in the combined inbox, messages from each individual account are color-coded along the left side.) Unread messages are solid black with a bright orange email icon; messages you've read appear slightly shaded and with a shaded icon. Each message displays the sender's name and email, the subject of the message, and the first line of the message. You also see the date or time the message was received. Scroll down to view more messages.

3. Tap the message you want to read. The message opens on the next screen.

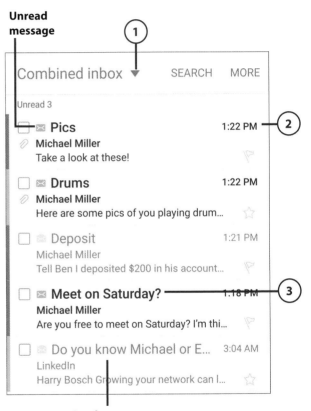

Unread message

Combined inbox ▼   SEARCH   MORE

Unread 3

✉ **Pics**   1:22 PM
  Michael Miller
  Take a look at these!

☐ ✉ **Drums**   1:22 PM
  Michael Miller
  Here are some pics of you playing drum...

☐ ✉ Deposit   1:21 PM
  Michael Miller
  Tell Ben I deposited $200 in his account...

☐ ✉ **Meet on Saturday?**   1:18 PM
  Michael Miller
  Are you free to meet on Saturday? I'm thi...

☐ ✉ Do you know Michael or E...   3:04 AM
  LinkedIn
  Harry Bosch Growing your network can l...

Read message

4 Tap Delete to delete this message after you've read it.

5 Tap the back arrow to return to the inbox.

6 Tap Reply to write a response to this message. (If the message was sent to multiple recipients, send your reply to all of them by tapping Reply All.)

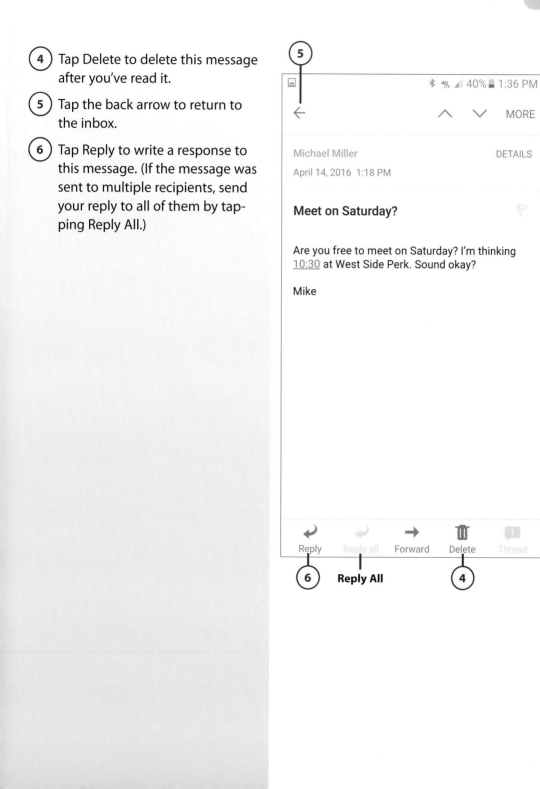

7 You see the reply screen, with the sender's name or email address already added to the To field and the original message displayed beneath. Use the onscreen keyboard to type your reply.

8 Tap Send to send the email.

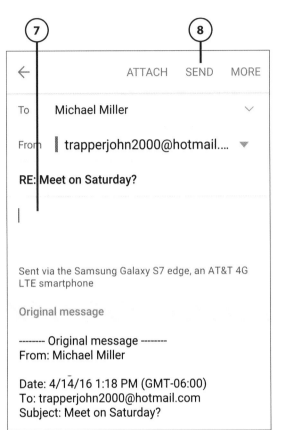

Delete from the Inbox

Sometimes you don't need to read a message to know you want to delete it. To delete a message directly from the inbox, drag the message header to the left.

Create a New Message

It's also easy to create and send a new email message. You can enter the recipient's email address manually or automatically send to anyone in your contacts list.

1 From the inbox screen, tap the New Message icon to open a new message.

2 If you have multiple email accounts, tap the From down arrow to select which email account you want to send from.

3 Tap in the To box and type the recipient's email address.

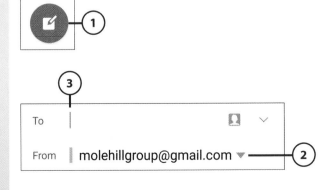

4 The Email app displays matching contacts. Tap a name to select it, or finish typing the name. If you want to send to more than one person, separate address with semicolons (;) or…

5 Tap the Add Recipient icon to display your contacts list.

6 Tap to select one or more recipients for this text.

7 The recipients' names appear at the top of the screen. Tap Done to return to the new message screen.

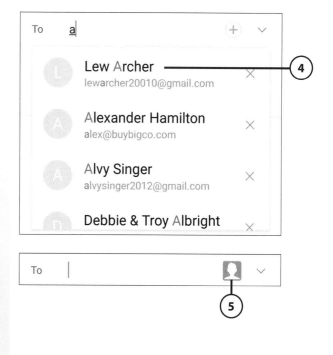

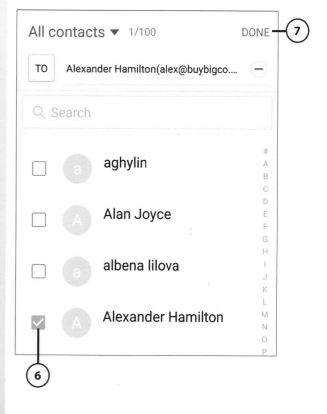

8 Tap in the Subject box and type the subject of this email.

9 Tap in the box beneath the Subject box and type your email message.

10 Tap Send to send the message.

←   ATTACH   **SEND**   MORE

To   Alexander Hamilton   ⌄

From   molehillgroup@gmail.com ▾

Subject

Sent via the Samsung Galaxy S7 edge, an AT&T 4G LTE smartphone

Send Photos and Other Attachments

You can send photos and other files stored on your phone via email. To send a file, you attach it to your message; these files are called *attachments*.

1 From within a new message, tap Attach to open the Attach panel.

2 To attach a photo, tap to select the Gallery tab.

3 Tap to select the item(s) you want to attach.

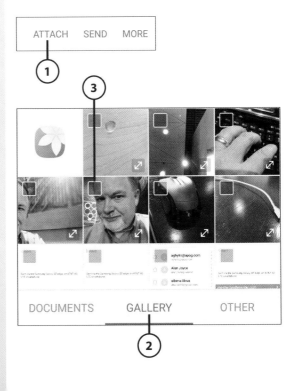

ATTACH   SEND   MORE

DOCUMENTS   GALLERY   OTHER

4 To attach a different type of file, tap the Other tab.

5 Tap the type of file you want to attach and then continue to select a specific item.

6 The files you selected are added to your email. If you decide not to attach an item, tap the minus (–) sign.

7 Finish creating the message as normal and then tap Send.

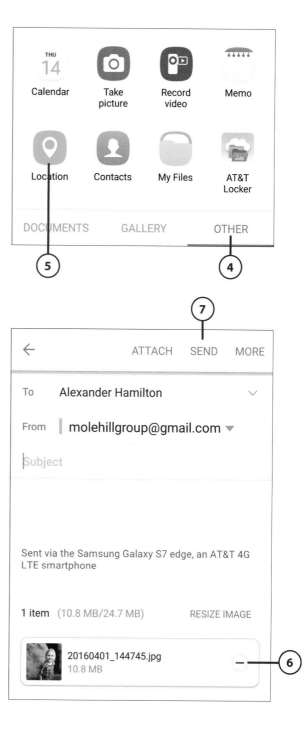

It's Not All Good

Sending Photos via Mobile Data

Photographs and videos attached to email messages are typically very large files. That may be fine when you're sending email when connected to Wi-Fi, but when you're sending email over a mobile data connection, those large files can quickly eat up the available data on your data plan. It's easy to send a handful of pics of your grandkids, or a video or two when you're on vacation; if you're not connecting via Wi-Fi, those attachments could use a lot of your available data, and possibly send you over the limit.

A good rule of thumb is to wait until you have a Wi-Fi connection to send photos, videos, and other large attachments via email. That way you won't overuse your mobile data plan, and keep your costs down.

View and Save Attachments

Photos are not displayed by default in email messages you receive. You have to tap to view photos and other files sent to you by others.

1 Messages that include attachments are noted with a paper clip icon in the inbox. Tap to open the message.

2 Tap the down arrow to see all attached files.

3 Tap to view a specific file.

4 Tap Save to download the file to your phone.

It's Not All Good

Viruses and Malware

While your smartphone is a lot safer than your personal computer, it can still become infected with viruses and other malicious software (collectively dubbed *malware*). The most common way for malware to spread is via infected files sent as email attachments.

If you tap to open an infected file attachment, your phone could become infected with that particular malware. For this reason, I recommend that you *never* tap to open any file attachment you weren't otherwise expecting. It's always possible that someone has purposefully or inadvertently sent you a bad file, and if you don't open it, you won't be infected.

So if you're expecting a friend or colleague to send you a file or photo via email, it's generally okay to open it. But if you get sent a file you weren't expecting, just delete the entire email. Better safe than sorry!

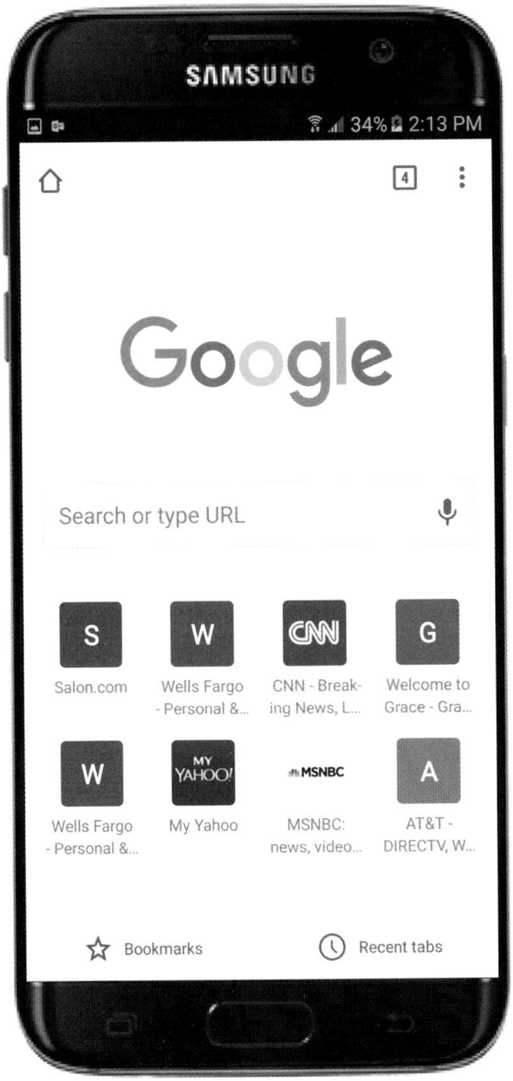
SAMSUNG
34% 2:13 PM
4
Google
Search or type URL
S
Salon.com
W
Wells Fargo - Personal &...
CNN
CNN - Breaking News, L...
G
Welcome to Grace - Gra...
W
Wells Fargo - Personal &...
MY YAHOO!
My Yahoo
MSNBC
MSNBC: news, video...
A
AT&T - DIRECTV, W...
Bookmarks
Recent tabs

In this chapter, you see how to use the Chrome web browser to browse and search the Web. Topics include the following:

→ Browsing the Web with Google Chrome
→ Working with Your Home Page
→ Using Tabs
→ Bookmarking Favorite Pages
→ Making the Web More Readable
→ Searching the Web with Google

Browsing and Searching the Web

Your Samsung Galaxy S7 or S7 edge smartphone is so much more than a regular phone. When you connect it to the Internet, either via Wi-Fi or your mobile carrier, it's a full-fledged computer and web browser that you hold in the palm of your hand. In fact, many people use their smartphones more than their computers to connect to the Internet. It's easy to see why!

Browsing the Web with Google Chrome

To browse websites on the Internet, you need an app called a web browser. Your Galaxy S7/S7 edge comes with two web browsers installed—Samsung's default browser, called Samsung Internet, and the Google Chrome browser. Samsung Internet is set as your phone's default browser (see the Internet icon at the bottom of the Home screen), although you can reset the default to Chrome.

Make Chrome Your Default Browser

Both Samsung Internet and Google Chrome work in a similar fashion, but Google Chrome is both more popular and more versatile than Samsung Internet. I recommend you switch from the default Samsung Internet browser and make Chrome your default browser app.

1. Swipe down from the top of the screen to view the notification panel.

2. Tap Settings to open the Settings screen.

3. Tap to select the Device tab.

4. Tap Applications to open the Applications screen.

5. Tap Default Applications.

6. Tap Browser App.

7. Tap to select Chrome.

Home Screen Shortcut

You can find a shortcut to Google Chrome in the Google folder located either on your Home screen or the Apps screen. Use the techniques discussed in Chapter 6, "Installing and Using Apps," to place a Chrome shortcut directly on the Home screen or in the Favorite Apps area.

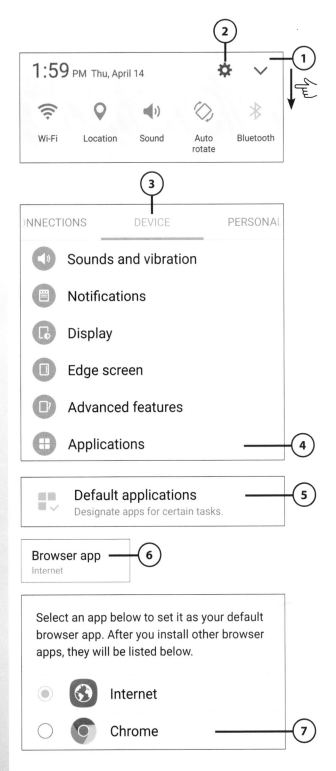

Launch Google Chrome

Chrome

The version of Chrome on your smartphone is very similar to the version you might be using on your personal computer, but it's customized to the smaller phone display.

To use Google Chrome to browse the Web, your phone must be connected to the Internet. If you don't have a Wi-Fi network or hotspot nearby, your phone automatically connects using your mobile carrier's data network.

Connecting to the Internet
Learn how to connect to the Internet in Chapter 5, "Connecting to the Internet and Cellular Networks."

(1) From any Home screen, tap the Chrome icon to open Google Chrome.

(2) The first time you launch Chrome, it opens to Chrome's New Tab page. If you've previously used the browser, it opens your last open page.

Home   **Omnibox**   **Menu**

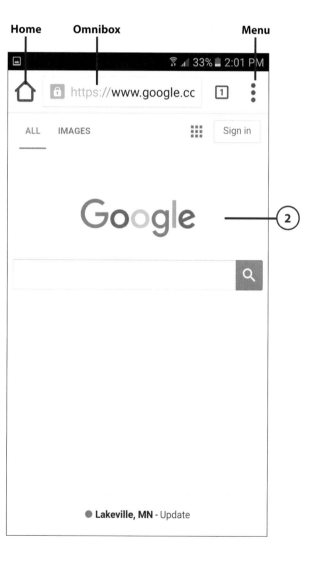

Enter a Web Address

To go directly to a given website or web page, you must enter the web address of that page into the Omnibox at the top of the browser screen.

1. Tap within the Omnibox to display the onscreen keyboard. If the Omnibox is not visible (it slides up when not in use), drag down the web page until it appears.

2. Enter the address of the web page you want to visit.

3. As you type, Chrome might suggest matching web pages. Tap any page to go to it *or...*

4. Finish entering the full address and then tap Go on the keyboard to go to that page.

5 The web page appears onscreen. Swipe up to scroll down the page.

6 If a page has trouble loading, or if you want to refresh the content, you can reload the page. Begin by tapping the Menu button.

7 Tap the Reload button.

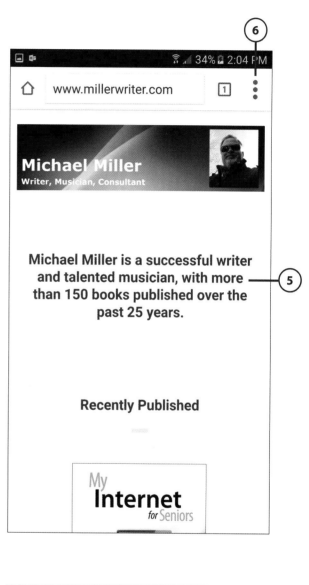

>>>Go Further
WEB ADDRESSES

A web address is called a Uniform Resource Locator, or URL. Technically, all URLs start with either **http://** or (for secure sites) **https://**. You don't need to type this part of the URL, however; Chrome assumes it and enters it automatically.

The main part of most web addresses starts with **www** followed by a dot, then the name of the website, then another dot and the domain identifier, such as **com** or **org**. As an example, my personal website is **www.millerwriter.com**.

To make things easier, Samsung's onscreen keyboard includes a **www.** key you can use to start the URL. As you enter the rest of the address, this key changes to a **.com** key you can tap to finish things off.

Use Web Links

Pages on the Web are often connected via clickable (on your phone, tappable) links, called web links. A web link can be within a page's text (typically underlined or in a different color) or embedded in an image. Tap a link to go the linked-to page.

(1) On the current web page, tap the web link.

(2) The linked-to page displays.

(1)

It's a problem the workplace has tried to ignore: hearing loss among the millions of boomers still on the job.

☰ MENU **AARP** Real Possibilities 🔍

Celebrating the Adventures of Hearing ——(2) Loss

For those with hearing loss, most career and social obstacles have to be navigated in a more strategic way

by Katherine Bouton, December 24, 2015

💬 Comments: 9

Revisit Past Pages

How easy is it to return to a web page you've previously viewed? Chrome keeps track of all your web browsing history, and revisiting a page is as easy as tapping it in the History list.

(1) Tap the Menu button.

(2) Tap History to display the History screen.

(3) Tap the page you want to revisit.

Working with Your Home Page

You can configure Chrome to display a Home page when it launches or when you tap the Home button.

Set Your Home Page

Your phone carrier might have created a default Home page for you. (For example, AT&T sets its own home. att.com page as your Home.) You can keep this page or set a different Home page.

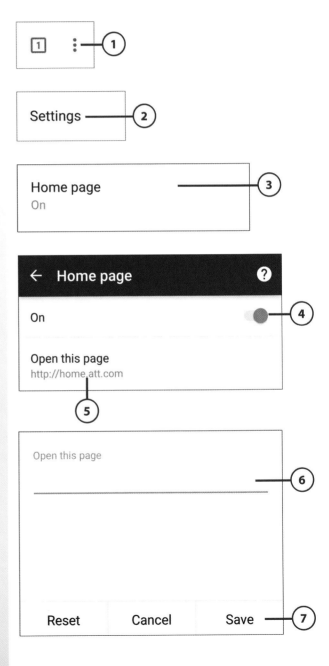

1. Tap the Menu button.

2. Tap Settings to display the Settings screen.

3. Tap Home Page to display the Home Page screen.

4. Tap On the switch at the top of the page.

5. Tap Open This Page.

6. Enter the address of your desired Home page into the top box.

7. Tap Save.

Go to Your Home Page

Your Home page is never more than a tap away. Just tap the Home button and the Home page displays.

Home button ———

Using Tabs

Chrome is a tabbed browser, which means you can open several web pages at the same time, all in different tabs. You then switch from page to page by selecting different tabs within the browser.

Display Tabs as Tabs

By default, each tab displays as a separate app on your Galaxy S7 or S7 edge. In this default mode, if you want to switch between open tabs, you have to tap the Recents key to view all running apps and then tap the app thumbnail that's running the tab you want.

Many users find this default behavior confusing, and would rather have all tabs available within the browser. You can make this happen by reconfiguring the proper setting.

(1) From within the browser, tap the Menu button.

(2) Tap Settings to display the Settings screen.

(3) Tap Merge Tabs and Apps.

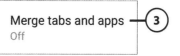

(4) Tap Off the switch at the top of
the screen. (To return to tabs-as-
apps operations, return to the
Merge Tabs and Apps screen and
tap On the switch.)

(5) You are cautioned that Chrome
will separate tabs and apps.
Tap OK.

Open a New Tab

When you separate tabs and apps,
Chrome displays a Tabs button at the
top of the screen. The number within
this button tells you how many tabs
you have open. You use this button to
open new tabs and switch between
tabs.

When you open a new tab, you see
Chrome's New Tab page. This page
includes a Google search box and
thumbnails that link to your most-
visited web pages.

(1) Tap the Tabs button. All open
tabs now appear in a stack.

(2) Tap the New Tab (+) button.

(3) The new tab opens and displays
the New Tab page.

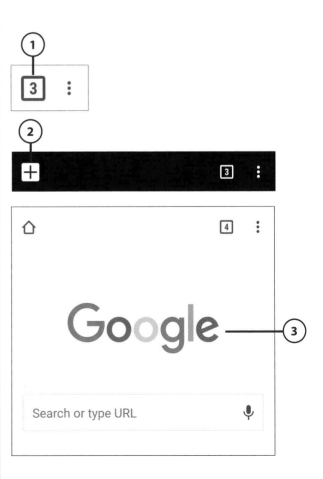

It's Not All Good

Too Many Tabs

If you're like me, you go from one page to another in rapid succession. The temptation is to do so in separate tabs, and then leave all those tabs open. Before you know it, you end up with a half-dozen or more open tabs—which is not a good thing.

Not only are a lot of open tabs confusing to navigate (which page is where?), each tab you have open uses system resources. If you keep a half-dozen or so tabs open in the background, your phone's battery will drain much more quickly.

The best solution is to limit yourself to no more than two or three open tabs at a time. If you need to open another one, close an open one first. It's a lot more manageable!

Open a New Incognito Tab

Sometimes you want to visit web pages that you don't want others to see. Maybe you're shopping for a birthday present for your spouse that you want to keep secret. Maybe you want to view content that you simply want to keep private. To accommodate your need for privacy, Chrome offers Incognito browsing, a private browsing mode. Incognito mode is totally anonymous; the pages you visit in this mode are not tracked or stored in your browser history.

(1) Tap the Menu button.

(2) Tap New Incognito Tab.

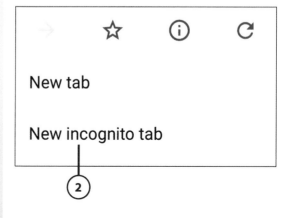

(3) A new Incognito tab opens. You can browse in this tab as you would normally.

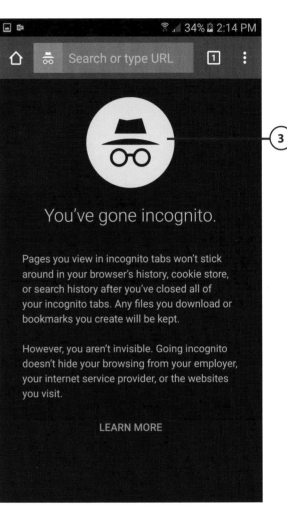

(3)

Switch Between Tabs

When you have several different web pages open in different tabs, it's easy to switch back and forth between pages.

(1) Tap the Tabs button.

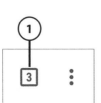

(**2**) You now see all your open tabs in a stack. Tap the tab you want to view.

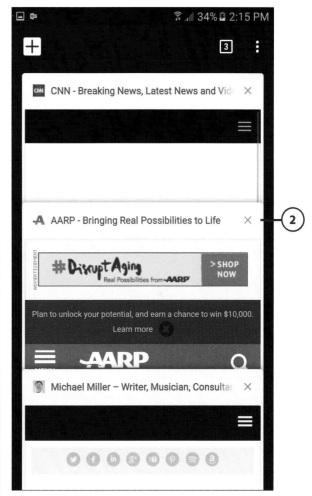

Close a Tab

Closing a tab is equally easy.

(**1**) Tap the Tabs button.

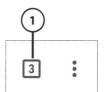

(2) Tap the X for the tab you want to close.

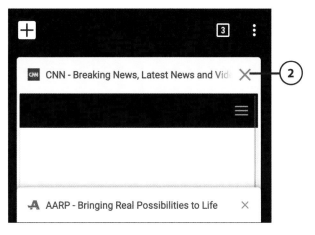

Bookmarking Favorite Pages

When you find a web page you like and expect to revisit, you can save that page as a *bookmark*. To return to the page, you don't have to re-enter the URL—just click the bookmark!

Create a Bookmark

Bookmarking a web page is as easy as tapping an icon.

(1) Open the page you want to bookmark and then tap the Menu button.

(2) Tap the star icon.

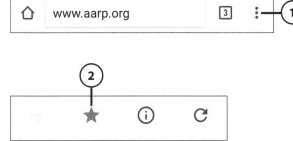

Revisit a Bookmark

When you want to revisit a book-marked page, just tap the item in your bookmark list.

(1) Tap the Menu button.

(2) Tap Bookmarks to display your bookmark folders.

(3) Tap the bookmark for the page you want to view. The page now opens in the Chrome browser.

3 ⋮ —(1)

→ ★ ⓘ ↻

New tab

New incognito tab

Bookmarks ———(2)

≡ **Bookmarks** 🔍 ✕

A AARP - Bringing Real Possibilities... ⋮ —(3)

A major Batman v. Superman cliff... ⋮

D Diamond Comic Distributors, Inc ⋮

C Comic Art & Graffix Gallery ⋮

P PTG Author Connection ⋮

H HP Home ⋮

>>>Go Further
SYNCHRONIZING BOOKMARKS—AND MORE

When you use the Chrome browser after signing into your Google Account (and you're always signed in on your S7 or S7 edge), the pages you visit and bookmark are stored in your Google Account, online. When you open a Chrome browser on another device, such as your personal computer, you see the same browsing history and bookmarks on that device. (As long as you're signed into your Google Account, of course.)

This synchronization works both ways. Any new pages you visit using the PC version of Chrome also appear in your history when you next open Chrome on your smartphone. Likewise, any bookmarks you add when browsing Chrome on your PC appear when you access bookmarks on your smartphone.

This synchronization is a great way to maintain continuity between all the different devices you use. It's like using the exact same version of Chrome no matter which device you're using!

Making the Web More Readable

As our eyes age, we sometimes have trouble reading smaller type. Unfortunately, a lot of web pages are designed with very small type—especially on smartphone screens. Although sites well-designed for mobile use automatically resize the type for smaller screens, other sites become almost unreadable when viewed on your smartphone. Fortunately, there are ways to make these websites more readable.

Zoom Into a Page

The first thing you can do on many websites is to zoom into the page. This enlarges the entire page—which means you might need to drag your finger left and right to view the entire width.

(1) Press two fingers together on the screen and then spread them apart to zoom in.

(2) In some instances, you can zoom into a picture or other onscreen item by double tapping it.

(3) Press two fingers apart on the screen and pinch them together to zoom back out.

Rotate the Screen

The other way to make some web pages more readable is to rotate your phone so that your screen is horizontal (landscape orientation). This makes the web page wider, with larger type.

(1) Rotate your phone 90 degrees to the left or right.

(2) The web page enlarges to fill the width of the horizontal screen.

Searching the Web with Google

Google is not only the company behind the Chrome browser; it's also the most popular search engine in the world. You use a search engine, such as Google, to search for items and information on the Internet.

Enter a Query

You can query Google from Google's home page (www.google.com) or directly from the Chrome browser's Omnibox.

1. From within the Chrome browser, tap in the Omnibox to display the onscreen keyboard. Alternatively, you can go to **www.google.com** and tap within the search box there.

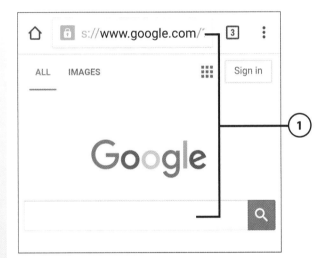

2 Start typing your query.

3 As you type, Google offers various search suggestions. Tap any suggestion to begin your search *or...*

4 Finish typing your query and tap the Go button on the keyboard.

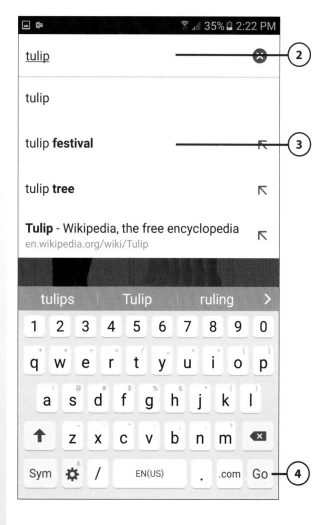

5 Google displays its search results. Tap a link to go to that web page.

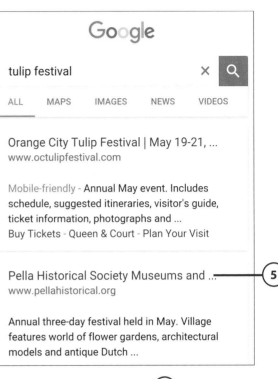

Fine-Tune Your Search Results

A Google search results page includes a list of links that match what you were searching for. You can tap to go directly to any listed web page, or use various Google features to fine-tune your search results.

1 By default, Google displays web page results. Display news results instead by tapping the News tab.

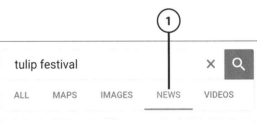

(2) Display matching images by tapping Images.

(3) Display additional search tools by scrolling the bar underneath the Omnibox to the left and then tapping Search Tools.

(4) Different types of search results offer different types of search tools. For Web results, tap Any Time to filter the results by time—Any Time, Past Hour, Past 24 Hours, and so forth.

(5) For image results, you can filter results by color, type (Face, Photo, Clip Art, Line Drawing, or Animated), or time.

---

(2)

tulip festival   ✕ 🔍

ALL   MAPS   IMAGES   NEWS   VIDEOS

ottawa   skagit valley   seattle   istanbul

---

tulip festival   ✕ 🔍

BOOKS   FLIGHTS   APPS   SEARCH TOOLS — (3)

ANY TIME ▾   ALL RESULTS ▾

(4)

---

tulip festival   ✕ 🔍

BOOKS   FLIGHTS   APPS   SEARCH TOOLS

COLOR ▾   TYPE ▾   TIME ▾

(5)

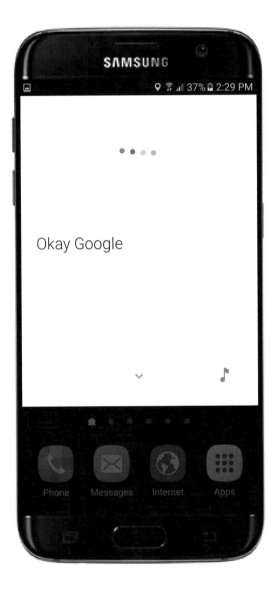

In this chapter, you are introduced to controlling your phone and finding online information using voice commands. Topics include the following:

→ Controlling Your Phone with Samsung's S Voice
→ Doing More with OK Google

Controlling Your Phone with Voice Commands

You're probably used to using your fingers to control your phone. This dates back to the old rotary dial days, of course, when you needed to insert your index finger into the dial to make things work. Same thing in the touchphone days, when you had to push the buttons with your finger.

Now that we're working with smartphones and touchscreens, your fingers are as necessary as ever. Unless, that is, you know how to control your phone by talking to it. That's right, you can use voice commands not only to control your Samsung Galaxy S7 or S7 edge, but also to search the Internet and find all sorts of information. It's a little like having your own HAL9000 (from the movie, *2001: A Space Odyssey*) in the palm of your hand.

Controlling Your Phone with Samsung's S Voice

In addition to the normal touchscreen interface, Samsung built voice control functionality into your Galaxy S7 phone. It's called S Voice, and you can use it to control basic phone operations as well as search the Internet for various types of information.

S Voice uses a natural language user interface to answer questions, make recommendations, and perform various operations. That means you can talk to it in plain English, and S Voice understands what you're asking and performs the appropriate operation. In a way, it's like the Siri personal assistant that Apple includes with its competing iPhones; you ask S Voice a question or tell it what to do, and it does what you've asked.

You can use S Voice to dial voice calls, dictate text messages, create tasks and events, play music, set alarms, and generate driving directions. You can also ask S Voice informational questions that can be answered based on information found on the Internet. Ask S Voice how far it is to the moon, or how old Kenny Rogers is, or how many miles there are in a kilometer. (Or is it vice versa?)

Set Up S Voice for the First Time

S Voice is activated by default on your new Samsung smartphone. Before you use it, however, you need to configure it to recognize your voice.

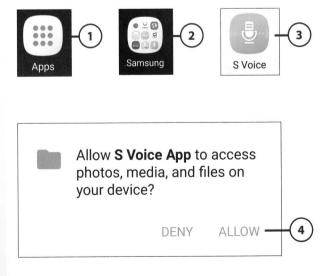

(1) From your phone's Home screen, tap Apps to open the Apps screen.

(2) Tap to open the Samsung folder.

(3) Tap S Voice.

(4) The first time you launch S Voice, you're prompted to let the S Voice App access photos, media, and files on your phone. Tap Allow.

Allow **S Voice App** to access photos, media, and files on your device?

DENY   ALLOW

(5) Tap Next.

(6) You see a screen of legal information. Tap to check I Agree and then tap Next.

(7) You are now prompted to record the wake-up command. Choose a phrase, such as "Hi there," "Hello S Voice," or "Honey, I'm home." Tap Start and say your phrase four times.

(8) Your setup is now complete. Tap Done to continue using your phone.

NEXT > —(5)

(6)

☐ I agree

NEXT >

🖼 📶 39% ⚡ 2:32 PM

← Set wake-up command

Set wake-up command

- Your command should be 3-5 syllables long.
- Speak at a constant speed.
- Speak loudly and clearly in a quiet place.

8-12 inches

LATER   START—(7)

RETRY   DONE—(8)

Configure S Voice Options

By default, S Voice works when you start speaking to it. There are, however, some settings you might want to configure.

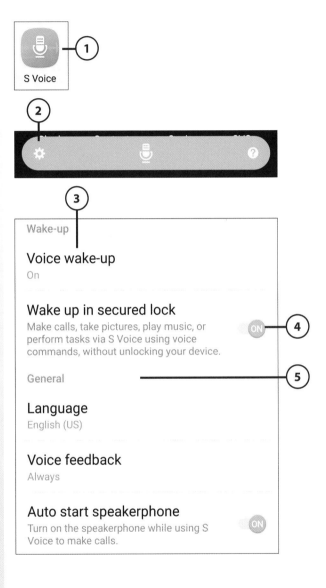

1. From your phone's Home or Apps screen, tap S Voice.

2. From the S Voice command bar at the bottom of the screen, tap Settings to display the S Voice Settings screen.

3. By default, you can wake up S Voice by speaking the phrase you previously set. To turn off this functionality or change your wake-up command, tap Voice Wake-Up then make the appropriate changes.

4. By default, you can use S Voice to make calls, take pictures, and perform other tasks without first unlocking your device. To turn off this functionality, go to the Wake Up in Secured Lock section and tap Off that switch.

5. Configure any of the other settings in the General section, as desired. (The default settings work fine for most people.)

Add to Home Screen

If you use S Voice a lot, you might want to add a shortcut for the app to your Home screen. Open the Samsung folder, then tap and drag the S Voice icon up to your Home screen of choice.

Learn S Voice Commands

After you've set up S Voice, it's time to start using it—by talking to your phone. The following table details the commands you speak to initiate various operations.

Operation	Voice Command	Example
Control Wi-Fi and Bluetooth settings	Turn *setting* on/off	"Turn Wi-Fi off"
Find information	What or How or Why or When	"What is the largest ocean?" or "How old is George Clooney?"
Get directions	Navigate	"Navigate to art museum"
Hear news headlines	Read the news	"Read the news"
Local listings	Find	"Find coffee shops"
Memo	Memo	"Memo *Buy milk*"
Music	Play	"Play *Proud Mary*" or "Play artist *Frank Sinatra*"
Open app	Open	"Open Calculator"
Post social network update	*Network* update	"Twitter update *Who remembers Perry Mason?*" or "Facebook update *Had a wonderful vacation glad to be heading home*"
Record voice	Record voice	"Record voice"
Schedule	New event	"New event *Collin's soccer game June twentieth at six pm*"
Search	Google	"Google *senior living in Arizona*"
Search contacts	Look up	"Look up *Olivia Jones*"
Set alarm	Set alarm	"Set alarm for seven thirty am"
Set timer	Set timer	"Set timer for five minutes"
Task	Create task	"Create task *Star project due August second*"
Text message	Text	"Text Caleb the message *I'm on my way home*"
Voice dial	Call	"Call Bob"
Weather forecast	What is the weather	"What is the weather for today?"

Give S Voice a Command

Using S Voice is as easy as tapping the screen and speaking your command.

1. From your phone's Home or Apps screen, tap S Voice to display the command bar at the bottom of the screen.

2. Speak a command or ask a question.

3. If you asked a question, S Voice speaks the answer and displays the answer onscreen.

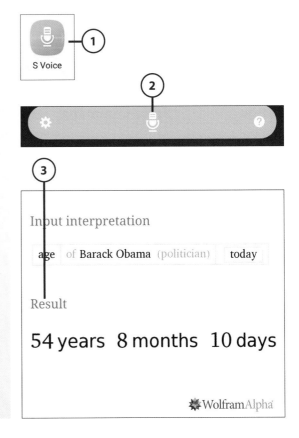

Doing More with OK Google

S Voice is pretty nifty, but there's an even better voice control app available from Google—and built into your phone.

Google's voice operation functionality is called OK Google, because that's what you say to activate it. You can use OK Google to set alarms and reminders, create events, check your schedule, dial voice calls, check your voicemail, dictate text messages, send emails, post to social networks, play music, search for web pages and images, shoot pictures, record videos, look up travel plans, track packages, check weather, calculate tips, define words, convert between units, solve math problems, and more. Practically anything you can do from Google's search site, you can do from your phone using voice commands.

You operate OK Google from the Google Search widget that's preinstalled on your phone's main Home screen.

Google Now

OK Google is part of the Google Now app, included in the Google folder of your Samsung S7/S7 edge. Google Now is an intelligent personal assistant, like Apple's Siri, that taps into the power of Google Search. It offers information personalized to your needs and organizes that information into onscreen "cards." Launch Google Now by tapping the Google Now shortcut in the Google folder.

Learn OK Google Commands

You use OK Google to initiate voice searches and voice commands, by saying "OK Google." The following table details some of the more popular voice commands you can use.

Operation	Voice Command	Example
Calculate a tip	What's the tip	"What's the tip for thirty-seven dollars?"
Check the weather	What's the weather	"What's the weather like tomorrow" or "Do I need a jacket today?"
Check voicemail	Listen to voicemail	"Listen to voicemail"
Check your schedule	What's my day look like or When is event	"What's my day look like tomorrow?" or "When is my next meeting?"
Control Wi-Fi and Bluetooth settings	Turn on/off	"Turn on Wi-Fi"
Convert between units	What is first unit in second unit	"What is twenty-two miles in kilometers?"
Create a Google Calendar event	Create a calendar event	"Create a calendar event for lunch with Joan at Five Guys, Friday at noon"
Define a word	What does word mean	"What does defenestrate mean?"

Operation	Voice Command	Example
Find a movie in a theater	What movie is playing *or* Where is *movie* playing	"What movies are playing this weekend?" or "Where is *The Avengers* playing?"
Find a radio station from Google Play	Play some music	"Play some music"
Find information	Where *or* How *or* When *or* What	"When was Abraham Lincoln killed?" *or* "How far is it to the moon?"
Find nearby places	Where is	"Where is the nearest coffee shop?"
Find new music	What songs	"What songs does Taylor Swift sing?"
Find the time	What time is it	"What time is it in Paris?"
Flashlight	Turn on/off my flashlight	"Turn on my flashlight"
Get directions	Navigate to *or* Directions to	"Navigate to the post office" *or* "Directions to Tenth and Main, Brownsburg, Indiana"
Identify a song	What's this song	"What's this song?"
Learn about a TV show	What's on TV	"What's on TV?"
Look up travel plans	Show me *or* Where is	"Show me my flights" *or* "Where is my hotel?"
Make a restaurant reservation	Book a	"Book a table for two at Luigi's on Friday night at eight pm"
Plan your trip	What are	"What are some attractions in San Diego?"
Play music	Play	"Play the Beach Boys" or "Play *California Dreaming*"
Post to a social network	Post to *network*	"Post to Facebook that I'm playing with my grandkids"
Read a book from Google Play	Read	"Read *To Kill a Mockingbird*"

Operation	Voice Command	Example
Record a video	Record a video	"Record a video"
Search for images	Show me pictures	"Show me pictures of pickup trucks"
Search within apps on your device	Search for *thing* on *app*	"Search for Italian food on Yelp"
See your upcoming bills	My bill(s)	"My bills" *or* "My electric bill"
Send a Hangouts chat message	Send a Hangouts message	"Send a Hangouts message to Jacob"
Send an email	Send an email	"Send an email to Megan, subject *Meeting*, message, *Remember that the next meeting is changed to next Tuesday*, full stop"
Set a reminder	Remind me	"Remind me to take out the trash"
Set an alarm	Set an alarm	"Set an alarm for seven thirty am"
Solve a math problem	What is	"What is one hundred forty-three divided by fifteen?"
Start a Hangouts video call	Start a video call	"Start a video call with Alethia"
Take a photo	Take a picture	"Take a picture"
Text message	Text	"Text Hayley that I'm on my way"
Track a package from a Gmail order confirmation	Where's my package	"Where's my package?"
Translate words or phrases	How do you say	"How do you say house in Chinese?"
Voice dial	Call	"Call Susie"
Watch a movie from Google Play	Watch	"Watch *Frozen*"

Give an OK Google Command

Using OK Google is much like using S Voice; tap the screen and speak a command.

(1) From your phone's Home screen, tap the Microphone icon in the Google Search widget, or just say "OK Google."

(2) Google listens for your voice command. Speak a command or ask a question.

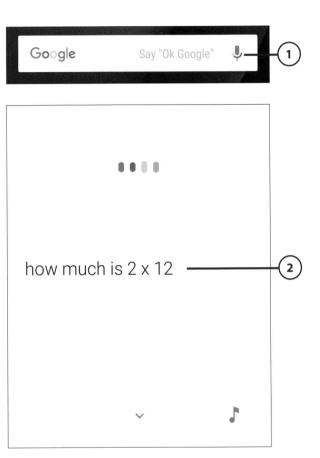

3 If you asked a question, OK Google speaks the answer and displays the answer onscreen.

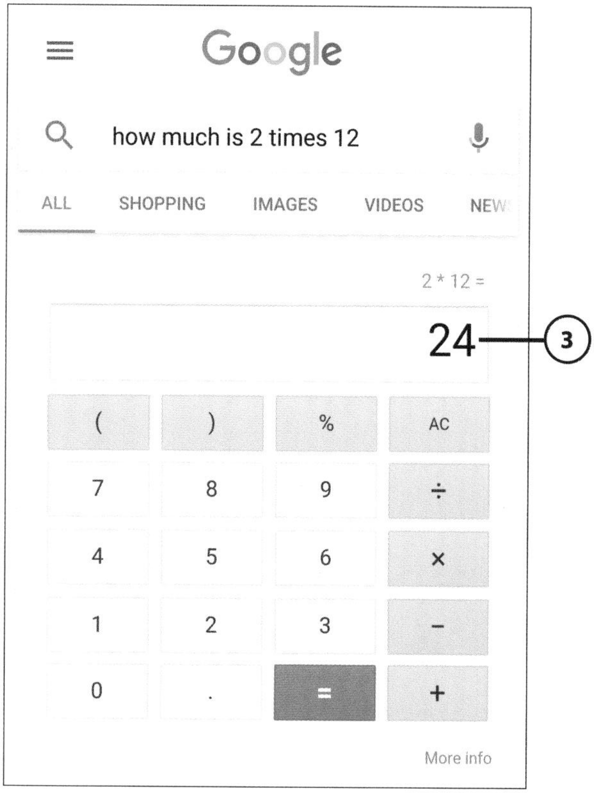

Google

how much is 2 times 12

ALL   SHOPPING   IMAGES   VIDEOS   NEW

2 * 12 =

24 — **3**

(	)	%	AC
7	8	9	÷
4	5	6	×
1	2	3	−
0	.	=	+

More info

Google Hangout

Skype video chat

In this chapter, you see how to make video calls with Google Hangouts and Skype. Topics include the following:

→ Using Google Hangouts
→ Using Skype

Video Chatting on Your Phone

In addition to making traditional voice calls, you can also use your new Samsung Galaxy S7 or S7 edge to make video calls. That's right, the age of video calling is here, and you can do it on your phone!

Using Google Hangouts

Video calling is a great way to keep in touch with distant friends and family. If you can't be there in person, you can talk via video chat on your smartphone. It's just like being there—and, because you do it over the Internet, it's completely free.

One of the most popular video calling apps comes from Google. Google Hangouts lets you make one-on-one video calls as well as participate in group video chats. You can even use Google Hangouts to make voice calls and text message with others.

Hangouts

In Google parlance, a Hangout can be either a text or video chat. Instead of calling them chat sessions, Google calls them Hangouts. So that's that.

Make a Video Call

The Google Hangouts app is prein-stalled on your Samsung smartphone. When you're logged into your Google Account (which you are by default), it's easy to call someone else who's using the same app on their phone or computer.

1. From your phone's Home screen, tap the Apps icon to open the Apps screen.

2. Tap to open the Google folder.

3. Tap the Hangouts icon to open the Google Hangouts app.

4. You see the most recent Hangouts in which you've par-ticipated. To resume talking with someone in a previous Hangout, tap that Hangout.

5. Start a new Hangout by tapping the New Chat (+) icon.

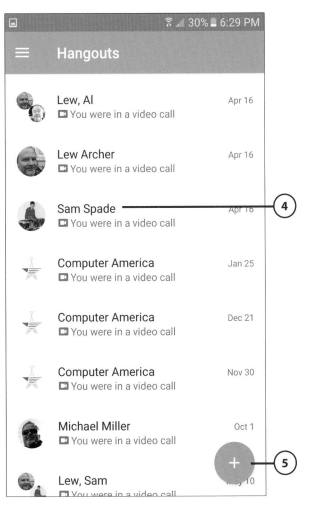

6 Tap New Video Call.

7 Tap the name of a person that you want to chat with.

8 Tap the video camera icon at the top of the screen. Google calls the other person to start a Hangout.

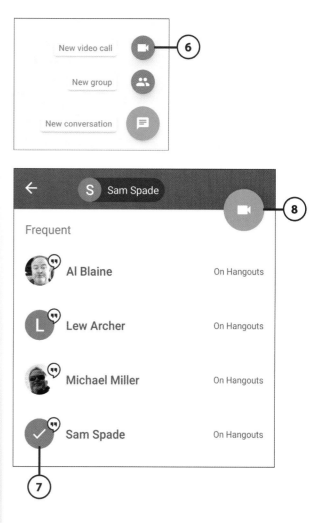

(9) When the other person answers, you see that person's picture across the middle of the screen. Your picture appears at the bottom right. Start talking!

9

Your picture

10 Tap the screen to display the Hangout controls at the top and bottom of the screen.

11 Tap the microphone button to mute the sound. Tap the microphone button again to unmute.

12 Tap the camera button to hide your video from the other person. Tap the camera button again to make your video visible.

13 Tap the red disconnect button to leave the Hangout.

Add to Home Screen

If you use Google Hangouts a lot, you might want to add a shortcut for the app to your Home screen. Open the Google folder then tap and drag the Hangouts icon up to your Home screen of choice.

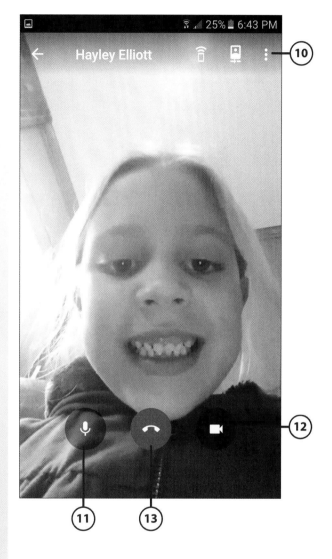

Add People to a Group Call

You can include multiple people in a group video Hangout. This is great for virtual meetings or impromptu family reunions.

(1) Start a video Hangout with the first person you're talking with and then tap the screen to show the Hangout controls.

(2) Tap the Menu button.

(3) Tap Add People.

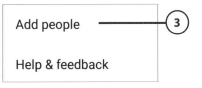

(4) From your list of contacts, tap to select the person or people you want to add to your Hangout.

(5) Tap the video camera icon.

(6) When the person answers the call, she is added to the Hangout. Her picture appears at the bottom of the screen, and whomever is talking at the moment appears in the large video window. Switch to display a specific participant's video by tapping that person's thumbnail at the bottom of the screen.

Participate in a Text Chat

You can also use Google Hangouts to participate in text chats. A text Hangout is like an exchange of text messages, but using the Google Hangouts service.

(1) Tap the New Chat (+) icon.

(2) Tap New Conversation.

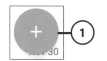

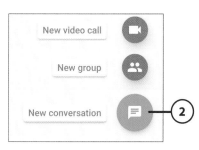

(3) Tap the name of a person that you want to chat with. This displays a new Hangout screen.

(4) Tap within the Write Message box at the bottom of the screen and type your message.

(5) Tap the Send button.

(6) Your message appears on the right side of the screen. The other person's messages appear on the left. Continue messaging to participate in the conversation. When you're done, just quit— there are no buttons you need to tap to end the conversation.

Voice Calls

You can also use Google Hangouts and Skype to make voice calls. Just tap the telephone icon to initiate a voice call with another registered user.

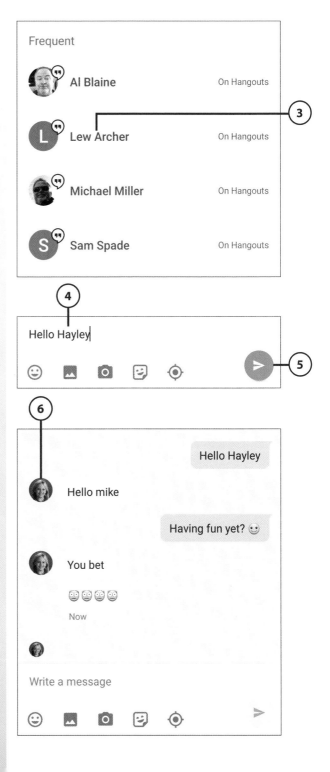

Using Skype

Google Hangouts is a popular app, especially among Google and Android users. But the most popular video chat service today is Skype.

To use Skype, you need to install the Skype app. You can do this from the Google Play Store; just search for Skype and then choose to download and install it. It's free.

Signing Up and Logging On

When you first install the Skype app, you're prompted to either log on with an existing Skype account (which you might have, from your computer) or create a new account. Follow the onscreen instructions to do so.

Make a Video Call

Skype automatically searches your phone's contacts list for those people who also have Skype accounts. You can then call any of these people directly—as long as you're both online at the same time. (And, in the case of people connecting via computer, that they have a webcam operating.)

1. From your phone's Home screen, tap the Skype icon to open the Skype app.

2. Tap the People tab to see all your Skype contacts.

3. Tap the name of the person you want to talk with.

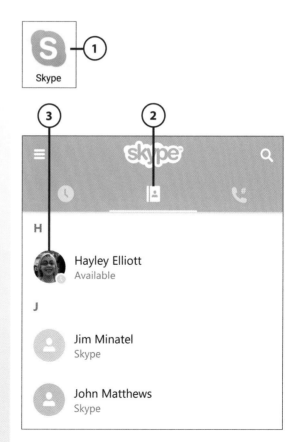

4 If you have not yet connected with this person on Skype, you're prompted to do so. (Otherwise, skip to Step 7.) Tap the Connect on Skype button.

5 Accept or edit the invitation message.

6 Tap the check mark to send the message. The other person must accept your contact request before you can chat with him.

7 On the next screen, tap the video camera icon to initiate a video call.

8 The person you're talking to appears on your phone's screen. A smaller thumbnail of you appears at the bottom right. Start talking!

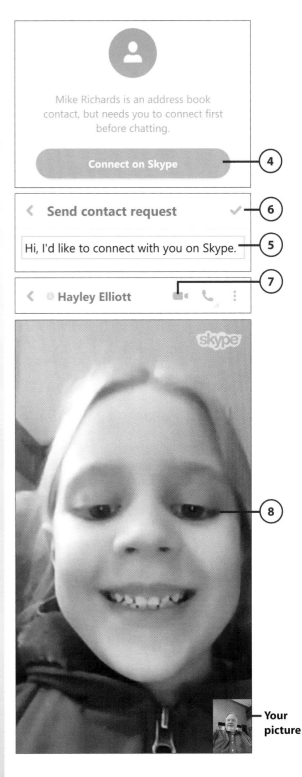

Mike Richards is an address book contact, but needs you to connect first before chatting.

Connect on Skype — 4

< **Send contact request** ✓ — 6

Hi, I'd like to connect with you on Skype. — 5

7

< ⦿ **Hayley Elliott**

8

— **Your picture**

9 Tap the screen to display the Skype controls.

10 Tap the microphone button to mute the sound. Tap the microphone button again to unmute.

11 Tap the camera button to hide your video from the other person. Tap the camera button again to make your video visible.

12 Tap the red disconnect button to leave the call.

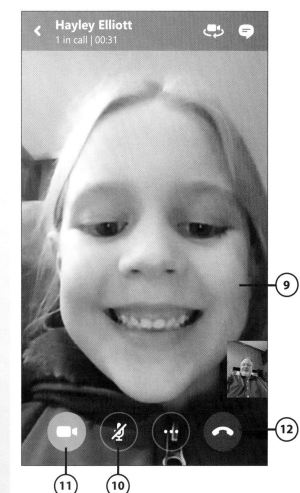

Participate in a Text Chat

Finally, you can use Skype to text message with other users.

1 From within the Skype app, tap the People tab.

2 Tap the name of a person that you want to chat with.

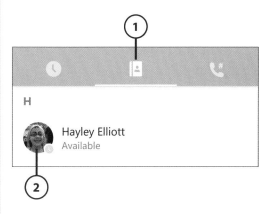

3 Tap within the Type a Message Here box at the bottom of the screen and type your message.

4 Tap the Send button.

5 Your message appears on the right side of the screen. The other person's messages appear on the left. Continue messaging to participate in the conversation. When you're done, just quit—there are no buttons you need to tap to end the conversation.

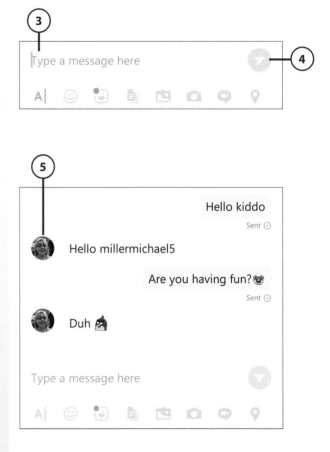

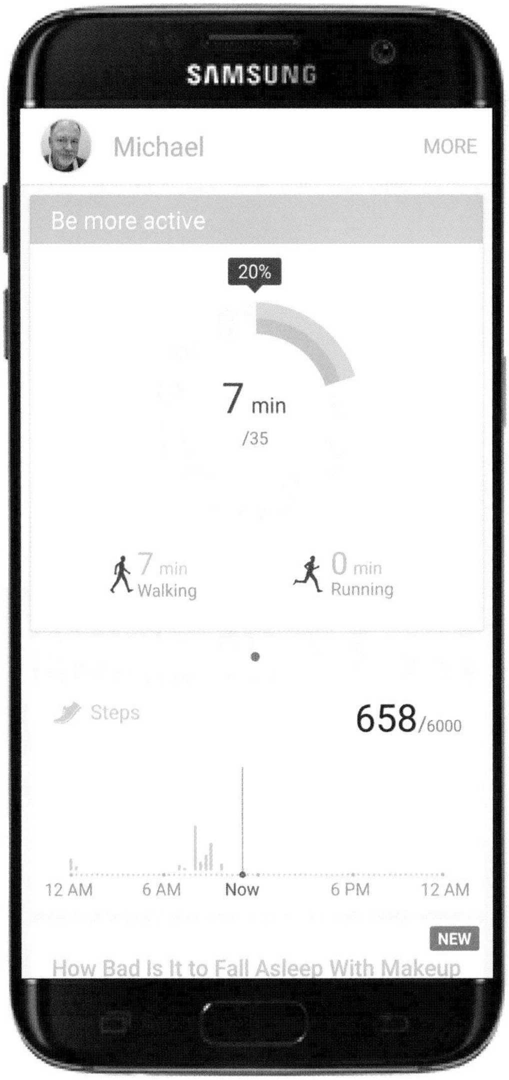
SAMSUNG
Michael
MORE
Be more active
20%
7 min
/35
7 min
Walking
0 min
Running
Steps
658/6000
12 AM
6 AM
Now
6 PM
12 AM
NEW
How Bad Is It to Fall Asleep With Makeup

In this chapter, you get suggestions on how to use your new Galaxy S7 and S7 edge to live healthier and manage your medicines and medical conditions. Topics include the following:

→ Setting Up the S Health App
→ Tracking Your Vital Statistics

Monitoring Your Health

Samsung cares about your health—really. The company's S7 and S7 edge smartphones include a built-in heart rate monitor, which you can use just by placing a finger on the back of the case. Even better, Samsung includes the S Health app, which works in conjunction with the heart rate monitor to track and analyze your heart rate and other medical conditions.

Setting Up the S Health App

You use Samsung's S Health app to plan and track a variety of health goals and medical conditions. S Health can track your exercise regimen, sleep patterns, and meals—as well as your heart rate, blood pressure, blood glucose levels, and weight.

Best of all, S Health is free—and already installed on your Galaxy S7 or S7 edge. It's a fun and easy way to stay as healthy as you can, all from the screen of your new smartphone.

Get Started with S Health

When you first use the S Health app, you need to configure it for your own personal use.

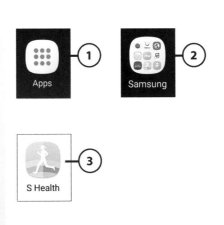

(1) From the Home screen, tap Apps to open the Apps screen.

(2) Tap to open the Samsung folder.

(3) Tap to open the S Health app. The first time you open the app you're prompted to agree to the app's privacy policy; you may also be prompted to set up or create a new Samsung account. Follow the onscreen instructions to proceed.

Add to Home Screen

If you use S Health a lot, you might want to add a shortcut for the app to your Home screen. Open the Samsung folder, then tap and drag the S Health icon to your Home screen of choice.

Configure Your Profile

To get the most out of S Health, you need to tell the app a little bit about yourself—including your gender, birthday, height, and weight.

(1) From within the S Health app, tap the profile picture or image at the top-left corner. Your My Page profile opens.

(2) Tap Profile to open the screen for editing.

(3) Tap Name to enter your name.

(4) Tap the camera icon and select the desired image to add a profile picture.

(5) Tap Male or Female in the gender section.

(6) Tap to enter your birthdate in the Birthday section.

(7) Tap to enter your height in the Height section.

(8) Tap to enter your weight in the Weight section.

(9) Tap the icon in the Activity Level section that best represents how active you are. If you're not at all active, tap one of the icons on the left. If you are very active, tap one of the icons on the right.

(10) Tap Save.

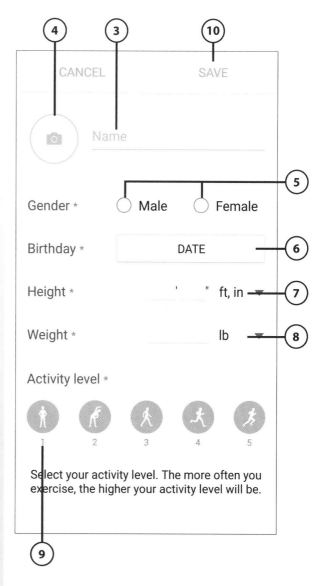

Select Activities to Manage

You need to tell S Health which activities you want to track.

1. At the top of the main screen of the S Health app you see a graphical representation of your current day's activity. If this is your first time using the app, you see zero activity.

2. Scroll down to see tiles for specific activities.

3. Scroll to the very bottom of the screen and tap + Manage Items.

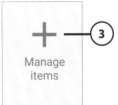

4 Tap to select the Trackers tab. (It might be selected by default.)

5 Tap On those activities and items you want to track—everything from walking and running to food and water, from weight and sleep to heart rate and blood pressure. Tiles are added to the main screen for those items you select.

6 Tap to select the Goals tab.

7 Tap to select any of the stated goals—Be More Active, Eat Healthier, or Feel More Rested.

4

TRACKERS	GOALS	PROGRAMS

Screen grid

Steps — ON

Walking — ON **5**

Running — OFF

Cycling — OFF

Hiking — OFF

Sports — OFF

Food — OFF

7   **6**

TRACKERS	GOALS	PROGRAMS

Be more active

Eat healthier

Feel more rested

8. For each goal you select, enter specific goals.

9. Tap Start.

My Health Technology for Seniors

Learn more about managing your personal health and fitness in the book *My Health Technology for Seniors*, written by Lonzell Watson, available where you purchased this book.

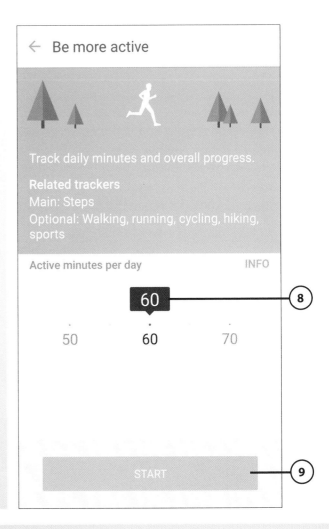

← Be more active

Track daily minutes and overall progress.

Related trackers
Main: Steps
Optional: Walking, running, cycling, hiking, sports

Active minutes per day   INFO

60   8

50   **60**   70

START   9

>>>Go Further

OTHER HEALTH AND FITNESS APPS

Many other companies offer health-related apps that help you turn your Galaxy S7 or S7 edge into a full-fledged portable medical tracker. You can use your smartphone to manage your prescriptions (including alerting you when it's time to take your meds), track blood sugar and blood pressure, organize your medical charts and visits, and even look up detailed information about various medical conditions and medications.

There are also fitness and yoga and dieting apps to help you live healthier, and apps you can activate if you ever have a medical emergency. Just search the Google Play Store and you'll be pleasantly surprised by what's available.

In addition, you can connect all manner of fitness bands, smart watches, and the like to your phone via Bluetooth, and use those devices to monitor and feed information to S Health and other fitness apps. If you're serious about exercise and fitness and monitoring your health, there are a lot of options out there for you.

Tracking Your Vital Statistics

There are all sorts of statistics and activities you can track with the S Health app. We'll look at a few of the more common ones.

Monitor Your Pulse

Here's something cool and useful—your Galaxy S7 or S7 edge has a heart rate monitor built in. You can use this feature to monitor your pulse—but first, you have to enable heart rate tracking.

(1) Scroll to the bottom of the main screen and tap + Manage Items.

(2) Tap to select the Trackers tab.

(3) Scroll to the bottom of the screen and tap On the Heart Rate switch.

(4) Tap the back arrow to return to the main screen.

+

(1)

Manage
items

(4)

← Manage items

(2)

TRACKERS   GOALS   PROGRAMS

Food   OFF

Water   OFF

Caffeine   OFF

Weight   OFF

Sleep   OFF

Heart rate   ON   (3)

5 You see a new Heart Rate tile on the main screen. Tap Measure.

6 When prompted, place your index finger on the heart rate monitor on the back of your phone. Try to keep still and calm while the device monitors your pulse rate.

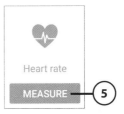

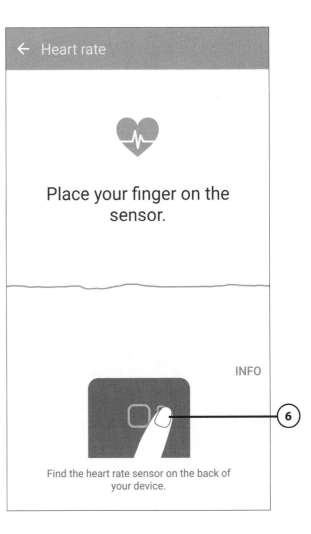

(7) S Health displays your measured heart rate.

(8) At the bottom of the screen, tap to select your current status: General, Resting, After Exercise, Excited, Tired, In Love, Surprised, Sad, Angry, Fearful, Unwell, or Before Exercise.

(9) Tap Save.

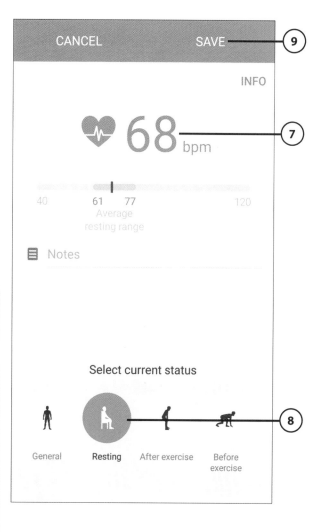

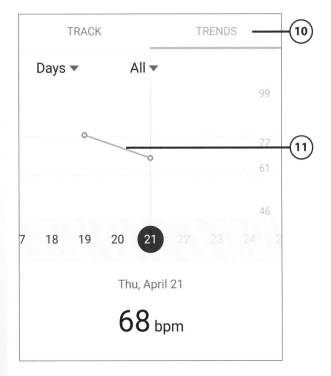

10 Tap Trends on the main Heart Rate screen.

11 You see a graph of your recent heart rate measurements.

Track Your Blood Pressure

As you've just seen, your Galaxy S7 or S7 edge can both record and track your heart rate. The S Health app can also track (but not measure) your blood pressure levels over time.

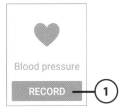

1 Add the Blood Pressure tile to the main screen of the S Health app, and then tap that tile to open the Blood Pressure screen.

(**2**) Enter your current blood pressure reading by tapping to select the Track tab.

(**3**) Tap Record Manually.

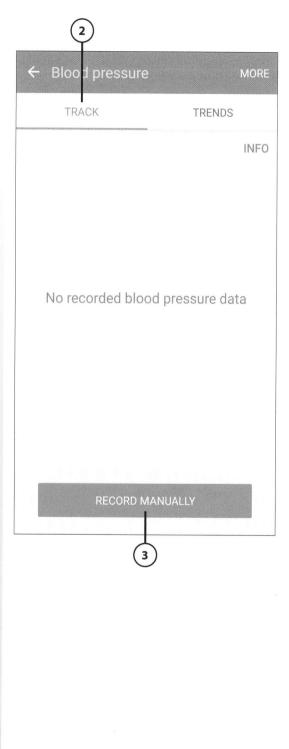

4 If you're entering a reading taken previously, tap the date control and enter a new date and time.

5 Tap and drag the appropriate controls to enter your systolic reading.

6 Tap and drag the appropriate controls to enter your diastolic reading.

7 Tap to enter your pulse rate, optional.

8 Tap Save. You see the reading you just entered.

9 Tap to select the Trends tab. You see a graph of your blood pressure readings over time.

Track Automatically

By default, you have to enter blood pressure, blood sugar, and other data manually. You can, however, connect external measurement devices to your smartphone to input this data automatically.

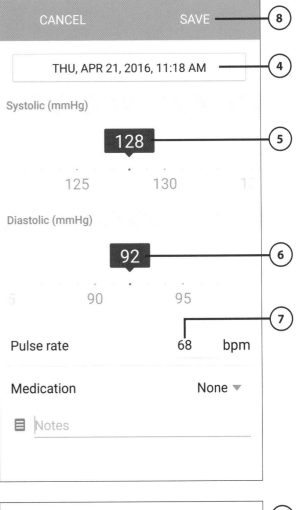

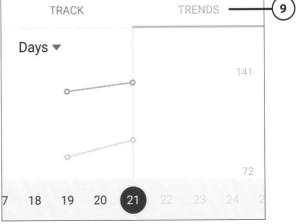

Track Your Food Intake and Calories Consumed

Another useful feature of the S Health app is its ability to track your daily food intake and calculate the calories you consume.

(1) Add the Food tile to the main screen of the S Health app, and then tap that tile to open the Food screen.

(2) Tap to select the Track tab.

(3) Tap the icon for the meal or snack you're recording.

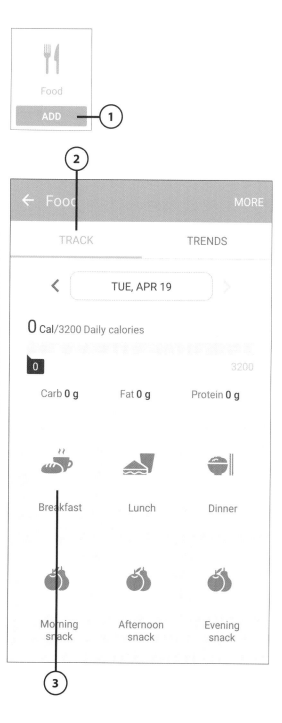

(4) Tap to select the Search tab then enter the name of the food you ate into the Search box *or*….

(5) Tap to select the Frequent tab and tap the check mark by the food you ate *or*….

(6) Tap to select the My Food tab and tap the check mark next to one of your favorite meals. (This only appears after you've added some foods.)

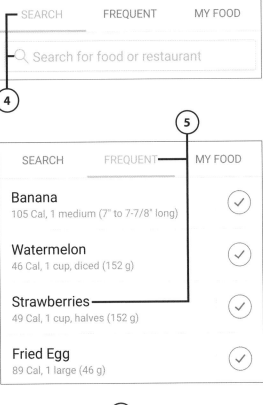

7 Examine the details of this meal. Add another food or drink item to the meal by tapping Add Food Item.

8 If this is a meal you eat often, tap Add to My Food.

9 Tap Done.

10 The calorie count for this meal and the total calories so far today are displayed on this day's track page.

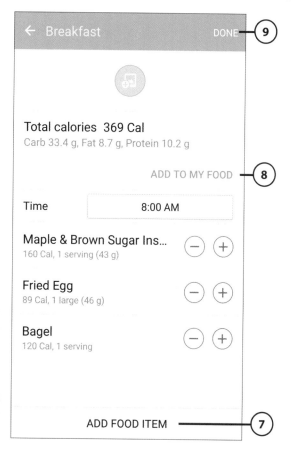

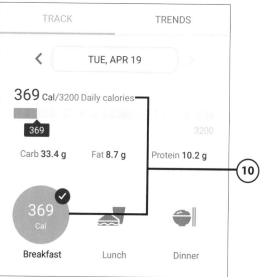

11 Tap to select the Trends tab. You see a graph of your calorie consumption over time.

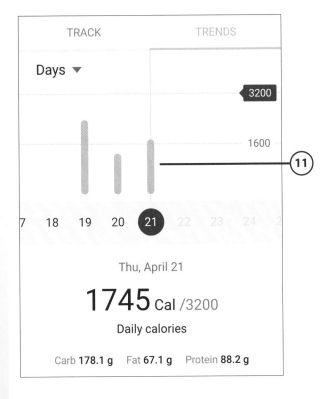

Track the Steps You Take

The S Health app includes a built-in pedometer for counting the steps you take. All you have to do is activate the pedometer and then start walking!

1 If the Steps tile is not currently on the main screen of the S Health app, add it now and then tap the tile to display the Steps screen.

2. Tap to select the Track tab. This displays a graph of the steps you've taken today. The distance you've walked and calories burned are displayed beneath the graph.

3. Tap the Trends tab. This displays a day-by-day graph of the steps you've taken.

Track Other Exercise

Walking is a rather low-impact type of exercise. If you're into more vigorous exercise and sports, the S Health app can track those, too. Just open the Manage Items screen and tap On those activities you want to track. Tiles for those activities will be added to the main screen; tap a tile to track and monitor that activity.

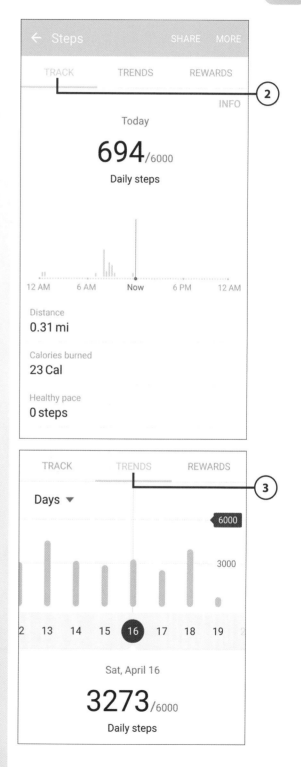

>>>Go Further
ORGANIZE YOUR TILES

Any goals you've activated in the S Health app are tracked at the top of the main screen. Tap and swipe left and right to scroll through progress graphs for multiple goals.

Beneath this section of the main screen are tiles for each activity or condition you're tracking. If you're tracking a lot of items, you'll have a lot of tiles displayed. To organize these tiles, tap and drag a tile to move it to a new position. You might like to put your exercise-related tiles all together, your meal-related tiles together, and the tiles that track your various health readings together.

In this chapter, you learn how you can manage your daily activities with Samsung's Calendar app. Topics include the following:

→ Viewing Your Calendar
→ Creating Appointments and Events
→ Creating a To-Do List

Managing Your Calendar

What do you have to do today? You can use your Galaxy S7 or S7 edge to manage your day-to-day activities, using the phone's built-in Calendar app. This chapter shows you how.

Viewing Your Calendar

Samsung includes the Calendar app with every new Galaxy S7 and S7 edge smartphone. You use this app to view calendars and track your appointments and activities.

Change the Calendar View

The Calendar app can display yearly, monthly, and weekly views. Choose the view that's right for you.

1. From the Home screen, tap the Calendar icon to open the Calendar app.

2. By default, the Calendar app displays a monthly calendar of the current month. To highlight the current day, tap Today at the top of the screen.

3. Swipe left on the screen to view the next month.

4. Swipe right on the screen to view the previous month.

5. Tap the down arrow by the month at the top of the screen to change the calendar view.

6. Select the view you want—Year, Month and Agenda, Week, Day, or Tasks.

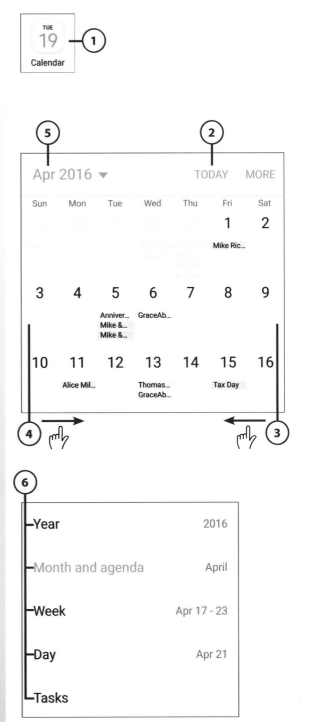

View Calendar Items

You add activities and appointments to the basic calendar and can then view upcoming events. (This example uses Month and Agenda view, but it works the same with other views.)

1. From within the Calendar app, tap a day on the calendar to view a pop-up with events for that day or…

2. View a list of events for a given day by tapping that day on the calendar and then swiping up from the bottom of the screen.

3. Tap an event to view details about that event.

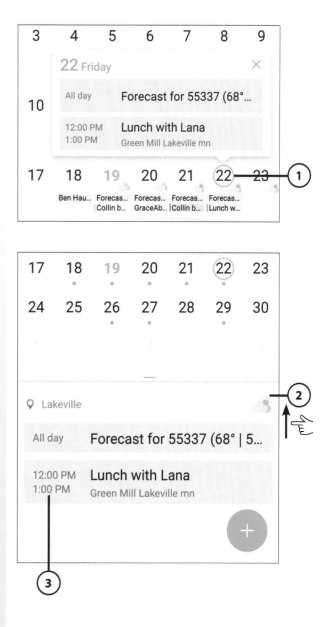

④ You now see the item's details—start time, end time, location, and such. To delete this event, tap Delete.

Start time   Event title   Calendar   End time

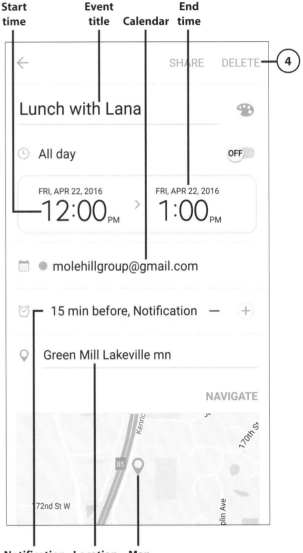

SHARE   DELETE —④

Lunch with Lana

🕐 All day   OFF

FRI, APR 22, 2016   FRI, APR 22, 2016
12:00PM > **1:00**PM

📅 ● molehillgroup@gmail.com

⏰ ─ 15 min before, Notification   ─   ＋

📍 Green Mill Lakeville mn

NAVIGATE

72nd St W

Notification   Location   Map

Creating Appointments and Events

You use the Calendar app not just to display yearly, monthly, and weekly calendars, but also to create and track events on those calendars. An event might be a meeting or an appointment, or maybe a friend's birthday or your anniversary.

Create a New Event

You can set a new event to start and end at a specific time, or you can create an all-day event.

| 24 | 25 | 26 | 27 | (28) | 29 | 30 |

Alec Ha... Greg La...   Jan Fre...
GraceAb...

(**1**) From the monthly or weekly view, tap the day you want the event to occur.

(**2**) Tap the green + button to open the new event screen.

(**3**) Enter the name of this event or appointment into the Title box.

CANCEL   SAVE

(**4**) Tap the color palette icon to assign a color to this event.

Title

(**5**) If this is an all-day event, tap On the All Day switch. Otherwise, leave this switch in the Off position.

All day   OFF

(**6**) Tap the Start control and set the start time, along with AM or PM.

THU, APR 28, 2016   THU, APR 28, 2016
8:00 AM > 9:00 AM

(**7**) Tap the End control and set the end time, along with AM or PM.

(**8**) By default, you'll receive an alert about this event 10 minutes in advance of the start time. To delete this alert, go to the notification section and tap – (minus).

molehillgroup@gmail.com

15 min before, Notification – +

(**9**) If you want to add another alert for this event, go to the notification section and tap + (plus).

Location   MAP

(**10**) Enter a location for this event by tapping Location and then entering an address, room number, or the like.

Repeat   Invitees   Notes   Privacy   Time zone

(**11**) Tap Save to save this event.

Create a Repeating Event

Events can repeat. For example, you can schedule a golf game to occur every Saturday at 10:00 a.m., or schedule a phone call to family on the first Wednesday of every month.

(1) Create a new event then tap Repeat.

(2) Tap how often this event recurs, from Daily to Yearly.

(3) For more detailed recurrences, tap Customize.

(4) By default, recurring events repeat forever. To change this, tap the Forever down arrow and then tap either Until or Repetitions.

Invite Others to an Event

You can use the Calendar app to schedule group meetings, by inviting others to a given event.

(1) Create a new event then tap Invitees to display a new section on the screen.

(2) Tap to enter individual email addresses *or...*

(3) Tap the Contacts icon to display the Contacts screen and select one or more invitees from your Contacts list.

(4) When you tap Save, invitations will be emailed to the people you've invited.

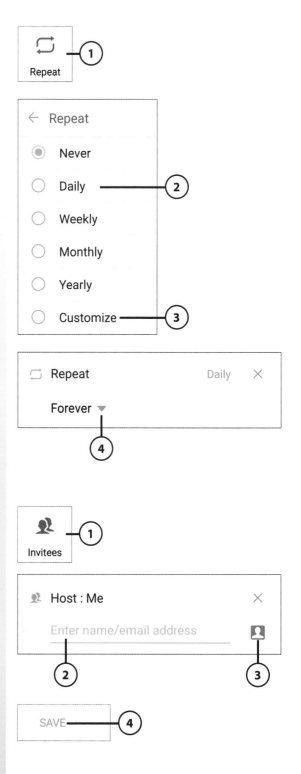

Creating a To-Do List

The Calendar app can also be used to manage your upcoming tasks, as a kind of digital to-do list.

Create a New Task

You create new tasks from the Tasks screen.

1. From any calendar screen, tap the date down arrow.

2. Tap Tasks to display the Tasks screen. A list of all current tasks opens.

3. Create a new task by tapping Enter New Task and using the onscreen keyboard to enter the task or name of the task.

4. As you type the name of the task, the screen changes to display additional options. If the task is to be completed today or tomorrow, click the Today or Tomorrow buttons.

5. If the completion date is further out, tap the Expand button.

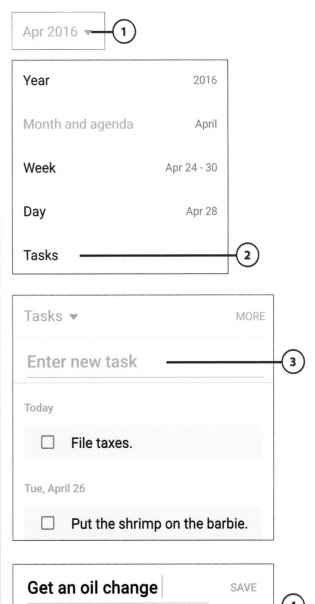

(6) Tap Set Date to display the Set
Date panel.

(7) Tap the date you'd like to have
this task completed.

(8) Tap Done.

(9) If you'd like to be reminded of
this task's due date, tap Reminder.

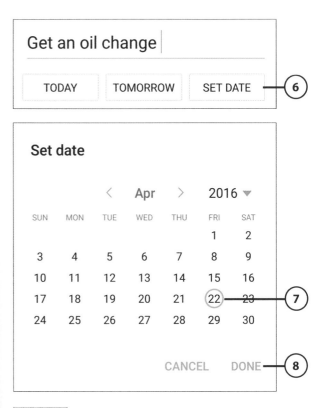

10 Tap the date and time you'd like to be reminded.

11 Tap Done.

12 If this is a particularly important task, tap Priority to display a new Priority section.

13 Tap the down arrow in the Priority section and select either High, Medium, or Low priority.

14 Tape Save to save this task.

Fri, Apr 22, 2016 12:57 PM

	‹	Apr	›	2016 ▼	
SUN	MON	TUE	WED	THU	FRI	SAT
					1	2
3	4	5	6	7	8	9
10	11	12	13	14	15	16
17	18	19	20	21	22	23
24	25	26	27	28	29	30

11   56   AM

12 : 57   PM — **10**

1   58

CANCEL   DONE — **11**

❗
Priority — **12**

CANCEL   SAVE — **14**

Get an oil change

🕐 (FRI, APR 22, 2016 —)

📅 ● My task

⏰ (FRI, APR 22, 2016 12:57 PM)   ✕

❗ Priority   Medium ▼ — ✕ **13**

Manage Your Tasks

After you've created a list of tasks, you can mark off tasks as you complete them.

1. From the Tasks screen, view details about a given task by tapping that task.

2. Swipe the task to the left to postpone a task's due date by one day.

3. Tap the task's check box to mark a task as completed.

4. Swipe a task to the right or tap Delete to remove a completed task.

Today

☐ File taxes.

Fri, April 22

☐ Get an oil change — ①

Tue, April 26

☐ Put the shrimp on the barbie.

Sat, April 30

☐ Wax the dog.

③ ④

SHARE   DELETE

②

☐ Get an oil change

🕐 FRI, APR 22, 2016 —

📅 ● My task

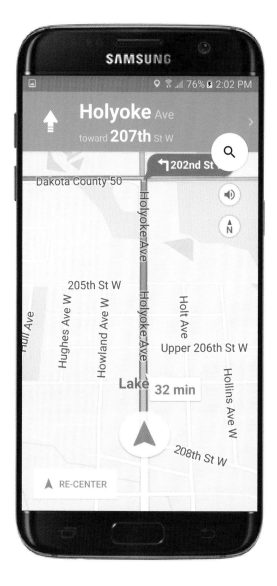

In this chapter, you discover how to find locations and generate driving directions using the Google Maps app. Topics include the following:

→ Viewing Maps
→ Finding Nearby Places
→ Generating Directions

Viewing Maps and Driving Directions

Your new Galaxy S7 or S7 edge comes with the Google Maps app preinstalled. You use Google Maps to find nearby homes and businesses, as well as to generate driving directions to places you want to go.

Viewing Maps

At its most basic, the Google Maps app displays maps of just about any location in the developed world. You can look at maps of your neighborhood, city, state, or country. You can even use Google Maps to view current traffic conditions—so you'll know which routes to avoid!

Display Your Current Location

Google Maps works with the GPS functionality of your phone to track and display your current location.

Turn On Location Tracking

To get full use and benefit of the Google Maps app, you need to turn on location tracking on your phone. Swipe down from any screen to display the notification panel, then tap On the Location icon.

1. From the Home screen, tap Apps to open the Apps screen.

2. Tap to open the Google folder.

3. Tap the Maps icon to open Google Maps.

4. By default, Google Maps uses your phone's GPS functionality to display your current location, as identified by a blue circle on the map.

5. Tap and drag the map in any direction to move around the map.

6. Return to your current location by tapping the Location icon at the lower-right corner of the map screen.

7. Zoom into the current location by tapping the screen with two fingers and then spread them apart.

8. Zoom out from the current location by pinching the screen with two fingers.

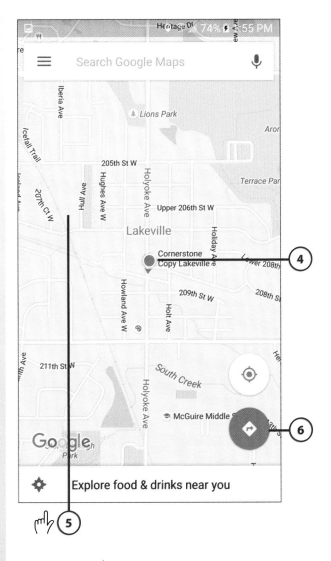

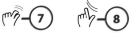

Add to Home Screen

If you use Google Maps a lot, you might want to add a shortcut for the app to your Home screen. Open the Apps screen then tap and drag the Maps icon up to your Home screen of choice.

Display Traffic Conditions

If you live in a busy metropolitan area, or even just an area prone to traffic jams and slowdowns, you can use Google Maps to display current traffic conditions on the map. Green means traffic is moving just fine, orange means traffic is slow, and red means traffic is heavily congested or stopped.

(1) From the main map screen, tap the Options button at the top-left corner.

(2) Tap Traffic.

(3) Current traffic conditions display on the map. (If no colors appear on a given road, that means no conditions are currently being reported.)

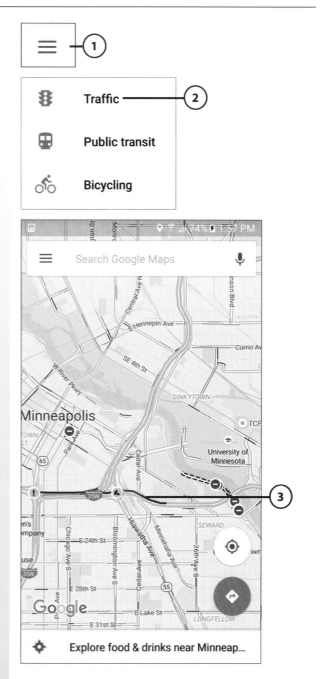

Change the Map Display

By default, Google Maps displays a typical street map. You can also choose to display public transit, bicycling, satellite, and terrain maps.

1. From the main map screen, tap the Options button at the top-left corner.

2. Tap the type of map you want to display.

▣	Traffic
▣	Public transit
⮷	Bicycling
▣	Satellite
▲	Terrain
◎	Google Earth

It's Not All Good

Draining the Battery

The Google Maps app is a lifesaver when you're not sure where you're going, or when you're travelling on a long trip. But know that the combination of the app and its use of location services puts a major drain on your phone's battery. Leave the Google Maps app running for an hour or more and you'll see your phone's battery level decrease significantly.

The solution is to either not use the app when you don't need it, or to keep your phone connected to your car's power. Do this with an external charger cable that connects to a 12 volt power outlet in your car. This way your phone will continually charge while you're driving, and the battery won't drain while you're navigating.

Finding Nearby Places

As you've discovered, it's easy enough to display a map of your current location. But what if you want to display a map of someplace else? Or find a restaurant or gas station nearby?

Enter a New Location

Google Maps can map street addresses, general location information (such as street intersections), cities and states, and even specific locations, such as museums, stadiums, and airports.

(1) From the main map screen, tap within the Google search box and enter the location you want to map. Enter a street address, street name, intersection ("Fifth and Main"), city, or state. You can also enter the name of a building or location, such as "Yankee Stadium," "O'Hare Airport," or "Golden Gate Bridge."

(2) Google displays a map of the general area, with the specific location pinpointed with a red pin.

(3) Generate driving directions to this location from your current location by tapping the Directions icon at the bottom right.

Voice Commands

If you're using Google Maps while driving, it is safer to speak your commands rather than type them. Tap the microphone icon in the Google search box and then speak the location you want to map, or the type of business or attraction you're looking for.

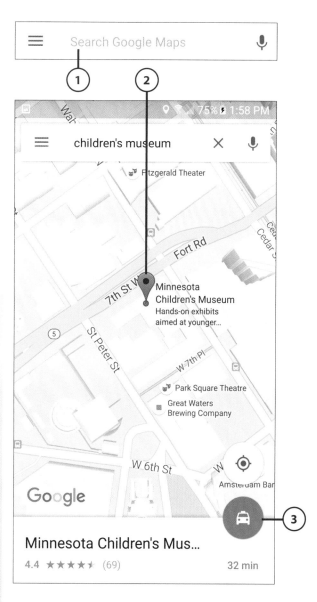

Find Nearby Businesses and Attractions

When you're traveling, you often want to find interesting and useful businesses and attractions near where you are. You might want to find nearby coffeehouses, restaurants, hotels, grocery stores, ATMs, or gas stations. Not surprisingly, Google Maps uses the power of Google to search for whatever it is you want—and then display the results on a map.

1) From the main map screen, tap within the Google search box to display a screen of search suggestions.

2) Tap Explore Food & Drinks to view suggested restaurants nearby.

3) Tap the appropriate icon to display nearby gas stations, groceries, pharmacies, and ATMs.

4) Tap More to see additional types of businesses.

5) Tap the type of business or service you're looking for or...

6) On the search suggestions screen, enter the type of business or service you want into the search box.

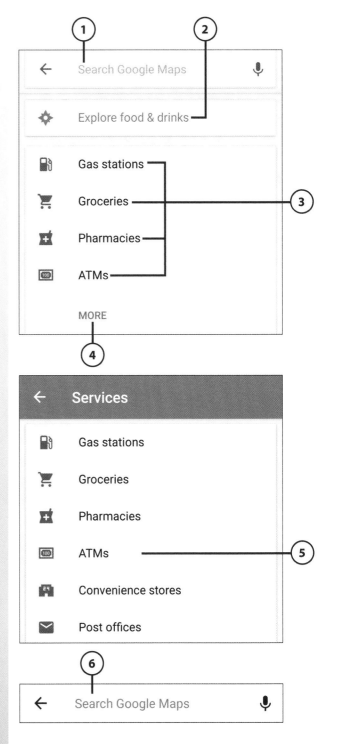

7 Matching businesses are displayed on the map and in a list on the bottom part of the screen. Tap an icon or listing to learn more about that business.

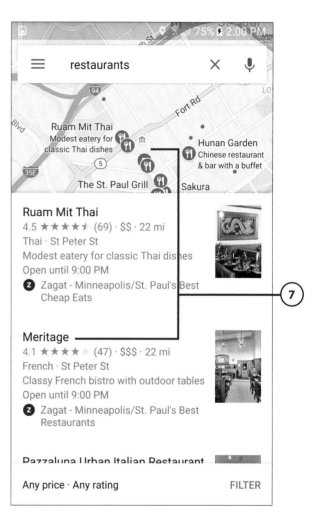

(8) Tap the Call icon to call that business from your phone.

(9) Tap the Website icon to display that business' website in the Chrome browser.

(10) Tap the Directions icon to display driving directions to this business.

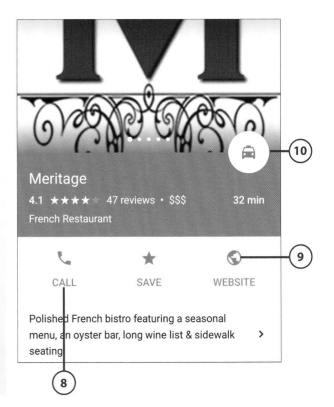

Generating Directions

If you don't know where it is that you need to go, you can use Google Maps to generate directions to get you there. Just follow the step-by-step (or turn-by-turn) instructions and you'll end up at the right place, every time.

Generate Driving Directions

To generate driving directions, all you have to do is tell Google Maps where you are and where you want to go.

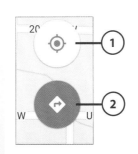

(1) From the main map screen, tap the Home icon to display your current location.

(2) Tap the Directions icon to display the Directions screen.

(**3**) Tap the car icon at the top of the screen to generate driving directions.

(**4**) Tap within the Choose Destination box and enter the end destination.

(**5**) Google now displays a map of what it feels is the best route to the destination. Optional routes are shown in gray on the screen; tap a route to view that route.

(**6**) Tap the bottom part of the screen to view the turn-by-turn directions.

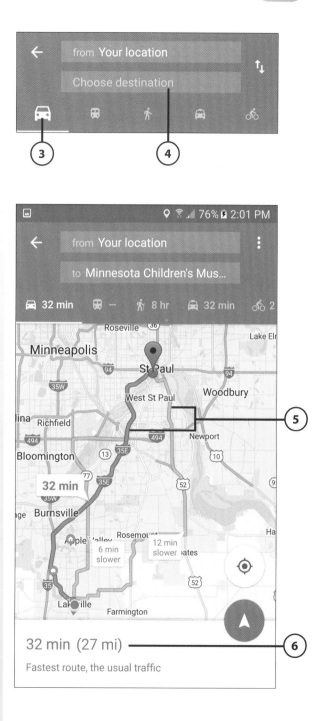

7. Tap the Start (up arrow) icon when you're ready to start driving.

8. Google Maps displays a zoomed in map of your current location, with the next turn highlighted at the top of the screen. The app's built-in voice speaks your first instructions.

9. Start driving and follow the driving directions. The map updates itself as you move, and the app speaks additional instructions as needed.

Coming Back Home

After you've arrived at a destination, Google Maps can generate directions for getting back home. Just re-open the directions screen and tap the reverse arrows between your current location and destination. The app now generates directions to your original location.

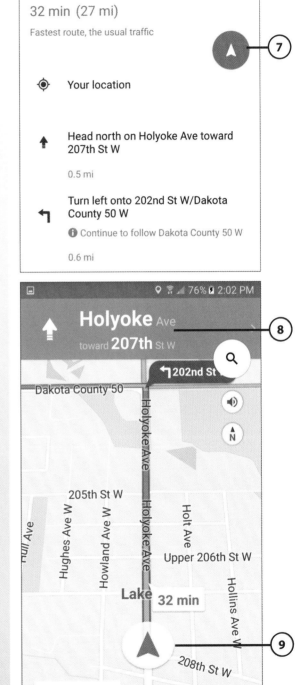

32 min (27 mi)
Fastest route, the usual traffic

7

◉ Your location

↟ Head north on Holyoke Ave toward 207th St W

0.5 mi

↰ Turn left onto 202nd St W/Dakota County 50 W
ⓘ Continue to follow Dakota County 50 W

0.6 mi

9 ⚡ 76% 2:02 PM

Holyoke Ave
toward **207th** St W

8

↰202nd St

Dakota County 50

Holyoke Ave

205th St W

Hull Ave

Hughes Ave W

Howland Ave W

Holyoke Ave

Holt Ave

Upper 206th St W

Hollins Ave W

Lake 32 min

9

208th St W

⬆ RE-CENTER

>>>Go Further

GOOGLE MAPS IN YOUR CAR

Google Maps is designed for use while you're driving. You can use the combination of Google Maps and your Galaxy smartphone much the same way you'd use a freestanding GPS navigation device. The screen provides turn-by-turn maps and directions while the app's voice directs you as to where to turn next.

If you have your phone synced to your car's audio system via Bluetooth, it gets even better. The voice commands sound through your car's speakers, and all you have to do is follow the instructions. The app even lets you know when you've arrived at your destination. (Learn more about connecting to your car via Bluetooth in Chapter 7, "Making Phone Calls.")

Generate Other Types of Directions

Google Maps isn't limited to generating driving directions. The app can also generate direction for mass transit, walking, and bicycling.

(1) From the main map screen, tap the Home icon to display your current location.

(2) Tap the Directions icon to display the Directions screen.

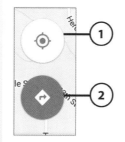

(3) Tap the Mass Transit icon to generate directions via mass transit (train, subway, or bus).

(4) Tap the Walking icon to generate walking directions.

Mass Transit

If you select Mass Transit, Google Maps displays a list of transportation options based on departure and arrival time. Tap the option that best meets your transportation needs.

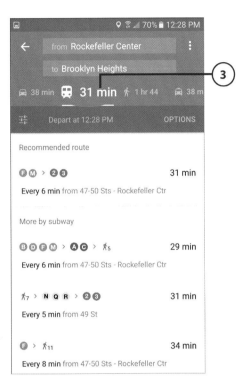

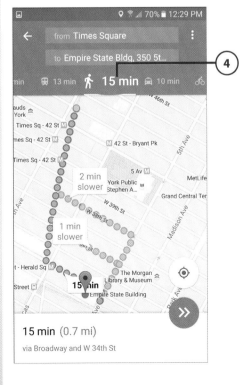

5 Tap the Bicycle icon to generate directions via bicycle paths and streets.

6 Tap the Uber button to see a list of active Uber drivers in your area, and their approximate rates.

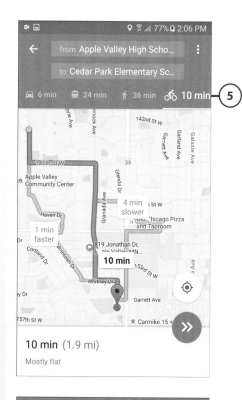

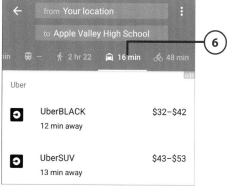

In this chapter, you find out how to shoot and share photos and videos with your Samsung Galaxy S7 or S7 edge. Topics include the following:

→ Shooting Photos with Your Smartphone's Cameras
→ Viewing and Organizing Your Photos
→ Editing Your Photos
→ Recording and Playing Videos
→ Sharing Your Photos and Videos

Shooting and Sharing Photos and Videos

Your Galaxy S7 or S7 edge has two high-quality cameras built in—one on the back, to shoot pictures of things you're looking at, and one on the front, to shoot pictures of you. These cameras can shoot still photographs or videos, and you can easily share the photos and videos you shoot, via email, text message, and even social media.

Shooting Photos with Your Smartphone's Cameras

Your smartphone's main camera is on the back of the unit, facing away from you. The other, front-facing camera is above the screen, facing toward you.

The main camera on the back of your phone is the best-quality camera of the two, with 12 megapixel (MP) resolution. You use this camera to take pictures of friends and family, events and attractions, landscapes and still lifes.

The front-facing camera takes good pictures, but not quite as good as the main camera, with 5MP resolution. Your phone automatically employs this camera when you make video calls. It's also used for taking selfies—photos of yourself.

Shoot a Photograph

You can shoot photos in portrait mode, with the phone held vertically, or in landscape mode, with the phone held horizontally. Taking a photo is as easy as aiming and then tapping the screen.

Camera

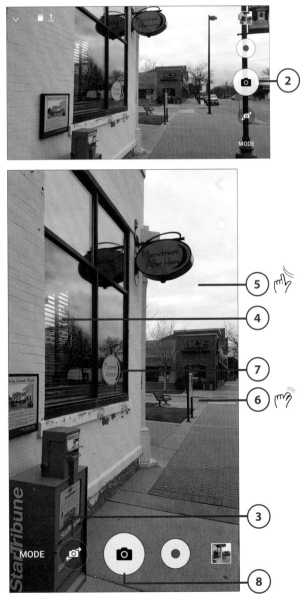

(1) On your phone's Home screen, tap the Camera icon to open the Camera app.

(2) Turn the camera 90 degrees left or right to shoot in landscape mode. The onscreen controls rotate with the camera.

(3) Tap the front/rear icon to switch between rear- and front-facing cameras.

(4) Aim at the subject and use your phone's display as the camera's viewfinder to compose your shot.

(5) Touch the screen with two fingers and spread them apart to zoom into the subject (make the subject appear larger).

(6) Pinch two fingers together on the screen to zoom out of the subject (make the subject appear smaller in the frame).

(7) Tap an area of your phone's screen to focus on the specific person or thing in that area.

(8) Tap the Camera icon to take the picture. The screen flashes slightly and you hear a shutter sound. The new picture is stored in your phone's Gallery.

Volume Keys

You can also take a picture by pressing the up or down Volume keys on the side of your phone.

Shoot a Selfie

Shooting a selfie is just like shooting a regular photo with the rear camera. The difference is that you use the front camera and typically stay in portrait mode, with the phone held vertically in your hand.

1. Open the camera app and tap the front/rear icon to switch to the front-facing camera.

2. When you use the front-facing camera, it automatically deploys Beauty mode, which subtly softens the picture for more of a glamour look. To fine tune this Beauty effect, tap the Beauty icon.

3. Soften the skin tone by tapping Skin Tone and then adjusting the slider left (for lesser effect) or right (for more effect.)

4. Add a spotlight effect by tapping Spotlight and then adjusting the top slider for the position of the spotlight and the bottom slider for the amount of the effect.

5. "Slenderize" your face by tapping Slim Face and then adjusting the slider to the right to increase the effect.

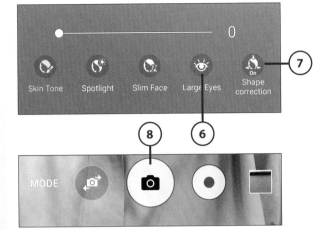

(6) Make your eyes look wider by tapping Large Eyes and then adjusting the slider to the right to increase the effect.

(7) If your face looks distorted (happens when you're too close to the lens), tap On the Shape Correction icon.

(8) Smile for the camera and then tap the Camera icon to take the picture.

Select a Shooting Mode

Your Samsung S7/S7 edge offers several shooting modes you can employ when taking a picture. You select a shooting mode before you take a picture.

When you're shooting with the front-facing camera, you have the following modes available:

Front-Facing Camera Modes

Mode	Description
Auto	Camera automatically determines best settings (default).
Pro	Enables you manually adjust the exposure, ISO, white balance, and color tone (for professionals).
Selective Focus	Enables you to change the focus of pictures after they've been taken.
Panorama	Creates a vertical or horizontal panorama from multiple single shots.
Video Collage	Creates short video collages.
Live Broadcast	Broadcasts your video live on YouTube.
Slow Motion	Records videos at a high frame rate for viewing in slow motion.
Virtual Shot	Creates multi-directional views of objects.
Food	Adjusts settings to capture the vivid colors of food.
Hyperlapse	Creates a time-lapse video.

When you're shooting a selfie with the rear-facing camera, you have the follow-ing modes available:

Rear-Facing Camera Modes

Mode	Description
Selfie	Adjusts settings to best shoot selfie photos (default).
Wide Selfie	Takes a wide-angle selfie shot to better fit more people in the picture.
Video Collage	Creates short video collages.
Live Broadcast	Broadcasts your video live on YouTube.
Virtual Shot	Creates multi-directional views of objects.

(1) From within the Camera app, tap Mode to view the available modes. Which modes are available depends on whether you're using the main or the front-facing camera.

(2) Tap the mode you want to use.

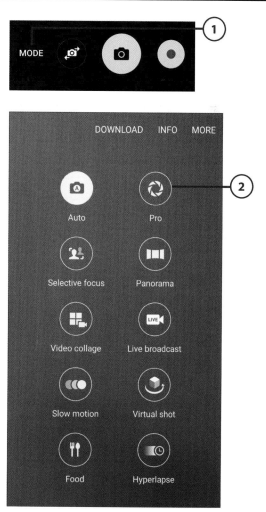

3 Depending on which mode you select, additional options or actions might be available. Follow the onscreen instructions to proceed.

4 Tap the Camera icon to take your picture in the selected mode.

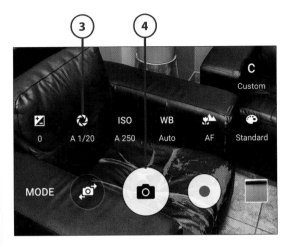

Download More Modes

You can download additional shooting modes for your phone's camera from Samsung's Galaxy Apps Store. Just tap the Download icon from the Modes screen.

Select Quick Settings

Your Samsung smartphone offers several settings you can configure to best optimize the pictures you take. The most useful of these are available as Quick Settings that appear across the top (in portrait mode) or side (in landscape mode) of your phone's screen/viewfinder. The available settings differ depending on which shooting mode you're in.

1 From the Camera app's main screen, tap the left arrow to display the Quick Settings.

2 Change the aspect ratio and resolution of your photos and videos by tapping the Picture Size icon and then selecting the desired setting.

3 Use the LED flash for the main camera by tapping the Flash icon. When you tap this icon, you cycle through three settings: On, Off, and Auto (automatic).

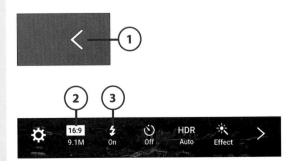

(4) Take a time-delayed photo by tapping the Timer icon and then selecting a time, from 2 to 10 seconds.

(5) Turn on the HDR effect by tapping
On the HDR icon.

HDR

HDR stands for High Dynamic Range, and
it uses multiple shots combined together
to create photos with greater contrast and
dynamic range than normal.

(6) Employ special photographic
effects (actually photo filters, such
as Film and Nostalgia) by tapping
the Effect icon.

Configure Other Camera Settings

There are several other settings you can
configure to personalize the way your
phone's camera functions.

(1) From within the Camera app, tap
Settings to display the Camera
Settings screen.

(2) Tap Video Size (Rear) and make a
new selection to adjust the resolution and aspect ratio of the videos
you shoot.

(3) Tap On the Motion Photo switch to
enable Motion Video, where your
phone takes a short video of what's
happening just before you take a
still picture. When you view a Motion
Photo picture, it appears to move
until it snaps into the final shot.

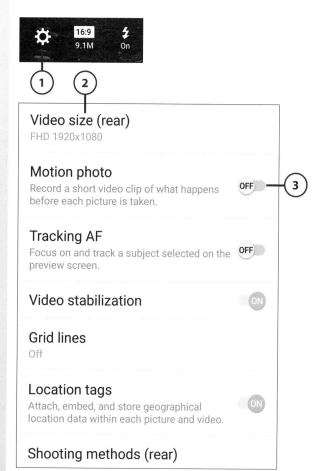

(4) Turn on auto-focus tracking, where you tap to select a subject and the camera keeps that subject in focus as it moves, by tapping On Tracking AF.

(5) Tap On Video Stabilization to turn on video stabilization, which helps to keep the picture steady when you're shooting videos.

(6) Tap On Grid Lines to display grid lines on the camera display to help you compose your pictures.

(7) Tap On Location Tags to enable GPS location tagging, where your location is automatically added to the shooting information (called *metadata*) that accompanies each photo.

(8) Tap On Shooting Methods (Rear) to enable voice control of the rear-facing camera for selfies.

(9) Tap On Review Pictures to have your phone automatically display each picture as you take it.

(10) Tap On Quick Launch to have your phone open the Camera app when you double-tap the Home key.

(11) If you're shooting in Pro mode, tap On Save as RAW File to save pictures without compression (in RAW format) for professional editing. (This mode also saves a copy of the picture in JPG mode, as well.)

(12) Tap Storage Location to determine where your photos are stored—on your phone or on your phone's SD card.

(13) By default, tapping the up or down Volume keys on the side of your phone takes a picture. To change this function so that tapping the Volume keys either records video or zooms in and out, tap Volume Keys Function and make a selection.

(14) Tap Off Shutter Sound to turn off the shutter sound your phone's camera makes when you take a photo.

(15) Tap Reset Settings to reset all your phone's setting to the factory defaults.

Review pictures
View pictures immediately after you take them.
`OFF`

Quick launch
Open Camera by pressing the Home key twice in quick succession.
`OFF`

Save as RAW file
Save pictures without compression in Pro mode. Each picture will be saved as both a RAW file and a JPG file. A viewer app is required to view pictures saved as RAW files. Burst shots cannot be saved as RAW files.
`OFF`

Storage location ———————————— **(12)**
SD card

Volume keys function ———————— **(13)**
Take pictures

Shutter sound `ON` ——— **(14)**

Reset settings ———————————— **(15)**

Viewing and Organizing Your Photos

The photos you take are automatically saved in your phone's Gallery app. You use the Gallery app to view photos, as well as manage the photos you've taken.

View Pictures in the Gallery

The Gallery app displays your photos either by Time, Albums, Events, or Categories.

(1) From your phone's Home screen, tap the Gallery icon to open the Gallery app.

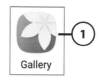

Gallery

(2) By default, the Gallery app displays various albums of your photos. To instead display your photos by Time (date and time taken), Events (that you create), or Categories (Pictures, Videos, or People), tap the down-arrow next to Albums and make a new selection.

(3) Tap an album thumbnail to display the photos within that album or category.

(4) Tap a photo to view it fullscreen.

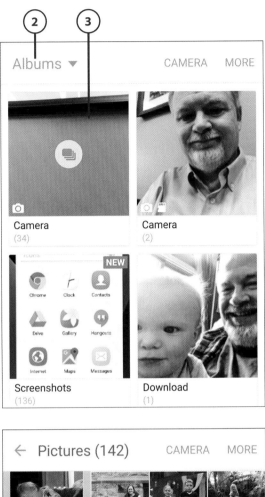

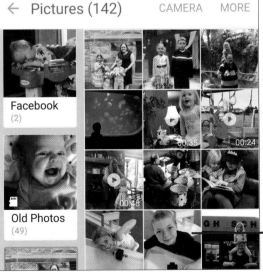

5 Swipe the screen to the left to move to the next photo in the album.

6 Swipe the screen to the right to move to the previous photo in the album.

7 Pinch two fingers together to zoom into the photo (make it larger). Alternatively, double-tap on the screen to zoom in.

8 Place two fingers on the screen and spread them apart to zoom out of the photo (make it smaller).

Manage Your Photos

The Gallery app offers various options for viewing and managing your photos.

1. When viewing a photo, tap the screen to display the viewing and editing controls.

2. Tap the Favorite (star) icon to make this photo a favorite (which makes it easier to recall in the future).

3. Tap the Auto Adjust icon to apply a quick fix to this photo.

4. Tap the Share icon to share this photo with others. (More on this in the "Sharing Your Photos and Videos" section, later in this chapter.)

5. Tap the Edit icon to edit the photo. (More on this in the "Editing Your Photos" section, later in this this chapter.)

6. Tap the Delete icon to delete this photo.

7. Tap More to display more options.

8 Tap Rotate Left to rotate the picture 90 degrees counter clockwise.

9 Tap Rotate Right to rotate the picture 90 degrees clockwise.

10 Tap Details to view details (what photographers call *metadata*) about this picture.

11 Tap Slideshow to launch a slide-show of photos in this album.

12 Tap Set as Contact Picture to set this photo as your contact (pro-file) picture.

13 Tap Set as Wallpaper to set this photo as your phone's wallpaper.

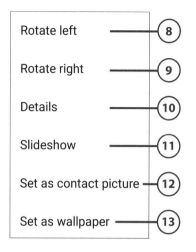

Create a New Album

Within the Gallery app, a photo album is essentially a folder where photos are stored. Photos you shoot are automatically stored in the Camera album. Images you download from the Internet or other sources are stored in the Downloads album. Screenshots you take are stored in the Screenshots album.

You can also create new albums to help you organize your photos.

1 From within the Gallery app, make sure you're viewing in Albums view.

2 Tap More.

3 Tap Create Album.

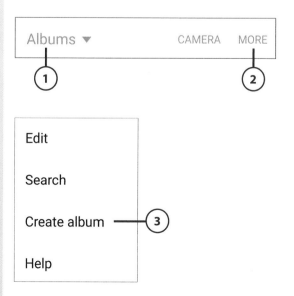

(4) Select where you want to create this album—on your phone
(Device) or on your SD card.

(5) Enter a name for the new album.

(6) Tap Create.

(7) You see the new album displayed
on the left of the screen, and your
photos are displayed on the right.
Tap to select those photos you
want to move to the new album.

(8) Tap Done.

(9) Tap Move when you're prompted
to copy or move the items.
(Unless you want the photos to
reside in both the original and
new albums, in which case tap
Copy.)

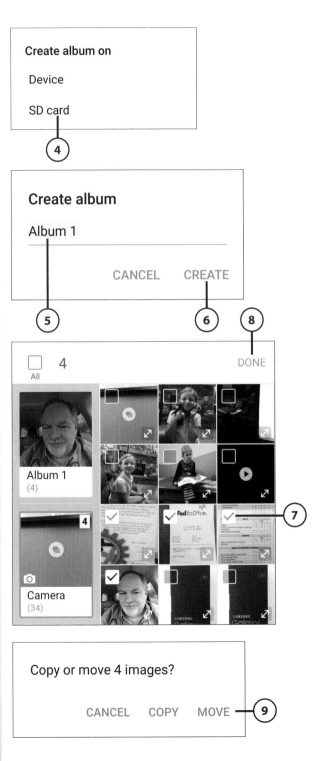

Delete Photos

You can tap the Delete icon to delete any photo you're currently viewing. You can also delete one or more photos from the host album or category.

(1) From within the Gallery app, open the album or category you want to view.

(2) Tap More.

(3) Tap Edit.

(4) Tap to select those photos you want to delete. Each selected photo appears with a check mark.

(5) Tap Delete.

(6) Tap Delete in the confirmation box.

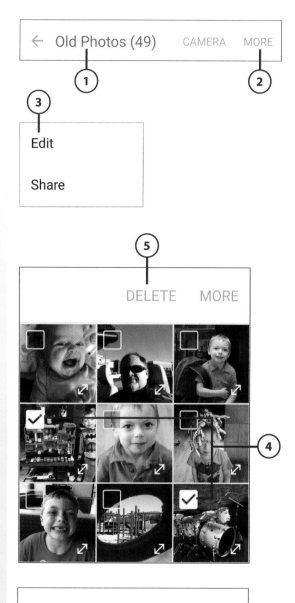

← Old Photos (49)   CAMERA   MORE

Edit

Share

DELETE   MORE

2 images will be deleted.

CANCEL   DELETE

>>>Go Further
GOOGLE PHOTOS

The Gallery app included with your Galaxy S7/S7 edge is a good photo storage/editing app. There are lots of similar apps available, however, that you might want to consider instead of the Gallery app.

One of the more popular photo storage/editing apps is Google Photos. Like the Gallery app, Google Photos lets you store and organize your photos in albums, as well as do basic touch ups and editing. (Also like the Gallery App, Google Photos is free.)

Where Google Photos really shines is its use of the cloud to store your photos. (In this instance, the cloud is a collection of Google servers on the internet.) Yes, it can store your photos on your phone or SD card, like the Gallery app. But it also uploads all your photos to the Google cloud, where they're accessible from any internet-connected device whenever you log into your Google account. This way you can take a picture on your phone and have it immediately available from your personal computer or tablet.

Google's cloud photo storage is also a great backup service. You can opt to delete the original photos from your phone, and they'll still be available via the cloud, using the Google Photos app on your phone or other device.

For this reason, many serious photo takers are switching from the Gallery app to Google Photos. It's what I personally use, and I suggest you check it out.

Editing Your Photos

The photos you shoot with the Camera app can be edited in the Gallery app. This way you can touch up your photos without having to use a third-party photo editing app—or transfer them to your computer to edit in Photoshop or a similar software program.

Employ Auto Adjust

Sometimes you take a photo that just looks a little off—the colors aren't quite right, maybe it's a little too light or too dark. For many photos, the Gallery app's Auto Adjust option can make these little changes for you, automatically. (And if you don't like the automatic changes, you can always undo them!)

1. Open the picture you want to edit, then tap to display the editing controls.

2. Tap Auto Adjust. The adjustments are made to the photo; if you don't like the results, tap Off Auto Adjust.

Rotate an Image

Even the smartest smartphone camera sometimes gets confused. You shoot a picture in landscape orientation and it displays rotated, in portrait mode. Fortunately, there's a quick fix for this problem.

1. Open the picture you want to rotate and then tap the screen to display the editing controls.

2. Tap More.

3. Tap Rotate Left to rotate the picture 90 degrees counterclockwise. Continue tapping this control to rotate the picture further.

4. Tap Rotate Right to rotate the picture 90 degrees clockwise. Continue tapping this control to rotate the picture further.

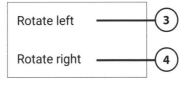

Crop a Photo

It's not uncommon to include more in the picture than what you wanted to focus on. In this instance, you want to crop the picture so that the important subject is larger in the frame, and the unnecessary edges are cropped off.

(1) Open the picture you want to crop and then tap the screen to display the editing controls.

(2) Tap Edit to display the quick editing panel at the bottom of the screen.

(3) Tap Adjustment to display the crop box and grid.

(4) Tap and drag any of the crop handles along the edges and corners until only that part of the picture you want to keep is included.

(5) Tap Apply.

Crop Ratio

To constrain your crop to a standard aspect ratio, such as 1:1 (square), 4:3, or 16:9 (widescreen), tap the Ratio icon and make a selection before cropping.

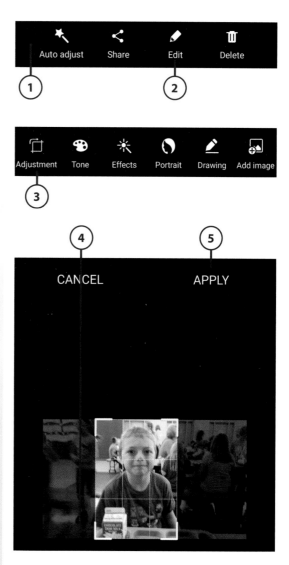

Perform Detailed Adjustments

The Gallery app includes the basic rotate and crop controls, as discussed in the preceding tasks, as well as some more detailed adjustments that enable you to spin and flip the images you shoot.

1. Open the picture you want to adjust and then tap the screen to display the editing controls.

2. Tap Edit to display the quick editing panel.

3. Tap Adjustment to display the adjustments screen.

4. Spin the picture (similar to rotate, but in smaller increments) by tapping and dragging the slider underneath the photo—right for clockwise, and left for counterclockwise.

5. Tap the Flip Horiz. icon to flip the picture horizontally (left to right).

6. Tap the Flip Vert. icon to flip the picture vertically (top to bottom).

7. Tap the Rotate icon to rotate the picture 90 degrees clockwise.

8. Crop the picture by tapping and dragging any of the crop handles.

9. Tap Apply to apply your changes.

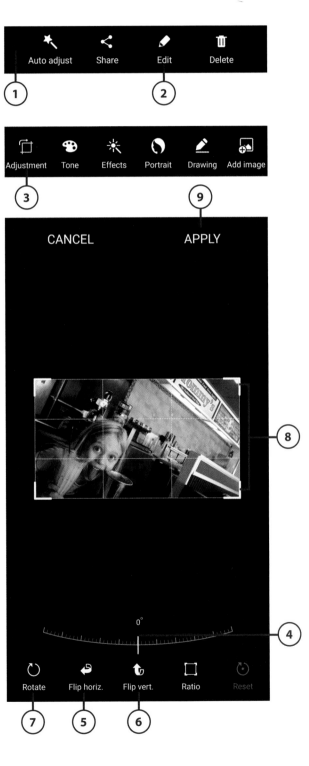

Adjust Brightness, Contrast, and Color

The Gallery app also enables you to adjust the brightness, contrast, color, and other tonal settings for your picture.

1. Open the picture you want to edit then tap the screen to display the editing controls.

2. Tap Edit to display the quick editing panel.

3. Tap Tone to display the photo editing controls.

4. Adjust the brightness by tapping Brightness and then dragging the Brightness slider—left for darker, right for brighter.

5. Adjust the contrast by tapping Contrast and then tapping to drag the Contrast slider.

6. Adjust the color saturation by tapping Saturation and then tapping to drag the Saturation slider—left for less color, right for more color.

7. Adjust the color tint by tapping Hue and then tapping to drag the Hue slider.

8. Adjust the color temperature by tapping Temperature and then tapping to drag the Temperature slider—left for cooler colors, right for warmer.

9. Tap Apply to apply your changes.

Apply Special Effects

Just as you can apply special effects when shooting a photo, you can also add effects during the editing process. In fact, there are more effects available in the Gallery app than in the Camera app.

1. Open the picture you want to edit and then tap the screen to display the editing controls.

2. Tap Edit to display the quick editing panel.

3. Tap Effects to display the effects screen.

4. All available special effects are displayed in a row at the bottom of the screen. Swipe this row left or right to access additional effects.

5. Tap to select the effect you want. The picture displays with that effect applied.

6. Adjust the intensity of an effect by tapping and dragging the slider left (for less intensity) or right (for more).

7. Tap Apply to apply the effect.

It's Not All Good

Changes Are Permanent

When you're done applying special effects or making other changes to a picture in the Gallery, you must tap Save on the next screen. When you do this, the edited picture overwrites the original version. You can't undo your changes after you've tapped Save. (You can, however, undo your changes before they're saved, by tapping Undo.) So make sure you like the changes before you save them!

Drawing and Collages

The Gallery app also lets you draw on your photos, by tapping Drawing from the quick editing panel. You can also add other photos to a single photo to create a photo collage; just tap Add Image from the quick editing panel.

Recording and Playing Videos

You can use either the main or front-facing camera on your Galaxy S7 or S7 edge to shoot videos as well as still photos. Many of the same controls are available when shooting video as when shooting photos.

Record a Video

You shoot a video much the same way you shoot a still photo, and with the same app—your phone's Camera app. Videos are recorded at the resolution and aspect ratio you've selected in the Camera app's settings, as described earlier in this chapter in the "Configure Other Camera Settings" task.

(1) On your phone's Home screen, tap the Camera icon to open the Camera app.

Camera

(2) Turn the camera 90-degrees left or right to shoot a widescreen picture. The onscreen controls rotate with the phone.

(3) Tap the front/rear icon to switch between rear- and front-facing cameras.

(4) Aim at the subject and use your phone's display as the camera's viewfinder to compose your shot.

(5) Tap the red button to begin recording. The elapsed time displays at the bottom of the screen, along with a flashing red dot.

(6) Touch the screen with two fingers and spread them apart to zoom into the picture.

(7) Pinch two fingers together on the screen to zoom out of the picture.

(8) Tap the Capture icon to capture a still photo while you're recording the video.

(9) When you're done recording, tap the large Stop button. The video is now processed and saved to your phone's Gallery.

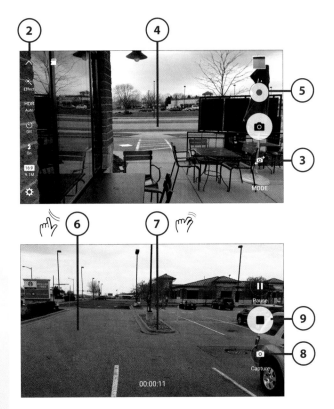

It's Not All Good

Widescreen Videos

Most viewers expect to see videos in widescreen format—*not* in portrait or vertical format. This means you do *not* want to hold your phone normally when shooting videos. Instead, rotate the phone 90 degrees left or right so that it's horizontal—and the picture you see onscreen is wider than it is tall.

>>>Go Further
SLOW MOTION

The Galaxy S7 and S7 edge offer a slow motion video shooting mode. With Slow Motion enabled, you record at a high frame rate, which enables you to play back parts of the video in slow motion.

You enable this slow motion effect *before* you start recording. Tap Mode and then tap Slow Motion. Record your video as normal.

After you're done recording, tap the thumbnail at the bottom right to review your video. Tap the screen to begin playback; use the controls at the bottom of the screen to indicate when and how long you want the slow motion effect to appear.

Play a Video

All the videos you record are stored in the Gallery app. Use this app to access and view your videos.

(1) From within the Gallery app, tap the down arrow at the top of the screen to display the menu of options.

(2) Tap Categories.

(3) Tap to open the Videos category.

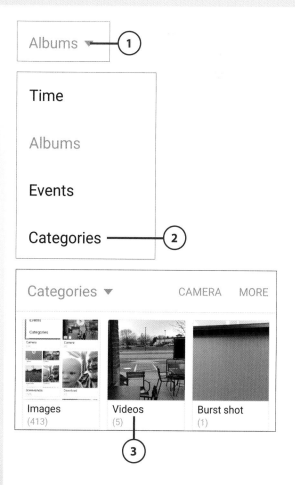

(4) You see all the videos you've recorded. Tap to open the video you want to view.

(5) Turn the phone sideways to view a normal widescreen video. Tap anywhere on the screen to begin playback.

(6) The video begins to play. Tap the screen to display the playback controls.

(7) Tap the Pause button to pause playback. The button changes to a Play button; tap the Play button to resume playback.

(8) Tap and drag the slider (sometimes called a "scrubber") to move to another portion of the video.

(9) Tap the previous button to play the previous video.

(10) Tap the next button to play the next video.

(11) Tap Pop-Up to display the video in a small window at the top of the screen while you work in other apps.

(12) Tap Full to have the video fill the entire screen of your phone.

(13) Tap More and then tap Delete to delete this video.

Sharing Your Photos and Videos

You can easily share the photos and videos you take in a number of different ways. You can share them via email, via text messages, and via various social media.

Shoot and Share a Photo or Video

Many times you take a picture and decide there and then that it's worth sharing. Maybe you want to text it to a friend or family member, or you want to post it to Facebook. It's easy to do.

1. Using the Camera app, shoot the photo.

2. Tap the thumbnail at the bottom of the screen to display the photo you just shot.

3. Tap the screen to display the controls at the bottom.

4. Tap Share to display the Share Via pane.

5. Swipe right and left to view other ways to share.

6. Tap how you want to share this photo.

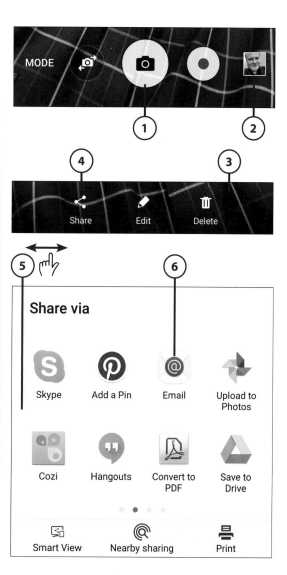

Follow the onscreen instructions to share the photo via the selected method.

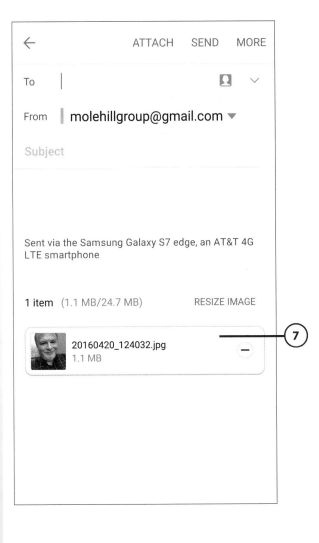

Share Items from the Gallery

You can also share any photo or video you've shot from the Gallery app.

 From within the Gallery app, open the album or category that contains the photo(s) or video(s) you want to share.

 Tap More.

 Tap Share.

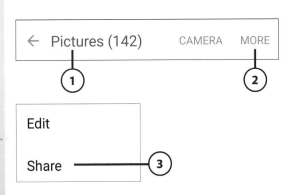

4 Tap to select the item(s) you want to share.

5 Tap Share to display the Share Via pane.

6 Tap the icon for how you want to share these items and then complete the sharing process accordingly.

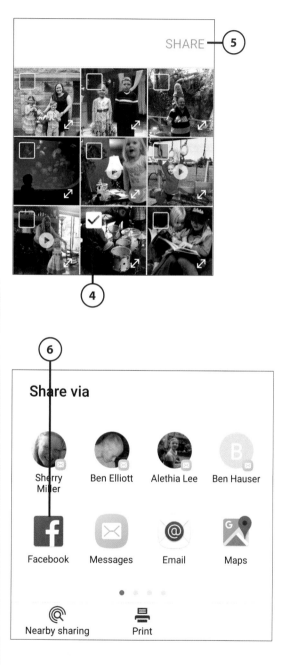

In this chapter, you walk through using your smartphone to listen to your favorite music. Topics include the following:

→ Listening to Streaming Music Services
→ Listening to Music Stored on Your Phone

Listening to Music

Back in the old days, we listened to music on record players in our living rooms. Then things got portable with transistor radios, both AM and FM. Later, Sony brought us the Walkman portable cassette player, and then came compact discs (and Sony's Discman portable CD player). It's been more than a decade since music went digital, thanks to the Apple iPod.

It's hard to believe, but iPods and other MP3 players are already passé. Instead, we now listen to music on our smartphones. Your Samsung Galaxy S7 or S7 edge has enough internal and SD card storage to hold a fairly large collection of downloaded digital music, or you can do like all the kids are doing and get your music online via streaming music services. The latter choice is particularly appealing, as you get access to just about any song you want without having to purchase and store anything.

Listening to Streaming Music Services

The music business is changing—again. We've all lived through several seismic changes in how our music is delivered, and now we're in the middle of another one.

Instead of buying music one track or album at a time, either online or in retail stores, more and more people are subscribing to online music services that let you listen to all the songs you want, either for free or a low monthly charge. These services, such as Pandora and Spotify, stream music in real time over the Internet to any connected device, including your smartphone. There's nothing to download, and nothing to store on your device.

Listen to Pandora Radio

Pandora Radio is much like traditional AM or FM radio, in that you listen to the songs Pandora selects for you, along with accompanying commercials. However, it's a little more personalized than traditional radio in that you create your own personalized stations. All you have to do is choose a song or artist; Pandora then creates a station with other songs like the one you picked.

You access Pandora from the Pandora app, available for free from the Google Play Store.

Free Versus Paid

Pandora's basic membership is free, but it's ad-supported. (You have to suffer through commercials as you listen.) To get rid of the commercials, pay for the $4.99/month Pandora One subscription.

(1) From the Home or Apps screen, tap the Pandora icon to open the Pandora app.

2. The first time you open the app, enter the email address for your Pandora account and then tap Log In.

3. If you don't yet have a Pandora account (the basic account is free), tap Sign Up and follow the onscreen instructions.

4. Tap to select the My Stations tab.

5. Tap Create Station to create a new station.

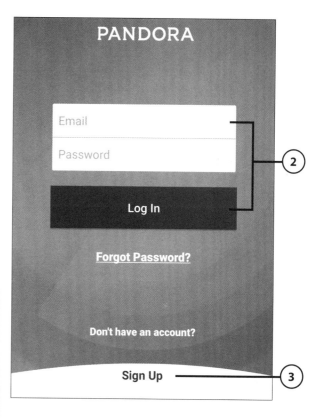

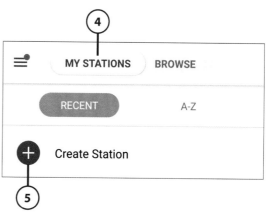

(6) Enter the name of a song, genre, artist, or composer into the box at the top of the screen.

(7) As you type, Pandora makes suggestions; tap the selection you want, or continue typing. The new station is created and starts to play.

(8) Tap the Pause button to pause playback. Tap Play to resume playback.

(9) Tap the thumbs-up icon to like the current song. Pandora will play more songs like this one.

(10) Tap the thumbs-down icon if you don't like the current song. Pandora skips to the next song, doesn't play the current song again, and plays fewer songs like it.

(11) Tap the next track button to skip to the next song without disliking it. (You can't repeat songs on Pandora, or return to songs you've just listened to.)

(12) Tap the up button above the playback controls to learn more about this song and artist.

(13) Tap the back arrow at the top of the screen to return to your station list.

← **Create Station**

creed — (6)

Top Hit

Creedence Clearwater Revival

Artists

Creed

Creedence Clearwater Revisited — (7)

47% 12:54 PM

← **Creedence Clearwater Revi...** 👍 — (13)

CREEDENCE CLEARWATER REVIVAL
BAYOU COUNTRY

20bit K2 SUPER CODING

Proud Mary ⌃ — (12)
Creedence Clearwater Revival

— (10)

0:06 — -3:03 — (9)

👎 👍 ❚❚ ⏭ — (11)
— (8)

14 Tap another station to switch to that station.

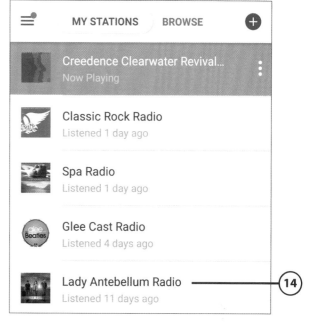

Local Radio Stations Online

If you'd rather listen to your local AM or FM radio station—or to a radio station located in another city —there are apps for that. The iHeartRadio and TuneIn apps offer free access to local radio stations around the world, over the Internet. Both apps can be downloaded for free from the Google Play Store.

Listen to Spotify Music

The other big streaming music service is Spotify Music. You listen to Spotify Music via the Spotify app, which you can download for free from the Google Play Store.

>>>Go Further

SPOTIFY PREMIUM

Spotify on your smartphone is a little different from Spotify on your computer. The computer version of Spotify lets you select individual songs to listen to. The mobile version, however, only lets you browse by artist or genre, not by song—unless, that is, you pay for a subscription.

Spotify charges $9.99/month for its Premium service. With the Premium service, you get the option of playing specific songs (which you don't have with a free membership). In addition, the Premium service removes ads that play if you have a free membership.

So, it might be worth it to pay for Spotify Premium on your smartphone. It's less valuable if you listen on a computer, but for smartphone listening, it makes the service much more useful.

1. From the Home or Apps screen, tap the Spotify icon to open the Spotify app.

2. The first time you open the app, tap Log In and enter your account information.

3. If you don't yet have a Spotify account (the basic account is free), tap Sign Up and follow the onscreen instructions.

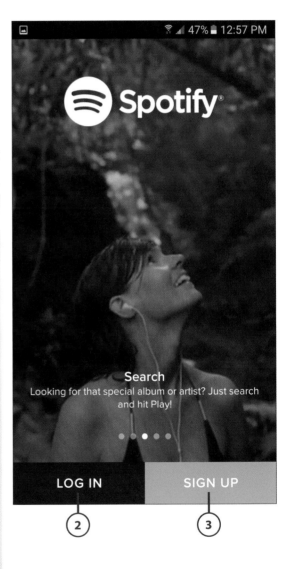

4 Curated playlists are organized by genre or type of music. Scroll down to a specific category and tap a playlist to open it.

5 Scroll down to see all the songs in the playlist.

6 Tap Shuffle Play to begin playback.

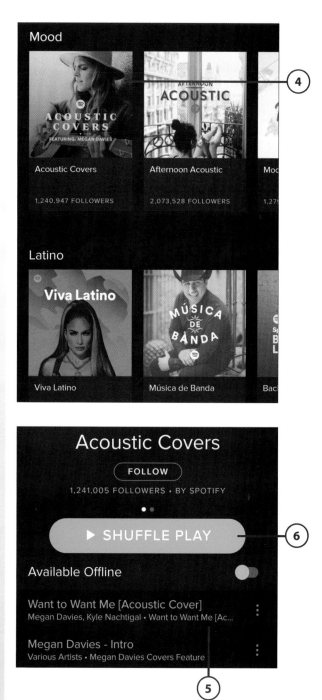

7 Tap the Pause button to pause playback —which then turns into a Play button. Tap the Play button to resume playback.

8 Tap the Next button to skip to the next track.

9 Tap the down arrow at the top left to return to the previous screen while playback continues.

10 Search for specific artists, songs, albums, or playlists by tapping the Options button and then selecting Search.

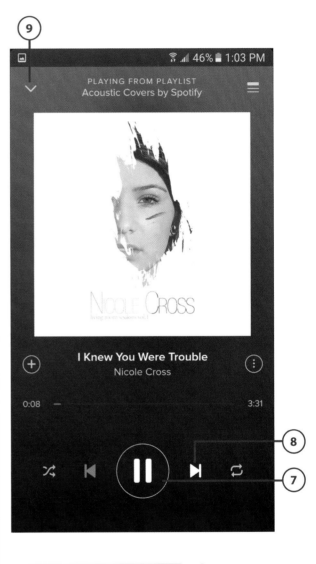

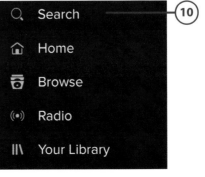

⑪ Enter the name of what you're looking for into the Search box. As you type, Spotify displays a list of suggestions.

⑫ Tap the artist you want, or continue typing. You see a playlist of related songs.

⑬ Tap Shuffle Play to begin playback.

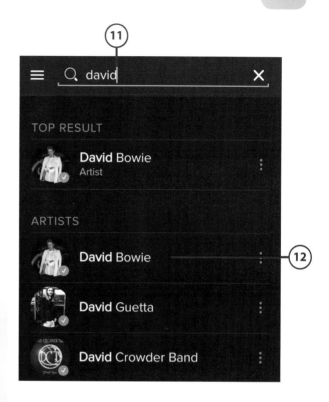

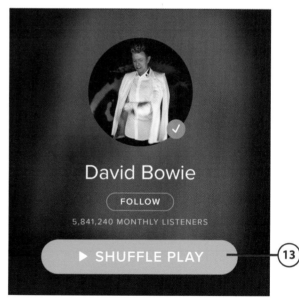

>>>Go Further

TRANSFERRING MUSIC FROM YOUR COMPUTER TO YOUR PHONE

You might have already purchased some digital music on your computer. You might have also "ripped" music from compact discs to store digitally on your PC. All that music is available to you on your phone, as soon as you copy it from one device to another.

There are many ways to copy digital music from your computer to your smartphone. For example, if you have a Windows PC, you can use the Windows Media Player (WMP) software on your PC to do the transfer. Just connect your phone to your PC with a USB cable, launch the WMP software on your computer, and then click the Sync tab. You can drag any and all tracks from your computer (displayed in the main part of the Windows Media Player window) to the Sync panel, and then click the Start Sync button. The music is copied to your phone—and, in the process, converted to the optimal file format for best storage and playback on your mobile device.

Listening to Music Stored on Your Phone

If you prefer to download rather than stream your music, there are many online music stores you can choose from, such as Google Play Music and Amazon Digital Music. You can purchase and download individual tracks or complete albums, and save them either on your phone or on your phone's SD card. (The latter is a better storage method.)

After you've purchased, downloaded, or copied music to your smartphone, you need an app that plays that music. There are lots of music player apps available from the Google Play Store:

• Fusion Music Player	Free
• Google Play Music	Free
• MediaMonkey	Free (Pro version $3.99)
• n7player Music Player	Free
• PlayerPro Music Player	$4.95
• Poweramp Music Player	$3.99 (free version also available)

We'll focus on using the Google Play Music app, as it's already installed on your Galaxy S7/S7 edge.

Play Music

Google Play Music is an app that lets you play music stored on your phone, purchase music from the Google Play Store, and listen to streaming music from the Google Play Music service. We'll focus on using the app to play music you've stored on your phone.

Play Music

☰ Listen Now

1. From the Home or Apps screen, tap the Play Music icon to open the app.

2. Tap the Options button at the top-left corner to display the menu of options.

3. Switch On the Downloaded Only option.

4. Tap Music Library to view the music stored on your phone.

🎧 Listen Now

Top charts

New releases

🎵 Music library ———— 4

((•)) Browse stations

Shop

Downloaded only ⬤ 3

(5) Tap the Playlists tab to view any playlists you've created. (More on playlists in a moment.)

(6) Tap the Artists tab to view your music by artist.

(7) Tap the Albums tab to view your music by album.

(8) Tap the Songs tab to view your music by individual song.

(9) Tap the Genres tab to view your music by genre.

(10) From within a given tab, tap the genre, artist, or album you want to listen to.

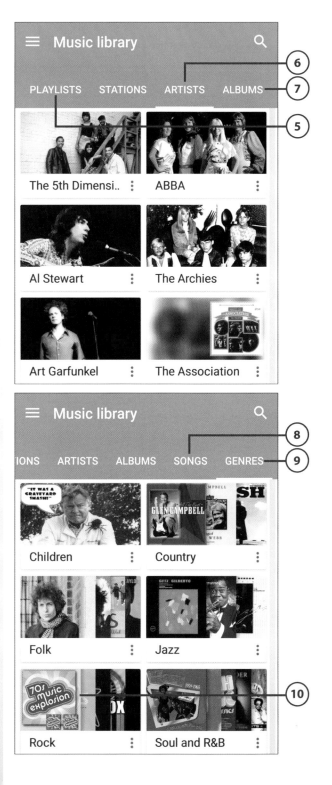

11 From within a genre or artist screen, tap All My Songs to view all the songs from that artist or genre.

12 Tap an individual album to view the songs in that album.

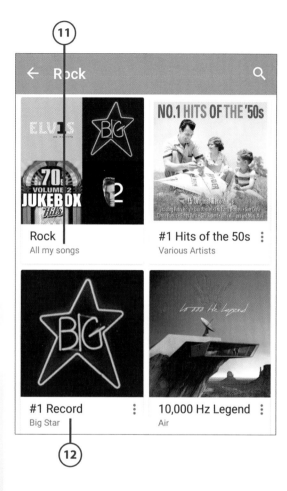

(13) Tap the big orange Play button to play all the songs.

(14) Tap an individual song to play that song.

(15) Tap the Pause button to pause playback. The Pause button turns into a Play button. Tap the Play button to resume playback.

(16) Swipe up from the bottom of the screen to view the current selection full screen, along with more playback controls.

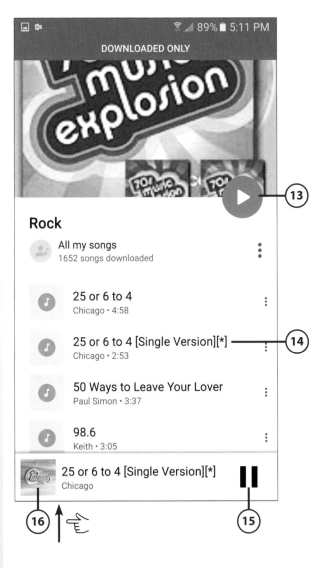

17 Tap the Repeat icon once to repeat all the songs in this album. Tap this button twice to repeat the current song.

18 Tap the Shuffle icon to shuffle the order of playback.

19 Tap the Pause button to pause playback. The Pause button turns into a Play button. Tap the Play button to resume playback.

20 Tap the Next button to play the next song.

21 Tap the Previous button to play the previous song.

Create and Play Playlists

You can create playlists of your favorite songs. A playlist can include tracks from multiple artists and albums.

1 To create a new playlist, find a specific song you want and then tap that song's Menu button.

2 Tap Add to Playlist to display the Add to Playlist panel.

(3) Tap the name of a playlist to add this song to an existing playlist.

(4) Tap New Playlist to display the New Playlist panel and create a new playlist.

(5) Enter a name for this playlist into the Name box.

(6) Enter an optional description of this playlist into the Description box.

(7) Tap Create Playlist. The song is added to the playlist. Repeat steps 1–3 to add other songs to this playlist.

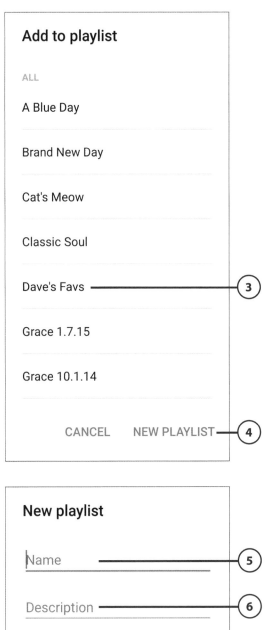

Add to playlist

ALL

A Blue Day

Brand New Day

Cat's Meow

Classic Soul

Dave's Favs ——————————— (3)

Grace 1.7.15

Grace 10.1.14

CANCEL   NEW PLAYLIST—(4)

New playlist

Name ————————(5)

Description ——————(6)

Public
Anyone can see and listen

CANCEL   CREATE PLAYLIST—(7)

8 To play a playlist, return to the Music Library screen and select the Playlists tab.

9 Scroll down the screen and tap the playlist you want to play.

10 Tap the orange Play button to begin playback.

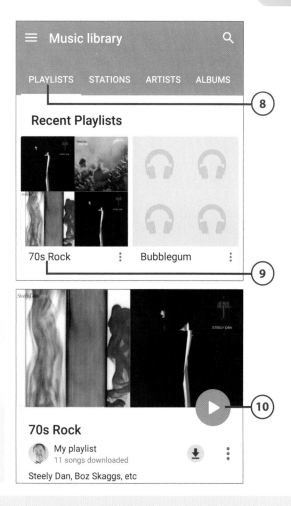

>>>Go Further
LISTENING TO SMARTPHONE MUSIC IN YOUR CAR

Many newer cars let you play music from your smartphone over the car's audio system. How this is done depends on the car.

Some cars let you connect your phone via USB. To do this, connect your phone's charger cable to the USB connector in your car and then switch your audio system to the auxiliary input. You might be able to control your phone's playback via your car's audio system, or you might have to start playback on your phone.

Other cars let you connect your phone via Bluetooth to the car's audio system. Follow your car's instructions to make the connection; you then should be able to use your car's audio system to control playback of Google Play Music, Pandora, and other music apps.

Netflix

Hulu

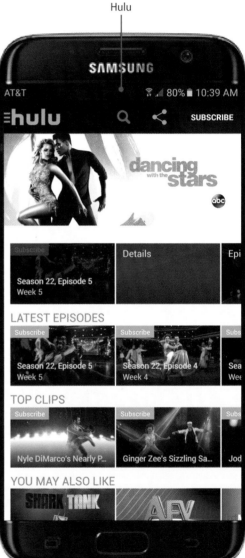

In this chapter, you learn how you can watch movies, TV shows, and other videos on your Samsung S7 or S7 edge. Topics include the following:

→ Watching TV Shows and Movies on Netflix
→ Watching TV Shows and Movies on Hulu
→ Watching Videos on YouTube

19

Watching TV Shows, Movies, and Other Videos

Watching TV in your living room is fine, but what if you want to entertain yourself when you're not in your living room? You can use your Samsung smartphone to watch a variety of TV shows and movies over the Internet, whatever room you're in—and even when you're in your car or away from home. It's all a matter of picking the right app and subscribing to the best video streaming service—Netflix, Hulu, or something different.

Watching TV Shows and Movies on Netflix

For a low $9.99/month subscription, you can watch all the movies and TV shows you want on Netflix—and there's a lot available. Netflix offers a mix of both classic and newer movies, as well as a surprising number of classic and newer television programs. There's also a surprising amount of original programming, including the series *Daredevil*, *Grace and Frankie*, *House of Cards*, *Orange is the New Black*, and *Unbreakable Kimmy Schmidt*. There's something there to please just about everyone.

To watch Netflix, you need to download and install the Netflix app on your smartphone, which you can do (for free) from the Google Play Store. You also need a Netflix subscription; you can sign up from either the Netflix app or website (www.netflix.com).

First Time Use

The first time you open the Netflix app, you're prompted to either create a new Netflix account or log into an existing one. Each subsequent time you open the app, it automatically logs in to this account and displays the appropriate content tailored exclusively to your viewing habits.

Watch a Movie or TV Show on Netflix

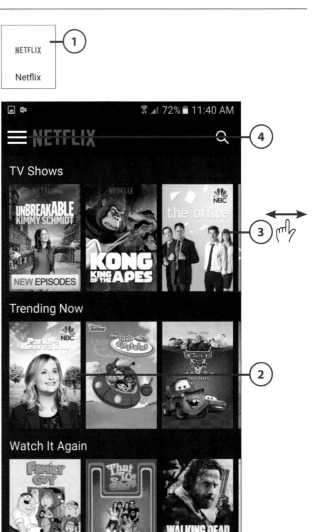

Netflix offers a variety of new and older movies for your viewing pleasure, as well as all manner of current and classic television programming. The selection varies from month to month, so keep looking for what's new!

1. From your phone's Home or Apps screen, tap the Netflix icon to open the app.

2. Netflix organizes its programming into various categories— Spotlight, TV Shows, Trending Now, Top Picks, Recently Added, and so forth. Scroll down to see additional categories.

3. Swipe left or right through any section to view more programming of that type.

4. To view programming by genre, tap the Options button.

(5) Tap the type of programming you want to watch—TV Shows, Action, Anime, Children & Family, Comedies, and so forth.

(6) To search for a specific movie or show, tap the Search (magnifying glass) icon to display the search panel.

(7) Use the onscreen keyboard to type the name of the movie or show into the Search box.

(8) As you type, Netflix displays matching suggestions. Tap one of these suggestions, or finish entering your search.

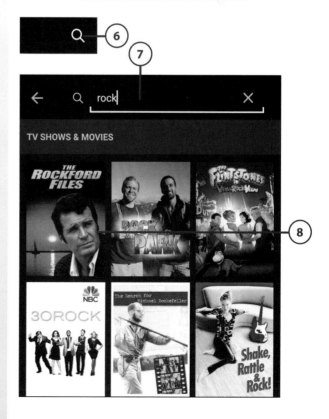

9 If you choose to watch a TV show, you typically can choose from different episodes in different seasons. Tap the Season down arrow to select a season; you see all the episodes from that season.

10 Tap an episode to begin watching it.

11 If you choose to watch a movie, tap the Play button at the top of the screen.

Playback Controls

When watching a video on Netflix, tap the screen to display the playback controls, which you can use to pause and otherwise control video playback.

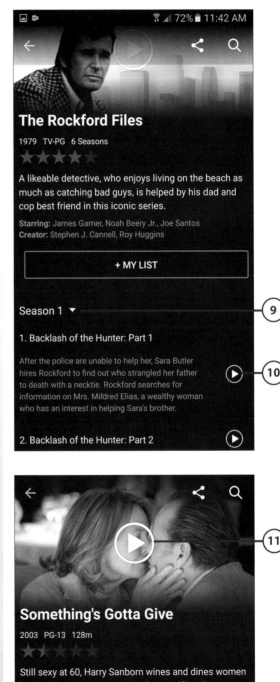

It's Not All Good

Too Much Data

Watching streaming video on Netflix, Hulu, and similar sites requires a lot of bandwidth; movie and TV shows contain a lot of data. So, you probably don't want to watch these apps when you're on a cellular connection, as it will quickly max out your data plan.

Instead, wait until you're connected to a solid Wi-Fi network or hotspot. Watching video over Wi-Fi won't affect your data plan at all.

Watching TV Shows and Movies on Hulu

If you want to watch current episodes of network TV shows, then Hulu is the app for you. Although Hulu does offer some movies and older TV programs, its real forte is newer programming.

The web version of Hulu, which you can watch on your computer, is free but limited. To watch Hulu on your smartphone, you need to subscribe to the Hulu service. Whereas the Hulu app is free (and downloadable from the Google Plus Store), a Hulu subscription runs you $7.99/month for a plan with limited commercials, or $11.99/month for a no-commercials plan. You can sign up either from the Hulu app or website (www.hulu.com).

First Time Use

The first time you open the Hulu app, you're prompted to either create a new account or log into an existing one. Each subsequent time you open the app, it automatically logs in to this account.

(1) From your phone's Home or Apps screen, tap the Hulu icon to open the app.

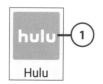

Hulu

(2) The Hulu app's home screen displays a variety of recommended programming, organized by type. Scroll down to view more.

(3) Swipe right or left in any section to view more options.

(4) Tap the Options button on the top left to browse for programs.

(5) Tap the type of programming you want to watch.

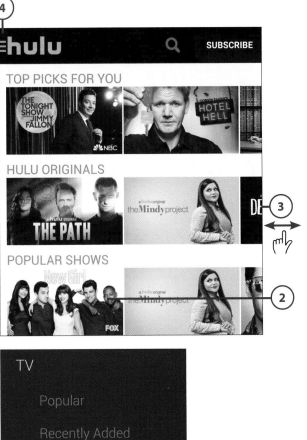

(6) Search for a specific program by tapping the Search icon to display the search panel.

(7) Enter the name of what you want to watch. As you type, Hulu displays suggested programs.

(8) Tap a program to view its screen.

(9) Tap an episode to view more details.

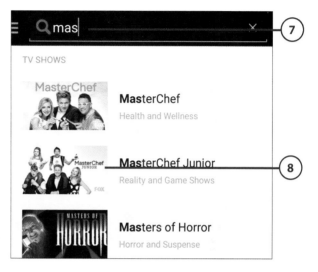

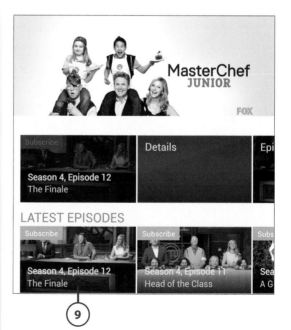

(10) Tap Play Video to begin watching this program.

Playback Controls

When watching a video on Hulu, tap the screen to display the playback controls, which you can use to pause and otherwise control video playback.

Watching Videos on YouTube

Then there's YouTube. If you haven't checked out YouTube yet, you're missing a lot. YouTube is a website (and accompanying app) that lets people upload their own videos to share those videos with other users. (It also has a lot of commercial videos available, including a ton of music videos both new and classic.)

YouTube is the place to find the latest "viral" videos—those videos that get super-popular when people share them with all their friends. Cat videos, baby videos, blooper videos, you name it—it's on YouTube.

How-To Videos

YouTube is also a great place to find advice and instruction. Whether you need to replace a garbage disposal or improve your golf swing, YouTube has instructional videos online to help you!

Watch YouTube

You watch YouTube videos from the YouTube app. You might have this app already installed on your Galaxy S7 or S7 edge; if not, you can download it (for free!) from the Google Play Store.

First Time Use

The first time you open the YouTube app, you might be prompted to sign in with your Google Account; if so, do so. (It's also possible that the app will automatically pick up your Google credentials from elsewhere on your phone.) After this, the app should automatically sign into your account whenever you launch it.

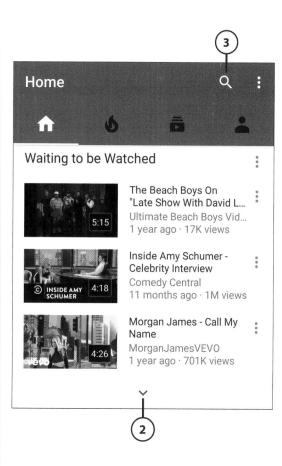

1. From your phone's Home or Apps screen, tap the YouTube icon to open the app.

2. The YouTube app's home screen displays a variety of recommended programming. Scroll down to view more.

3. Search for a video by tapping the Search button at the top of the screen; this opens a new Search YouTube panel.

4 Enter the name of what you want to search for. As you type, YouTube displays suggested searches.

5 Tap an item to view videos of that type.

6 Tap the video you want to watch.

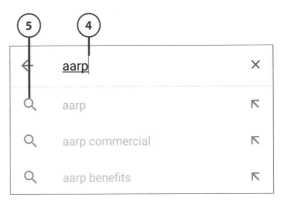

(7) Playback begins in at the top of the screen. To view the video full-screen, turn your phone sideways.

(8) Tap the screen to view playback controls.

(9) Tap the large Pause icon in the middle of the screen to pause playback. The icon now changes to a Play icon; tap this to resume playback.

(10) Tap and drag the scrub (slider) control to move directly to another part of the video.

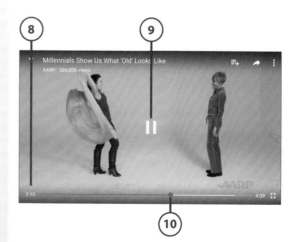

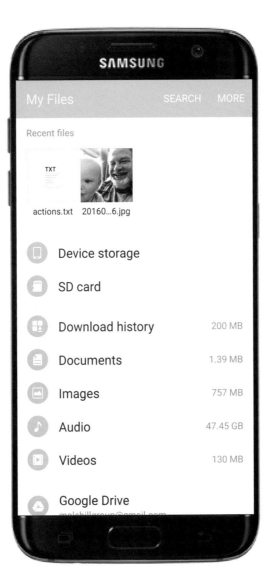

In this chapter, you learn about the files stored on your phone and how to manage them. Topics include the following:

→ Working with Removable MicroSD Storage
→ Viewing Device Storage
→ Using the My Files App
→ Storing Files on Google Drive
→ Transferring Files Between Devices
→ Backing Up Your Data

Copying Files To and From Your Phone—And Backing Up Your Important Data

Your Samsung Galaxy S7 or S7 edge is like a miniature computer that fits in the palm of your hand. Yes, it makes phone calls, but it also does just about everything a notebook or desktop computer does—including store important data in a collection of digital files.

All sorts of files are stored on your smartphone. Picture files, music files, video files, contact files, maybe even word processing and spreadsheet files. Plus all the system files necessary for your phone to run.

How, exactly, do you manage all these files? How do you copy files from your computer to your phone, and vice versa? And is there a better way to store these files than on your phone?

Read on to learn the answers to these questions—and more.

Working with Removable MicroSD Storage

The Galaxy S7/S7 edge lets you store files on the phone itself or on a removable MicroSD card. Storing some files on the MicroSD card can substantially increase the storage capacity of your phone. When you're talking about storing lots of large files—videos, photos, and music, especially—the SD card is the preferred storage device.

Insert a MicroSD Card

Most carriers do not include a microSD card with the S7/S7 edge phone. If you want to avail yourself of this additional storage, you need to purchase a microSD card (they're cheap), and then insert it into your phone.

Storage Capacity

MicroSD cards are available in varying capacities, from 8GB to 128GB. Obviously, the larger the card, the more files you can store. (Also, the larger the card, the higher the price!)

---

(1) Your Galaxy S7/S7 edge came with a small SIM/memory card removal tool in the box. Insert the pointed end of this tool into the hole for the SIM/memory card tray on the top edge of your phone and push until the tray pops out.

(2) Place the microSD card on the tray with the gold contacts facing down.

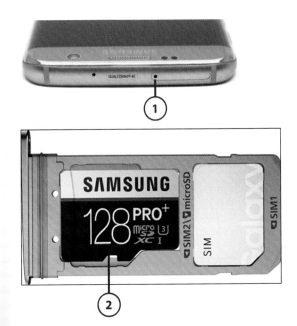

3 Slide the SIM/memory card tray back into the slot on the top edge of your phone.

Format a MicroSD Card

When you insert a new microSD card into your phone, you may need to format it before you can use it. (Some cards come preformatted; many don't.)

1 Swipe down from the top of any screen to display the notifications panel.

2 Tap Settings to display the Settings screen.

3 Tap to select the System tab.

4 Tap Storage to open the Storage screen.

5 Tap SD Card.

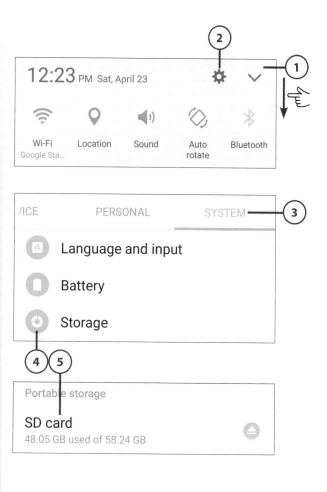

(6) Tap Format.

(7) Tap Format again. The card will be formatted.

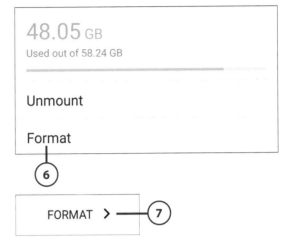

It's Not All Good

Files Are Deleted

You can also format a card you've already been using. Know, however, that when you format a microSD card, any files currently on that card will be deleted—permanently. Be sure you don't need these files before formatting the card and deleting them.

Remove a MicroSD Card

Before you remove a microSD card from your phone, you have to "unmount" it. This is necessary to prevent damage to the files stored on the card.

(1) Swipe down from the top of any screen to display the notifications panel.

(2) Tap Settings to display the Settings screen.

(3) Tap to select the System tab.

(4) Tap Storage to open the Storage screen.

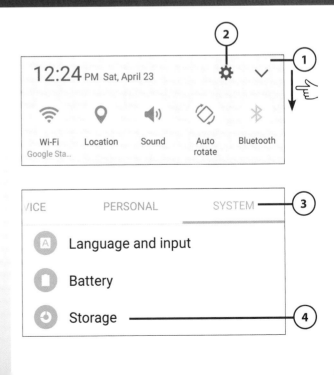

(**5**) Tap SD Card.

(**6**) Tap Unmount.

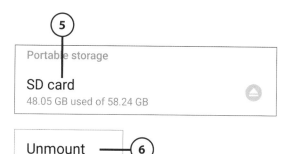

Portable storage

SD card
48.05 GB used of 58.24 GB

Unmount —— (**6**)

Viewing Device Storage

When you want to know how much storage space you've used—and how much you have free—turn to the System tab on the Settings menu.

View Storage Statistics

Your Samsung Galaxy S7/S7 edge keeps real-time statistics regarding how much storage space is used—and for which types of files.

(**1**) Swipe down from the top of any screen to display the notifications panel.

(**2**) Tap Settings to display the Settings screen.

(**3**) Tap to select the System tab.

(**4**) Tap Storage to open the Storage screen.

(**5**) You now see how much storage space is used for both internal storage (phone only) and the removable microSD card. Tap Internal Storage to view more details as to how the storage is used.

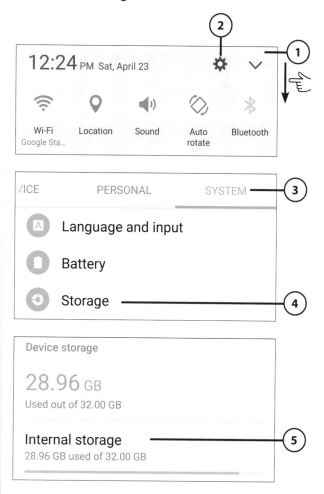

12:24 PM Sat, April 23

Wi-Fi   Location   Sound   Auto   Bluetooth
Google Sta...   rotate

VICE   PERSONAL   SYSTEM —— (**3**)

[A]   Language and input

[ ]   Battery

[ ]   Storage —————————————— (**4**)

Device storage

28.96 GB
Used out of 32.00 GB

Internal storage ———————————— (**5**)
28.96 GB used of 32.00 GB

(6) Wait a moment for the statistics to be updated, then view the Total Space, Available Space, System Memory, Used Space, and more storage statistics. To view more information about any type of storage, tap that item. For example, tap Used Space.

(7) You see how much space is used by Apps, Pictures and Videos, and Audio files. Tap a given item to view even more detail.

28.96 GB
Used out of 32.00 GB

Total space
32.00 GB

Available space
3.04 GB

System memory
8.68 GB

Used space
18.75 GB

Apps
18.24 GB

Pictures, videos
518 MB

Audio
835 KB

Using the My Files App

You manage your phone's files with the My Files app, which is preinstalled on all Samsung smartphones. This app lets you view and manage the files you have stored on your phone, your microSD card, and in the cloud (via Google Drive).

View and Manage Your Files

The My Files app is stored in the Samsung folder on the Apps screen. By default, it displays files by category—Images, Videos, Audio, and Documents.

Apps   **Samsung**   **My Files**

(**1**) From your phone's Home screen, tap the Apps icon to display the Apps screen.

(**2**) Tap to open the Samsung folder.

(**3**) Tap the My Files icon to open the My Files app.

(**4**) Tap to view files stored on your phone (Device Storage) or microSD card (SD Card) *or...*

(**5**) Tap the type of files you want to view—Documents, Images, Audio, or Videos. You can also tap to view recently downloaded files (Download History).

(**6**) Tap Storage Usage to view bar graphs of how much storage is used on your phone, microSD card, and in total.

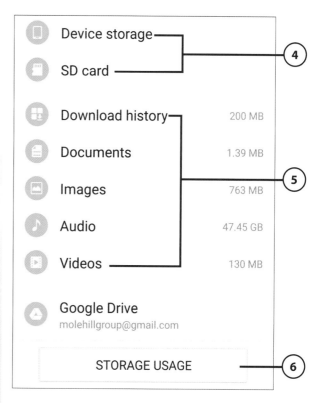

Device storage
SD card
Download history   200 MB
Documents   1.39 MB
Images   763 MB
Audio   47.45 GB
Videos   130 MB
Google Drive
molehillgroup@gmail.com

STORAGE USAGE

Change the File Display

By default, My Files displays the selected files in a list, with a thumbnail image for each file. You can choose to view more or fewer details about these files.

(**1**) From within the My Files app, tap to select the type of file you want to view.

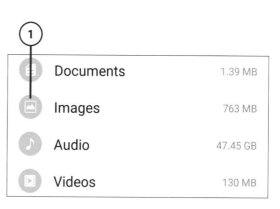

Documents   1.39 MB
Images   763 MB
Audio   47.45 GB
Videos   130 MB

(2) Tap More.

(3) Tap View As to display the View As pane.

(4) Tap Detailed List to view details (size and date) of each file.

(5) Tap Grid to view only file thumbnails, in a grid layout.

(6) Tap List to return to the default List view.

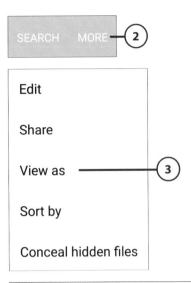

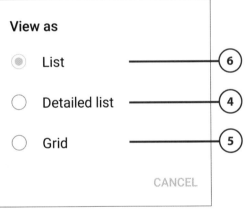

Change the Sort Order

By default, files are sorted in reverse chronological order, newest first. You can opt to sort your files by type, name, or size instead.

(1) From within the My Files app, tap to select the type of file you want to view.

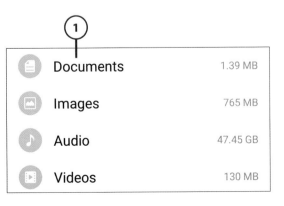

(2) Tap More.

(3) Tap Sort By to display the Sort By pane.

(4) Select how you want the files sorted—by Time, Type, Name, or Size.

(5) To change the sort from descending order to ascending order, tap Ascending.

(6) Tap Done.

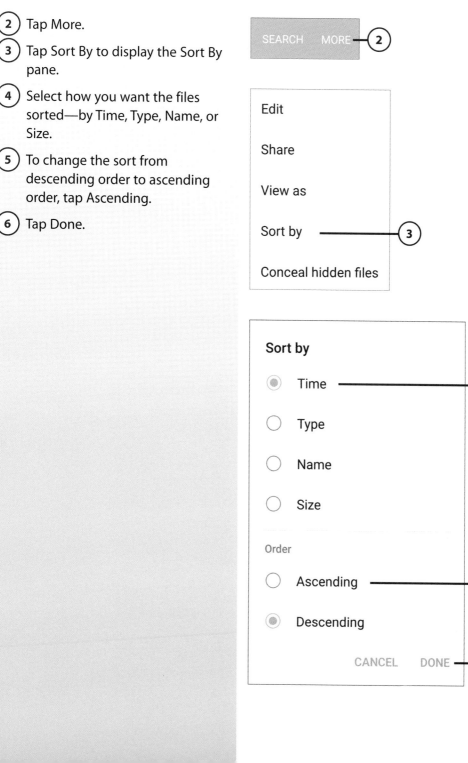

View Downloaded Files

The My Files app keeps separate track of files you download from the Web. Although these downloaded files are listed in their respective category (Images, Videos, Audio, or Documents), they're also listed on the Download History screen.

(1) From within the My Files app, tap Download History.

(2) You see your downloaded files, with the most recent listed first.

Download history   200 MB

— (1)

My Files > Download history

20160115_154416.jpg
Google Drive
372 KB   4/18/16 1:11 PM

20140831_133835.jpg
Downloaded from Google Photos
2.51 MB   4/18/16 12:32 PM

— (2)

View and Open Files

You can open image, video, audio, and document files directly from the My Files app. When you open a file, it opens in the appropriate app. (For example, when you open an image file, it opens in the Gallery app for viewing.)

The files on your phone are stored in individual folders. These are just like the folders on your computer, a convenient way to organize your files. Open a folder to view files stored within and then tap to open a particular file.

(1) From within the My Files app, tap Device Storage to display a list of the folders on your phone, or tap SD Card to view those folders on your microSD card.

(2) Tap a folder to see the files stored within.

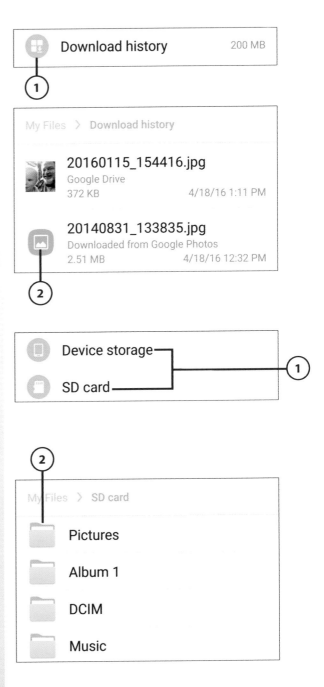

Device storage ⌐
                          (1)
SD card ⌐

(2)

My Files > SD card

Pictures

Album 1

DCIM

Music

Google Drive

The My Files app can also manage your files stored online in Google Drive. Read more about Google Drive later in this chapter in the "Storing Files on Google Drive" section.

(3) Tap to open a file in the appropriate app.

My Files 〉 SD card 〉 Pictures

    📁   Old Photos

    🖼️   20150905_143321.jpg

    🖼️   20160125_154115.jpg

    🖼️   20160125_154438.jpg

Delete Files

If you start to run low on storage space, you can use the My Files app to delete unused or unwanted files.

(1) From within the My Files app, navigate to the location that hosts the file(s) you want to delete.

(2) Tap More.

(3) Tap Edit.

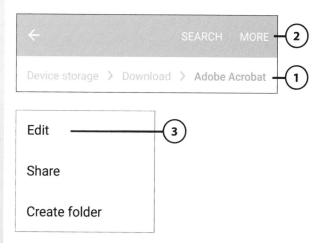

←   SEARCH   MORE —(2)

Device storage 〉 Download 〉 Adobe Acrobat —(1)

Edit ————(3)

Share

Create folder

(4) Tap to select the file(s) you want
to delete.

(5) Tap Delete.

(6) Tap Delete in the confirmation
box. The selected files are now
deleted.

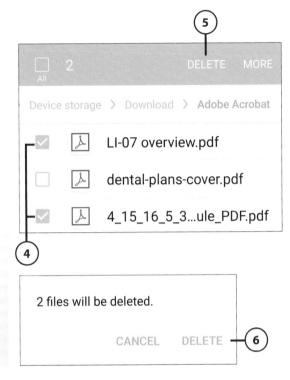

Storing Files on Google Drive

Your Samsung smartphone has a lot of available storage inside, and you can add
more by using a larger microSD card. Even with the relatively large amount of
storage available, however, it might not be enough to hold all the files you might
use. For example, if you have a lot of videos or photos, they take up a lot of storage space. Same thing if you want your phone to host a large music collection.
Over time, your phone's storage space will fill up.

The solution to this issue is to store at least some of your files somewhere else—
somewhere not physically on your phone but still accessible from your phone.
That somewhere is in what we call the cloud, which is a part of the Internet.
Several cloud storage services are available, but the one that's best integrated
into Samsung and other Android phones is Google Drive.

Use Google Drive from the My Files App

You can access Google Drive either from its own app or from the My Files app. It's the My Files integration that makes Google Drive especially useful for most users.

(1) From within the My Files app, tap Google Drive.

(2) You see all the files and folders you've previously uploaded. Tap a folder to view its contents.

(3) Tap a filename to open that file.

Signing In

The first time you access Google Drive, you are prompted to either sign into your Google Account or create a new account. If you do not yet have a Google Account, tap Add Account and follow the onscreen instructions. If you have a Google Account but are not yet signed into Google Drive, tap your Google Account name.

Use the Google Drive App

As practical as it is to access your Google Drive files from within the My Files app, you'll need to use the Google Drive app to perform more advanced operations, such as uploading and downloading files.

(1) From your phone's Home screen, tap the Apps icon to display the Apps screen.

(2) Tap to open the Google folder.

Google Drive
molehillgroup@gmail.com

(1)

My Files > Google Drive

📁 Presentations

📁 QuickBooks Miller

📁 TechSmith

📁 Work Files ———————— (2)

📁 Mom Pictures

🖼 20160411_160815.jpg

Ⓦ text_0

Ⓦ Untitled document ———— (3)

📄 This Week's News

(3) Tap the Drive icon to open the Google Drive app.

Drive

(4) You see all of the files and folders you've previously uploaded to Google Drive. Tap a folder to view the contents of that folder.

(5) Tap a filename to open that file.

≡   **My Drive**   🔍   ▦   ⋮

Folders   Name ↑

📁 Grace Band
    ⁂ Modified: May 13, 2015

📁 Higher Standards
    ⁂ Modified: May 18, 2015

📁 Mom Pictures
    ⁂ Modified: Jul 11, 2014

(4)

(5)

←   **Mom Pictures**   🔍   ▦   ⋮

Files   Name ↑

1958-1-Week-O...-Baby-Mike.jpg
⁂ Modified: Jul 10, 2014

1979 Miller-Family-Portrait.jpg
⁂ Modified: Jul 10, 2014

2004xmas05.jpg
⁂ Modified: Jul 10, 2014

Download a File from Google Drive

You can download to your phone any file stored on Google Drive so that you can use the file even if you don't have a connection to the Internet. You have to download one file at a time.

(1) From within the Google Drive app, tap the Menu button.

(2) Tap Select.

(3) Tap to select the file you want to download. You see a new panel at the bottom of the screen.

(4) Tap the Download icon. The file is downloaded to your phone into the Download folder.

Q ▦ ⋮ ──(1)

Sort by

Select... ─────────(2)

Select all

Folder actions

(3)

Files

✓ bebel.doc
Modified: Nov 9, 2010

Hello,
Modified: May 29, 2007

+

1 Item ✓ ⬇ 🔗 ⋮

(4)

Upload a File to Google Drive

If you have a photo or other file on your phone that you want to access from your computer, or share with other users, you can upload that file from your phone to Google Drive.

1. From within the Google Drive app, tap the blue + button to display the New panel.

2. Tap Upload.

3. Navigate to and tap the file you want to upload. The file is now uploaded to Google Drive.

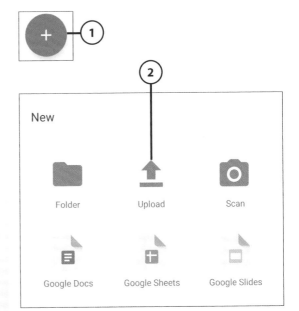

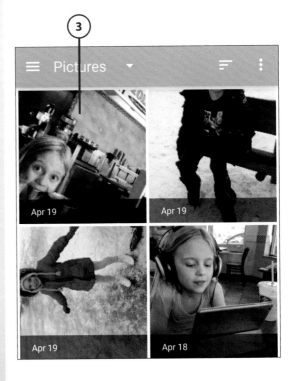

>>>Go Further

MICROSOFT ONEDRIVE

Another popular cloud storage service is Microsoft's OneDrive. In fact, some carriers include the OneDrive app (and 15MB of free storage) on their versions of the Galaxy S7 and S7 edge.

In terms of what it offers, OneDrive is very similar to Google Drive. You get massive amounts of storage online for your photos, videos, music, and documents. You can use OneDrive to store your original files or to make backup copies of files you store on your phone. You can access files stored on OneDrive from any device (smartphone, tablet, or computer) after you've signed into your Microsoft account.

If you don't have the OneDrive app on your phone, you can download it (for free) from the Google Play Store. Open the app, sign into your Microsoft account (or create a new one if you don't have one yet), and then follow the onscreen instructions to get going.

Transferring Files Between Devices

Sometimes you have some photos or music or whatever on your computer that you'd like to have on your phone. Other times you might have taken some pictures or videos on your phone that you'd like to transfer to your computer. How do you get those files from one device to another?

Connect Your Phone to Your Computer

The solution to the file transfer conundrum is to use the data cable that came with your phone and connect it to your PC.

(1) Connect the microUSB connector on one end of the data cable to the USB/charger jack on the bottom of the phone.

(**2**) Connect the USB connector on the other end of the cable to an open USB port on your computer.

(**3**) Swipe down from the top of your phone's screen to display the Notification panel.

(**4**) Tap the Connected As notification to display the Use USB For panel.

(**5**) If not yet selected, tap to select Transferring Media Files. Your two devices are now connected.

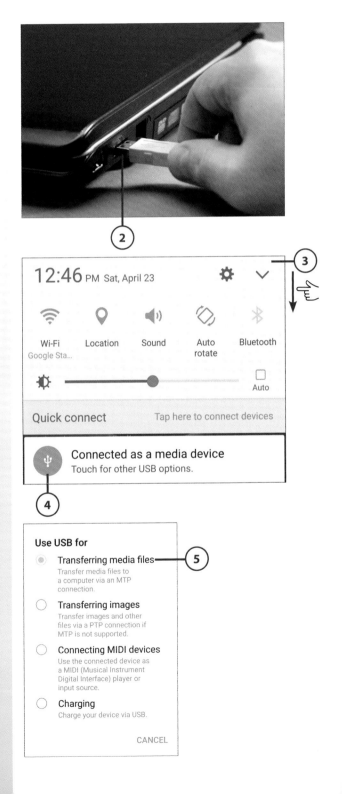

Copy Files from One Device to Another

After your phone is connected to your computer, you can use Windows Explorer or the Mac Finder to access and manage the files on your phone.

(1) On your computer, open Windows Explorer or the Mac Finder then click to open the Computer or This PC section.

(2) Click or double-click to select your phone, typically listed as "SAMSUNG-SM-G930" (for the basic S7) or "SAMSUNG-SM-G935" (for the S7 edge).

(3) To copy files to/from your phone's internal storage, double-click Phone. To copy files to/from the microSD card, double-click Card.

(4) Double-click to open the desired folder. Photos are typically stored in the DCIM and Pictures folders; music is typically stored in the Music folder; and videos are typically stored in the Movies folder.

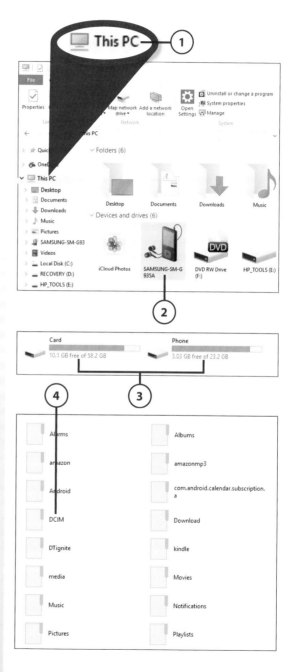

5 Copy a file from your phone by navigating to and right-clicking the file, and then selecting Copy. Then navigate to the desired location on your computer, right-click, and select Paste.

6 Copy a file from your computer to your phone by navigating to and right-clicking the file on your computer, and then selecting Copy. Then navigate to the desired location on your phone, right-click, and select Paste.

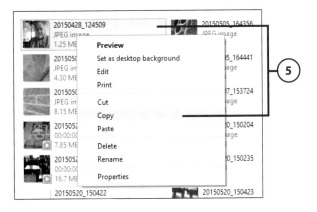

Backing Up Your Data

It's important to create backup copies of the data stored on your phone, in case your data is damaged or your phone is lost. In that contingency, you can restore the backed up data and be up and running again in no time.

Configure Data Backup

Your Samsung smartphone can be configured to automatically back up important data and settings to your Google Drive. All you have to do is enable this functionality.

(1) Swipe down from the top of your phone's screen to display the Notification panel.

(2) Tap Settings to display the Settings screen.

(3) Tap to select the Personal tab.

(4) Tap Backup and Reset.

(5) Tap Back Up My Data.

(6) Tap On the switch at the top of the screen.

(7) Tap the back arrow to return to the Backup and Reset screen.

12:59 PM Sat, April 23

Wi-Fi   Location   Sound   Auto rotate   Bluetooth
Google Sta...

DEVICE   PERSONAL   SYSTEM

Wallpaper

Themes

Home screen

Lock screen and security

Privacy and safety

Easy mode

Accessibility

Accounts

Backup and reset

Back up my data
Off

← Back up my data

On   ON

(8) Tap Backup Account to display the Set Backup Account panel.

(9) Tap the Google Account you want to use, or click + Add Account to add a new account. Your data and settings are automatically backed up to Google's servers using your Google Drive account.

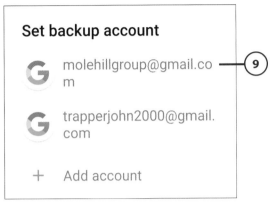

In this chapter, you discover tips for making your new Galaxy S7/S7 edge more secure. Topics include the following:

→ Creating a Safer Lock Screen
→ Locating a Lost or Stolen Phone
→ Paying Safely with Samsung Pay

Making Your Phone More Secure

How safe is your new phone—and everything stored on it? If someone were to steal your phone, how easy would it be for that person to access your important data?

If security worries you, don't fret—you can make your phone and your data more secure. It's a matter of making it more difficult for strangers to unlock your phone and access what's there.

Creating a Safer Lock Screen

The easiest and most effective way to make your phone more secure is to add some sort of protection to the Lock screen. That is, instead of simply swiping to the right to unlock, require some other action that keeps out unwanted visitors.

Add a PIN

The easiest and most common security option is to require a personal information number, or PIN, to unlock your phone. When you power up your phone or awaken the screen, you see a number pad; tap your PIN, and the phone unlocks. If someone tries to enter a different series of numbers, the phone remains locked and unusable.

(1) Swipe down from the top of the screen to display the Notification panel.

(2) Tap Settings to display the Settings screen.

(3) Tap to select the Personal tab.

(4) Tap Lock Screen and Security.

(5) Tap Screen Lock Type. If prompted, enter your current PIN or password.

Re-Enter

If you've previously selected an unlock method (such as a PIN or gesture) and want to change this method, you're asked to enter your PIN or password or gesture or whatever before you can select a new method.

(6) Tap PIN to display the Set PIN screen.

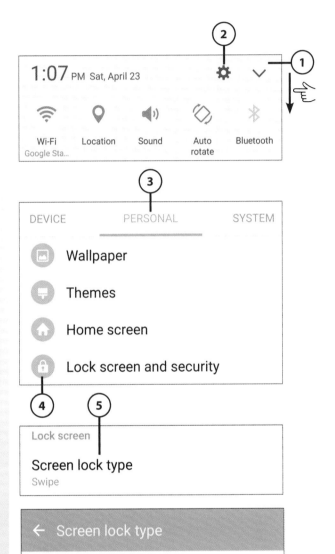

(7) Enter the numbers of your PIN. Your PIN must contain at least four numbers; the longer your PIN, the more secure it is.

(8) Tap Continue.

(9) Re-enter your PIN.

(10) Tap OK.

(11) If prompted whether to show notifications on the Lock screen, make a selection and then tap Done.

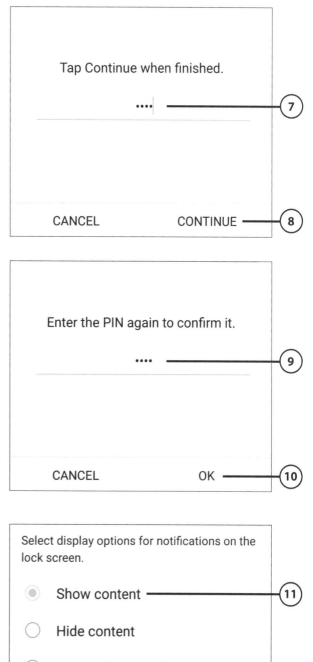

>>>Go Further

TOO LONG TO REMEMBER?

There's always a tradeoff between security and usability. The easiest way to unlock your phone is to swipe the Lock screen, but that's also the least secure method. Using a PIN is more secure than a swipe, but now you have to remember four or more numbers. A password is even more secure, but even harder to remember. And if you can't remember your PIN or password, you're locked out of your own phone!

The key is to select a method that offers the best compromise between security and ease of use. That's why I like using fingerprint login. No PINs or passwords to remember or for anyone to steal—and I always have my fingers with me!

If you decide to go with a PIN or password, create one that you're likely not to forget. And go ahead and write it down—as long as you keep it separate from your phone, in a secure place. Never, *never* tape your PIN or password to the back of your phone. That defeats the purpose of having one!

Unlock with a Password

Using a PIN to secure your Lock screen provides a good, but not great, level of security. For increased security, use a longer alphanumeric password instead of a relatively short numeric PIN.

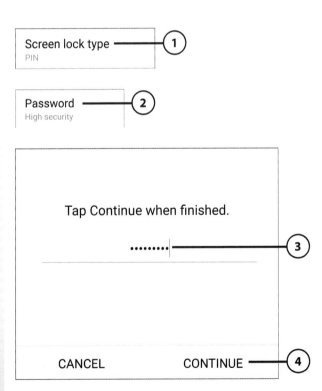

1. From the Lock Screen and Security screen, tap Screen Lock Type. If prompted, enter your current PIN or password.

2. Tap Password to display the Set Password screen.

3. Enter the desired password. Your password must contain at least four characters, including at least one letter. The longer and more complex your password, the more secure it is.

4. Tap Continue.

More Secure

Make your password something only you know, and something others can't guess. For this reason, don't use public information (such as your mother's maiden name, children's names, or birthdate) as a password. Aim for something complex and obscure enough that it can't be easily guessed.

(**5**) Re-enter your password.

(**6**) Tap OK.

(**7**) If prompted whether to show notifications on the Lock screen, make a selection and then tap Done.

Unlock with a Gesture

You can also opt to unlock your phone with a gesture across the screen. This method is easier for you to use on a day-to-day basis, but unfortunately it's also less secure than using a PIN or password.

(**1**) From the Lock Screen and Security screen, tap Screen Lock Type. If prompted, enter your PIN or password.

(**2**) Tap Pattern to display the Set Pattern screen.

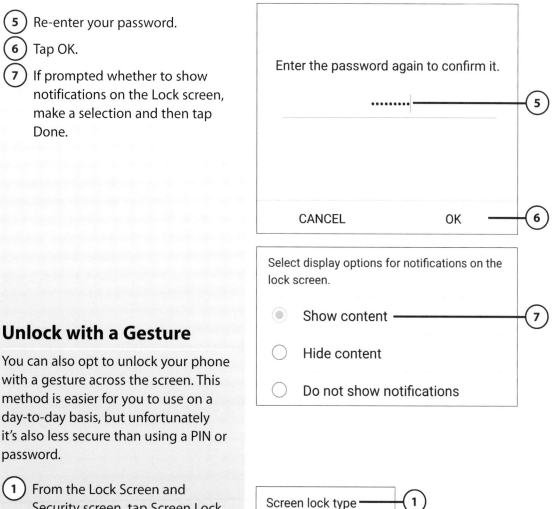

3 This screen features a grid of nine dots. Use your finger to trace a unique pattern from one dot to another. Make the pattern as simple or as complex as you're comfortable with; a simpler pattern is easier to duplicate, of course, but a more complex one might be more difficult to enter consistently.

4 Tap Continue.

5 Redraw the pattern to confirm it.

6 Tap Confirm.

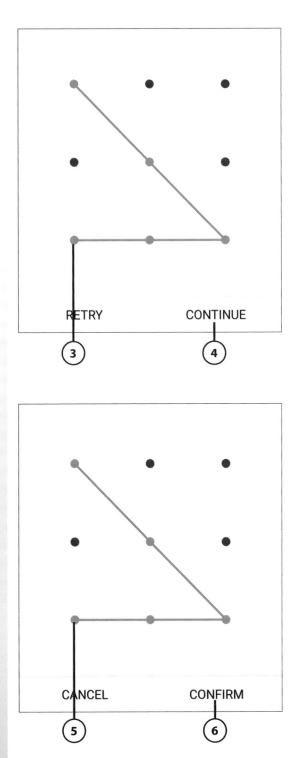

7 If prompted whether to show notifications on the Lock screen, make a selection and then tap Done.

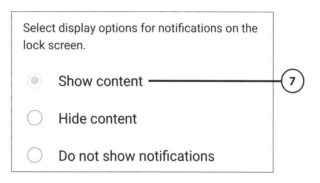

Select display options for notifications on the lock screen.

- ● Show content ———————— **7**
- ○ Hide content
- ○ Do not show notifications

Use Fingerprint Recognition

Your Samsung S7/S7 edge offers a newer, high-tech way to secure and unlock your phone—fingerprint recognition. And because no two fingerprints are alike, this approach might be the best security method of all.

After you've configured your phone for fingerprint recognition, you unlock it by placing your thumb or finger (whichever you registered) on your phone's Home key. Your phone "reads" your fingerprint, matches it to the one stored, and—assuming it matches—unlocks your phone. It's extremely easy and extremely effective.

1 From the Lock Screen and Security screen, tap Screen Lock Type.

2 Tap Fingerprints.

3 Before you register your fingerprint, you must set an alternate security method. Tap either Pattern, PIN, or Password as you wish, then enter the desired pattern, PIN, or password.

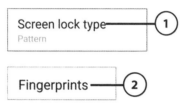

Screen lock type ———— **1**
Pattern

Fingerprints ———— **2**

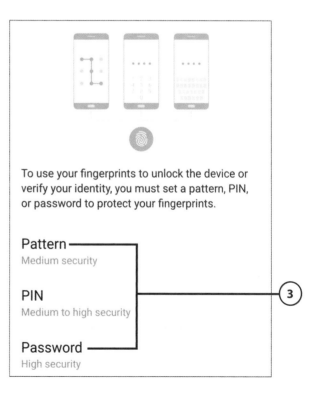

To use your fingerprints to unlock the device or verify your identity, you must set a pattern, PIN, or password to protect your fingerprints.

Pattern ————
Medium security

PIN ———————————— **3**
Medium to high security

Password ————
High security

4 You are now prompted to place your thumb or index finger on your phone's Home key. Do this quickly and then lift it off.

5 Your progress is noted onscreen. Repeat step 4 while moving your finger slightly until the entire fingerprint is registered. This process takes several attempts.

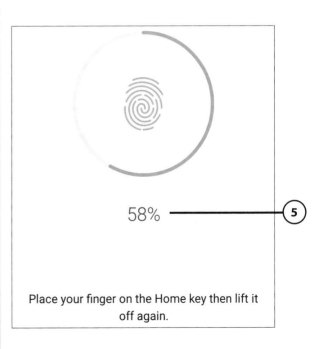

Place finger on Home key, lift it off, then repeat. Move finger upwards/downwards slightly between attempts.

58%

Place your finger on the Home key then lift it off again.

⑥ If prompted whether to show notifications on the Lock screen, make a selection and then tap Done.

> Select display options for notifications on the lock screen.
>
> ⦿ Show content ——————— ⑥
>
> ○ Hide content
>
> ○ Do not show notifications

Locating a Lost or Stolen Phone

What do you do if you lose your phone, or have it stolen? All is not lost; Samsung's Find My Mobile service lets you lock a lost or stolen phone so that no one else can access your data. You can even track a lost or stolen phone (using your phone's location services) and delete your data remotely.

Enable Find My Mobile

To use the Find My Mobile service, you must have a Samsung account. (If you don't yet have one, you can sign up during the activation process—it's free.) You also must have location services enabled on your phone for it to be tracked.

① From the Lock Screen and Security Screen, tap Find My Mobile.

② The next screen displays your Samsung account. Enter your password and tap Confirm.

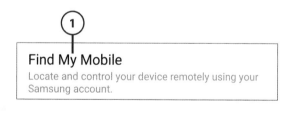

> ①
>
> **Find My Mobile**
> Locate and control your device remotely using your Samsung account.

> Confirm password
> _____
>
> Forgot your ID or password?
>
>
>
>
> ‹ CANCEL   CONFIRM ›

②

(3) On the Find My Mobile screen, tap On the Remote Controls switch.

(4) Tap On the Google Location Service switch.

(5) Tap SIM Change Alert.

(6) On the next screen, tap On the switch at the top of the screen.

(7) Enter a message into the Alert Message box that recipients will receive if someone tries to change or reactivate a stolen SIM card.

(8) Enter the phone number of the person you want to receive this alert into the Alert Message Recipients box.

(9) Tap Save.

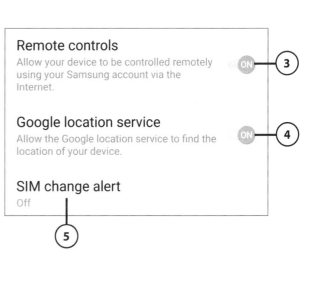

Remote controls
Allow your device to be controlled remotely using your Samsung account via the Internet. — ON — (3)

Google location service
Allow the Google location service to find the location of your device. — ON — (4)

SIM change alert
Off
— (5)

← SIM change alert   SAVE — (9)

On   ON — (6)

Enter a phone number to receive a text message when your device's SIM card is changed.

Alert message

Messages ———— (7)

Alert message recipients
Add a phone number including the country code.

Phone number   +
— (8)

CONTACTS

Access Your Phone Remotely

If your phone is lost or stolen, and you have Find My Mobile activated, you can go online from any computer or Internet-connected device to find it.

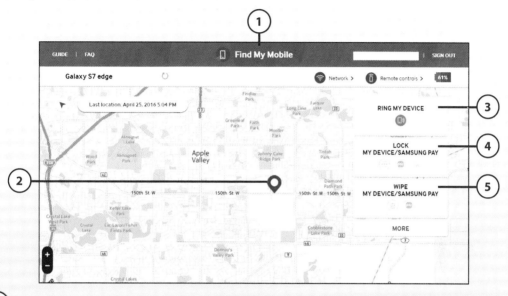

1. From any web browser, go to http://findmymobile.samsung.com and sign into your account.

2. Samsung automatically locates your mobile phone and displays its location on the map.

3. Make your phone ring (so you can find it if it's lost nearby) by clicking Ring My Device.

4. Lock your lost or stolen phone by clicking Lock My Device/Samsung Pay.

5. Delete the data stored on your phone, as a preemptive measure, by clicking Wipe My Device/Samsung Pay.

It's Not All Good

Wiping as the Last Resort

You should wipe your device of all data only as a last resort when you've exhausted all other options, and you fear that a thief might try to access your data without your permission. This option deletes all the data on your phone, so it won't be available to you should you later recover the phone.

Paying Safely with Samsung Pay

Tired of carrying cash in your wallet, or have too many credit cards to deal with? Then use Samsung Pay, a mobile payment system incorporated into your S7/S7 edge phone.

Samsung Pay lets you pay with your phone—no cash or credit cards to fumble with. It operates using near field communication (NFC), so all you have to do is hold your phone up to the scanning device at the checkout counter. Samsung Pay links to your preferred bank account or credit card, and funds are debited when you pay. It's convenient and very high tech.

Availability

Samsung Pay is currently accepted by many merchants in the U.S. and South Korea. More merchants are added daily, and the service is expected to roll out in other countries throughout 2016.

Set Up Samsung Pay on Your Phone

Before you can use Samsung Pay, you have to configure the Samsung Pay app with your payment information.

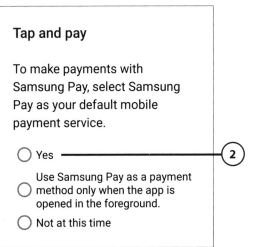

1. From the Home or Apps screen, tap the Samsung Pay icon to open the Samsung Pay app. When prompted, log into your existing or create a new Samsung account.

2. When prompted, tap Yes to select Samsung Pay as your default mobile payment service.

Tap and pay

To make payments with Samsung Pay, select Samsung Pay as your default mobile payment service.

○ Yes

○ Use Samsung Pay as a payment method only when the app is opened in the foreground.

○ Not at this time

(3) Tap to add a credit card or debit card. (If you've already added a card, you can add another card by tapping Add.) Follow the onscreen instructions to use your phone's camera to shoot a picture of the front of your card and then follow the onscreen instructions. Alternatively, tap Enter Card Manually to manually enter your card's information.

(4) Read the Terms of Service then tap Agree to All. You might be prompted to provide additional verification; follow the onscreen instructions to complete the validation process.

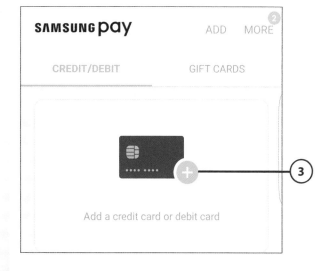

Set Up Simple Pay

You can pay via Samsung Pay without having to unlock your phone. This is called the Simple Pay function, and you use it by swiping up from the bottom of the screen when it's off—or from the Lock or Home screens when your phone is on.

To use Simple Pay, you first have to set it up.

(1) From within the Samsung Pay app, tap More.

(2) Tap Settings to display the Settings screen.

(3) Tap Use Simple Pay.

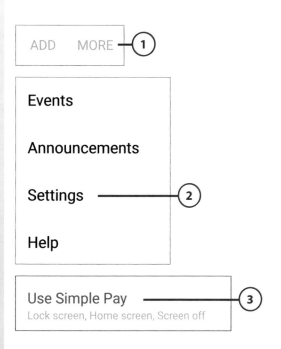

(4) Tap On where you want to access
Simple Pay—when your phone's
screen is off (Screen Off), from
the Lock screen, or from the
Home screen. (You can select any
or all of these three options.

Select where you want to access Simple Pay.

Lock screen   ON

Home screen   ON — (4)

Screen off   ON

Pay with Samsung Pay

You can use Samsung Pay at just about
any merchant that offers NFC or other
wireless payment options.

Samsung Pay — (1)

(1) Tap the Samsung Pay icon to
open the Samsung Pay app. (Or,
if you've activated Simple Pay,
swipe up from the bottom of the
screen.)

(2) When prompted, log in with your
Samsung password or fingerprint.

(3) From within the Samsung Pay
app, tap the credit card you want
to use. (This step is bypassed if
you use Simple Pay.)

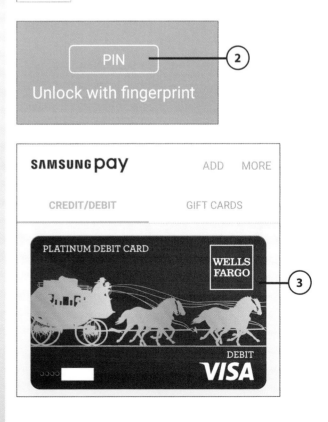

PIN — (2)

Unlock with fingerprint

SAMSUNG pay   ADD   MORE

CREDIT/DEBIT   GIFT CARDS

PLATINUM DEBIT CARD   WELLS FARGO

— (3)

DEBIT

VISA

4 Place the back of your phone against the NFC or card reader until the transaction is completed.

Email Receipt

When the payment is complete, a receipt is emailed to the email address you registered with your Samsung Account.

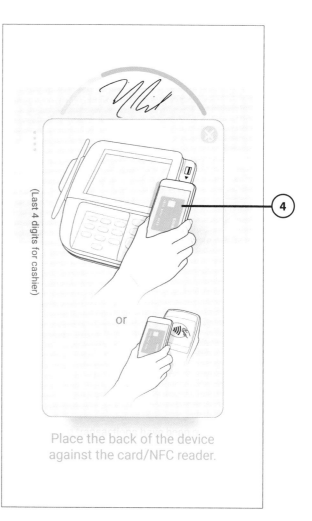

(Last 4 digits for cashier)

or

Place the back of the device against the card/NFC reader.

In this chapter, you discover how to keep your phone running in tip-top condition, and troubleshoot problems if they occur. Topics include the following:

→ Keeping Your Phone Up and Running
→ Troubleshooting Minor Issues
→ Rebooting and Resetting Your Phone

22

Fixing Common Problems

Your Samsung Galaxy S7 or S7 edge is a marvelous piece of technol-ogy—when it's working right. If you find your phone having trouble connecting to the Internet, or running slower than normal, or running out of battery charge, or even freezing up on you, then you probably think a lot less of that technological marvel in your hand.

What do you do if your phone is operating less than optimally? Read on to learn how to get the most out of your phone—and fix any issues that come up.

Keeping Your Phone Up and Running

Before we get into the problem-and-troubleshooting thing, let's look at what you can do to avoid problems, and keep your phone running in tip-top condition.

Maximize Battery Life

The one complaint that just about every smartphone user has is that the battery doesn't last long enough. That's a valid complaint; depending on how you use your phone, you might find the battery drifting toward 0% charge by the end of any given day. Fortunately, there are things you can do to maximize how much time you get on a charge.

- **Recharge your battery every night.** Don't let your battery get drained. Plug it in when you go to sleep at night so it'll be full and fresh when you turn it on the next morning.

- **Fast charge your phone when the battery is low.** You can top off your battery quite quickly, thanks to the Galaxy S7's Adaptive Fast Charging feature. Plug in for about a half hour and you recharge your battery up to the 50% level. (You have to use the quick charger that came with your phone, however, or a similar fast charger; regular charging units do not charge as rapidly.)

- **Examine battery usage.** Want to know how much power your phone is using—and which apps are draining your battery the fastest? Then open the Settings screen, select the System tab, and tap Battery. From there you can view detailed power usage statistics.

- **Decrease screen brightness.** One thing that drains your battery the most is your phone's screen. A brighter screen drains your battery more than a dimmer one, so adjust the screen brightness accordingly.

- **Turn off location services.** Your phone's GPS and location services can also be a big battery drain. That's because, when enabled, some apps (such as weather apps, I've found) constantly ping for the current location. All this location pinging drains your phone's battery, so disable location services to extend battery life.

- **Turn off Wi-Fi.** Wi-Fi is pretty much a necessity, but if you don't need it (when you're on a long automobile trip, for example), turn it off and you'll save a surprising amount of battery life.

- **Turn off Bluetooth.** Like Wi-Fi, Bluetooth uses a lot of power. If you're not connected to a Bluetooth device, turn off Bluetooth on your phone.

- **Turn off NFC.** Near field communications (NFC) is a great way to pay, but when you're not shopping, it still draws power. Unless you're shopping and ready to pay, turn off NFC to conserve battery life.

- **Close apps when you're done with them.** This is a big one. The apps on your phone theoretically are paused when you're not using them, but even a paused app can still draw some amount of power. That's especially true when the app keeps checking for updated information or your current location. When you're done using an app, tap the Recents key and close it out.

- **Avoid apps that use too much power.** Some apps just use more power than others. I've found that mapping apps, like Google Maps, are particular offenders, but other apps can also drain your battery faster than you'd think. Access the Battery screen (from the System tab on the Settings screen) to see which apps use the most power, and then use them less frequently.

- **Disable or uninstall apps you don't use.** Some preinstalled apps use power even when you don't run them. Disable these apps or, if you can, uninstall them. Less stuff on your phone makes your battery last longer.

- **Use Power Saving Mode when you're running low on juice.** When your battery dips toward the 25% range, it's time to take action. If you can plug in and recharge, great. If not, enter Power Saving Mode to turn off the color in the display and reduce other nonessential usage. It just might get you through to when you can recharge. Refer to Chapter 1, "Getting Started with Your Samsung Galaxy S7," for information on turning on Power Saving Mode.

By the way, your battery will become less efficient over time. If you started out getting 20 hours on a charge, a year later you may be down to 15 hours (or less!). That's normal; batteries lose charge the more you use them. When available battery life becomes unusably low, it's time to take your phone in and have its battery replaced.

Use a Performance-Enhancing App

Several companies offer apps specifically designed to free up unused memory and storage space on your phone, and thus increase your phone's performance. Run one of these apps to clear out any "junk" that take up space in your phone's memory and potentially slow down operation.

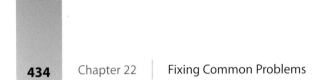

The following table details some of the most popular (and reputable) perfor-mance-enhancing apps.

Performance-Enhancing Apps

App	Cost
Avast Cleanup and Boost	Free
CCleaner	Free
Clean Master	Free
DU Speed Booster	Free
Mobi Cleaner	Free

Free Up Space by Deleting Unused Apps

As noted previously, disabling or uninstalling apps frees up some amount of memory and reduces power usage. Deleting unused apps also frees up storage space on your phone. When you need more space to install new apps or store more photos or music, you can find that space by deleting apps you don't use anymore. It's that simple.

Troubleshooting Minor Issues

Even if you take all the preventive steps recommended earlier in this chapter, it's still possible for your phone to act up every now and then. Fortunately, most issues you're likely to encounter are minor ones with relatively easy fixes.

You're Locked Out

Here's a common one. You go to enter the PIN or password to unlock your phone, and you get it wrong. And again. And again. And before you know it, your phone won't let you unlock it at all.

Your phone locks itself solid when you enter the wrong PIN or password more than three times in a row. At this point, you're likely to see an onscreen message that tells you the PIN is locked and you need to enter a PUK (phone unlock key). What do you do now?

A PUK is an 8-digit number linked to your phone's SIM card. (You may also need a PUK if you've enabled SIM card locking and forgotten that PIN.) Entering the PUK unlocks your phone and lets you set a new PIN.

Where do you find your phone's PUK? You need to contact your mobile carrier or log onto your account page on your carrier's website. After you obtain the PUK, enter it from your phone's Lock screen and, when prompted, create a new PIN. You should be good to go from there.

An Individual App Freezes

What do you do when you're using an app and it freezes? Close it! Tap the Recents button to display the stack of recent apps and then swipe away the frozen one. You should be able to restart the app from the Home or Apps screen and (hopefully) have it run properly.

Your Phone Freezes

What about if your entire phone freezes? Well, if your screen is frozen, you need to reboot it. Rebooting is covered later in this chapter in the "Rebooting and Resetting Your Phone" section, so turn there for details.

Your Phone Won't Turn On

If your phone won't turn on at all, the first thing to suspect is a discharged battery. Connect your phone to a power supply and try turning it on again. (You might need to wait a few minutes for the phone to receive a minimal charge.)

Remember, the proper way to turn on your phone is to press and hold the Power key on the right side of the unit. Just tapping the Home key on the front won't turn on a phone that's been powered off.

If your phone works when connected to a power outlet but not when it's running on battery then you have a dead battery. You need to replace it.

Your Phone Is Running Slow

If your phone is running slow, you probably have too many apps open. Tap the Recents key and close some of the apps you're not currently using.

If your phone continues to run slow, reboot it. This frees up any trapped memory and starts things off fresh.

Finally, if slow running is a constant problem, consider installing and using one of the performance-enhancing apps discussed previously in this chapter. They help you identify where your problems lie and help you clean up some of the junk you don't need.

Your Mobile Signal Is Weak

Your smartphone is still a phone, and mobile phones sometimes run into reception problems. When you have trouble connecting or staying connected to phone calls, the problem is probably your mobile carrier, not your phone.

Check the number of bars you have on the Home screen's status bar. If you only have one or two bars (or even none!) then you're not getting a strong enough signal. Try moving to another part of the room or to another room in your house. If that doesn't help, try moving to a totally different location. (For what it's worth, I've found I can improve my reception by moving from one end of my living room couch to the other!)

Cell signals are notoriously fickle, and some carriers have better coverage than others. If you continually have issues with weak signals in your home, consider changing carriers. You might find that Verizon has better coverage than AT&T in your area, or vice versa.

You Have Trouble Connecting to Wi-Fi

These days you'll spend a lot of time with your phone connected to a home or public Wi-Fi network. What do you do if your Wi-Fi signal cuts out unexpectedly—or if you can't connect at all?

First, make sure you're connected to the right network. In many locations you'll have multiple Wi-Fi networks or hotspots available. This may even be the case in your home, where you might see your own Wi-Fi network and those of your next-door neighbors. Make sure you're not connected to the wrong or weaker network.

If you have a consistently weak connection at home, try moving your Wi-Fi router. A router buried in one corner of your house will have trouble sending a signal to devices at the opposite end (or different floor) of the building. Put the router in a more central location—or, conversely, move your phone closer to the router.

If you have an unstable Wi-Fi connection, one that constantly drops due to poor signal strength, turn on your phone's Smart Network Switch. This will automatically switch you from a weak Wi-Fi signal to a stronger mobile data connection and let you stay connected to the Internet. Open the Notifications panel, tap and hold Wi-Fi, tap More, and then tap Smart Network Switch. When prompted tap On the switch.

Finally, if you're having connection problems with a particular Wi-Fi network, try rebooting your phone. Rebooting sometimes fixes connection problems like this, for whatever reason.

It's Not All Good

Water Is Not Good

Accidents will happen, and some of the most common phone-related accidents involve people getting their smartphones wet. We're talking dropping phones into sinks, puddles, pools, and even toilets. (Yes, toilets!)

In general, electronics and water don't mix. Samsung knows this, and made the Galaxy S7/S7 edge water resistant. Not water *proof*, mind you, but water *resistant*. That means that the electronics are fairly well sealed, enough to survive a brief dip in the potty or drop into a puddle. If you accidentally drop your phone into water, pick it up as quick as you can and use a towel to dry it off. (If you dropped it in the toilet, use another damp towel to wash it off, first.)

Because the phone isn't fully waterproof, it won't survive long periods underwater. So take your phone out of your shorts before you go swimming. That's just too much for the S7 to take!

Rebooting and Resetting Your Phone

Some problems are so severe that they require you to reboot your phone—that is, turn it off and turn it back on. Other problems are even more serious, and might require you to reset your phone to its original factory condition. If you need to reboot or reset, here's how to do it.

Reboot Your Phone

In the grand scheme of things, rebooting your phone isn't a big deal. It sounds more serious than it is; all it really means is that you power down your phone and then power it back up. It's quite easy.

(1) Press and hold the Power key on the right side of your phone to display the options panel.

(2) Tap Restart.

(3) Tap Restart again. The phone powers down and then immediately powers back up, displaying the Lock screen.

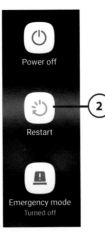

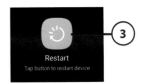

Reboot a Frozen Phone

If your phone is frozen or otherwise unresponsive, you can't reboot normally. In this instance, you have to perform what is called a *hard boot*. To do this, press and hold the Power key and the Volume down key simultaneously, for more than 7 seconds. The phone should now power off and then power back on.

Reset Your Phone's Settings

Sometimes it's the settings you've set that are causing your problems. You may be able to fix things by resetting all your settings to their default conditions.

Resetting your settings does *not* delete any data stored on your phones. It merely returns your phone to its factory default settings.

1. Swipe down from the top of any screen to display the Notifications panel.
2. Tap Settings to display the Settings screen.
3. Tap to select the Personal tab.
4. Tap Backup and Reset.

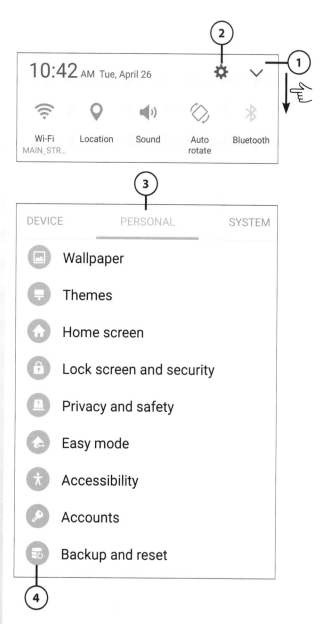

5 Tap Reset Settings.

6 Tap the Reset Settings button.

7 Tap Reset in the Warning box. Your phone's settings are now reset to factory defaults, and all your data and other files remain intact.

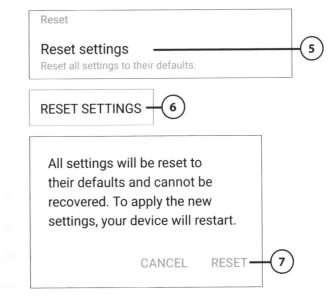

Reset Your Phone to Factory Condition

When your phone experiences recurring severe problems, there's a more extreme solution you can employ. The Factory Data Reset option not only resets all your phone's settings but it also deletes all your data—pictures, music…you name it. By deleting everything, your phone is returned to factory fresh condition.

That said, this is an extreme measure, to be taken only under extreme conditions. And, before you do it, you want to back up all your data and settings. We talked about backing up your data in Chapter 20, "Copying Files To and From Your Phone—And Backing Up Your Important Data," so turn there for instructions.

After your data is backed up, you can reset your phone.

It's Not All Good

Everything Is Deleted!

Performing a Factory Data Reset permanently erases all data from your phone. This includes your phone's settings, of course, but also your Google and Samsung account settings, email accounts and messages, photos, videos, music, and other documents and files. You should reset your phone only if all other measures are unsuccessful, and after you've backed up your data and settings.

1. Swipe down from the top of any screen to display the Notifications panel.

2. Tap Settings to display the Settings screen.

3. Tap to select the Personal tab.

4. Tap Backup and Reset.

5. Tap Factory Data Reset.

10:44 AM Tue, April 26			⚙	⌄
Wi-Fi	Location	Sound	Auto	Bluetooth
MAIN_STR...			rotate	

DEVICE   PERSONAL   SYSTEM

Wallpaper

Themes

Home screen

Lock screen and security

Privacy and safety

Easy mode

Accessibility

Accounts

Backup and reset

Factory data reset
Reset your device to its factory default settings. This will erase all data, including files and downloaded apps.

(6) Read the requisite warnings and then scroll down to the bottom of the screen. If you want to also format your phone's SD card (which deletes all data stored there), tap to select Format SD Card.

(7) Tap the Reset Device button.

(8) When prompted for your password or fingerprint, provide it and follow the remaining instructions to reset the phone.

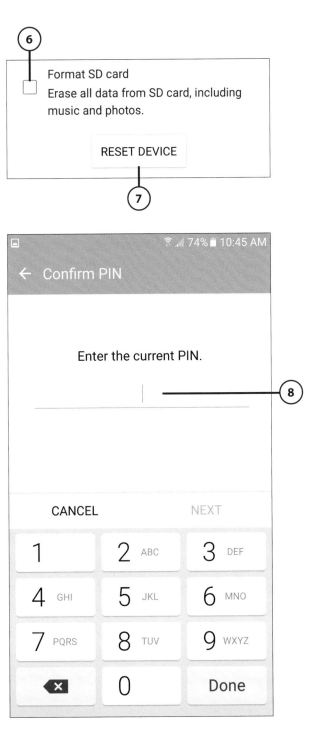

(6)

Format SD card
Erase all data from SD card, including music and photos.

RESET DEVICE

(7)

← Confirm PIN

Enter the current PIN.

(8)

CANCEL   NEXT

1   2 ABC   3 DEF

4 GHI   5 JKL   6 MNO

7 PQRS   8 TUV   9 WXYZ

⌫   0   Done

Glossary

1G First-generation analog wireless telephone technology.

2G Second-generation wireless technology, the first digital generation and the first to include data services.

3G Third-generation wireless telephone technology, noted for faster data rates.

4G Fourth-generation wireless telephone technology, with even faster data rates than the previous 3G.

Airplane mode Special smartphone mode that disables Wi-Fi and cellular functionality for use in flight.

Android Google's operating system for mobile phones and tablets. Samsung smartphones use the Android operating system.

app A software program that runs on a smartphone or other device.

application See *app*.

Back key On the Samsung Galaxy S7 and S7 edge, the "soft" key that you press to move back to the previous screen.

bandwidth The amount of data that can be sent over a connection in a given amount of time.

Bluetooth   A wireless protocol for exchanging data over short distances. Smartphones use Bluetooth technology to connect to wireless headsets and to in-car systems.

browser   See *web browser.*

caller ID   A feature that displays the caller's name and/or number when an incoming call is received.

calling plan   Services offered by a mobile carrier for a given charge. A calling plan typically includes all voice-related services, but typically not data services, which are often charged separately.

carrier   See *mobile carrier.*

cell phone   See *mobile phone.*

cellular network   A wireless network used for phone calls and data transmission, distributed over a range of geographic areas called cells.

cloud computing   A form of computing where files and applications are stored on a collection of Internet-based servers, instead of on local devices.

cloud storage   A means of storing files and other data on Internet-based servers, instead of on local devices.

coverage area   The geographic area within which a mobile carrier provides service.

data plan   Services offered by a mobile carrier for transmitting data and connecting to the Internet. Distinct from voice services offered in a typical data plan.

Easy mode   A special display mode that increases the size of text and icons onscreen, to improve accessibility.

Edge panels   On the Galaxy S7 edge, those panels that pull in from the right side of the screen and display specific types of data and information.

Edge screen   The curved areas on the sides of the Galaxy S7 edge smartphone, used to display auxiliary information.

front-facing camera   The camera that faces the user on a smartphone, typically located above the screen. Front-facing cameras are most often used to shoot selfies.

Home key   The large physical button located below the screen on the Galaxy S7 and S7 edge. Pressing the Home key returns the user to the Home screen.

hotspot   A public Wi-Fi network one can use to connect to the Internet. Typically found in coffeehouses, restaurants, hotels, and the like.

IMAP   Short for Internet Message Access Protocol, used by email apps to access messages stored on a central server.

iOS   The operating system used on Apple's iPhones and tablets.

iPhone   Apple's line of smartphones.

key   On Samsung phones, those physical or soft buttons used to perform specific operations, such as powering on or changing the volume.

landline   A wired telephone connection, like the type you have in your home.

LTE   Short for long-term evolution, a 4G wireless telephone technology.

main camera   See *rear-facing camera.*

memory card   A type of removable flash drive used to store digital data on smartphones, digital cameras, and similar devices.

microSD card   The type of removable flash memory card used to store photos, videos, music, and other data on the Galaxy S7/S7 edge.

MMS   Short for Multimedia Messaging Service, a means of sending images, videos, and other media along with text messages.

mobile   What Europeans call a *mobile phone.*

mobile carrier   A company that sells access to a wireless telephone network. Top carriers in the United States include AT&T, Sprint, T-Mobile, and Verizon.

mobile hotspot   A function that enables a smartphone to provide Wi-Fi services to nearby devices, and thus share an Internet connection with portable computers, tablets, and other phones.

mobile network   See *cellular network.*

mobile phone   A telephone that can make and receive calls wirelessly, over a cellular network.

mobile service provider   See *mobile carrier.*

Multi window   The functionality that enables display of two apps on the same screen.

NFC   Short for near field communications, a short-range standard for wireless data transfer. Typically used to share content between wireless devices and make retail payments wirelessly.

Notifications panel   The panel of icons that displays when you swipe down from the top of any screen on the Galaxy S7 and S7 edge. Contains shortcuts to various system settings and operations.

operating system   The underlying software that controls all the operations of a given electronic device. Samsung uses the Android operating system to control its Galaxy smartphones.

OS   See *operating system.*

PIN   Short for personal identification number, a numeric code used to provide secure access to a given device or service.

POP3   Short for Post Office Protocol 3, used by email apps to access messages stored on a central server.

Power key   The physical button on the right side of the Galaxy S7 and S7 edge, used to power the phone on and off.

PUK   Short for PIN unblock key, a numeric code used to reset a lost or forgotten PIN code.

rear-facing camera   The camera on the rear of a smartphone, used to take pictures of other people and subjects. This is often referred to as the phone's main camera.

Recent key   The soft key on the front of the Galaxy S7 and S7 edge that, when pressed, displays a stack of recent and open apps.

ringtone   The sound a phone makes when there is an incoming call.

Samsung Pay   The electronic payment service, provided by Samsung, that enables wireless payment at retail with your Galaxy S7/S7 edge smartphone.

SD (secure data) card   A type of flash memory card that stores digital data. The Galaxy S7/S7 edge uses a removable microSD card to store photos, videos, music, and other data.

selfie   A picture of oneself, typically taken with a smartphone's front-facing camera.

SIM   Short for subscriber identity module, the small removable card that contains identifying information necessary to operate a mobile phone.

smartphone   A mobile phone that, in addition to voice calling capability, includes a touchscreen and microprocessor that enable computer-like operation and Internet connectivity.

SMS   Abbreviation for Short Messaging Service, a means to send and receive text messages.

soft key   A flat area beneath the smartphone screen that functions as a key or button when pressed.

swipe   The action of moving your finger across a touchscreen to activate a function or operation.

tethering   The process of connecting a smartphone to a computer so that the computer can access the Internet via the phone's data connection.

text messaging   The process of sending text-based messages from one phone to another, via either SMS or MMS technology.

Twitter   A social network based on short (140-character) messages, called tweets.

USB   Short for Universal Serial Bus, a standard for wired connections between two electronic devices. Widely used to connect smartphones and peripherals to personal computers.

voice mail   An electronic service, similar to an answering machine, that enables callers to leave messages when calls are unanswered. Most mobile carriers offer voice mail service.

Volume keys   The two physical buttons on the left side of the Galaxy S7 and S7 edge that, when pressed, raise and lower the phone's volume.

web browser   An application used to access websites on the Internet.

Wi-Fi   Short for wireless fidelity, a technology that provides high-speed wireless data transmission between devices.

Wi-Fi hotspot   See *hotspot.*

wireless charging   The ability to recharge a smartphone or other devices without making a wired power connection.

wireless network   A public or private network that connects computers, smartphones, and other devices via Wi-Fi wireless technology.

Index

N

W

More Best-Selling **My** Books!

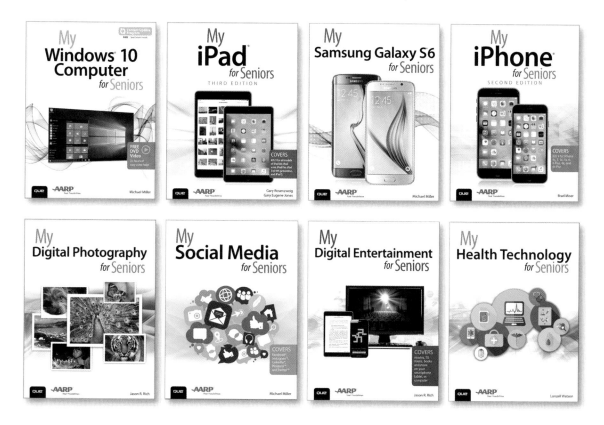

Learning to use your smartphone, tablet, camera, game, or software has never been easier with the full-color My Series. You'll find simple, step-by-step instructions from our team of experienced authors. The organized, task-based format allows you to quickly and easily find exactly what you want to achieve.

Visit quepublishing.com/mybooks to learn more.